FREE VIDEO  FREE VIDEO

Essential Test Tips Video from Trivium Test Prep!

Dear Customer,

Thank you for purchasing from Trivium Test Prep! We're honored to help you prepare for your CPCE exam.

To show our appreciation, we're offering a **FREE *CPCE Essential Test Tips* Video by Trivium Test Prep**.* Our video includes 35 test preparation strategies that will make you successful on your big exam. All we ask is that you email us your feedback and describe your experience with our product. Amazing, awful, or just so-so: we want to hear what you have to say!

To receive your **FREE *CPCE Essential Test Tips* Video**, please email us at 5star@triviumtestprep.com. Include "Free 5 Star" in the subject line and the following information in your email:

1. The title of the product you purchased.

2. Your rating from 1 – 5 (with 5 being the best).

3. Your feedback about the product, including how our materials helped you meet your goals and ways in which we can improve our products.

4. Your full name and shipping address so we can send your **FREE *CPCE Essential Test Tips* Video**.

If you have any questions or concerns please feel free to contact us directly at 5star@triviumtestprep.com.

Thank you!

- Trivium Test Prep Team

*To get access to the free video please email us at 5star@triviumtestprep.com, and please follow the instructions above.

CPCE
Study Guide 2024-2025

600+ Practice Questions and CPCE Exam Preparation

Elissa Simon

Copyright © 2023 by Trivium Test Prep

ISBN-13: **9781637983843**

ALL RIGHTS RESERVED. By purchase of this book, you have been licensed one copy for personal use only. No part of this work may be reproduced, redistributed, or used in any form or by any means without prior written permission of the publisher and copyright owner. Trivium Test Prep; Accepted, Inc.; Cirrus Test Prep; and Ascencia Test Prep are all imprints of Trivium Test Prep, LLC.

The National Board for Certified Counselors (NBCC) was not involved in the creation or production of this product, is not in any way affiliated with Trivium Test Prep, and does not sponsor or endorse this product. All test names (and their acronyms) are trademarks of their respective owners. This study guide is for general information and does not claim endorsement by any
third party.

Image(s) used under license from Shutterstock.com

Table of Contents

Online Resources vii

Introduction ix

1 Professional Counseling Orientation and Ethical Practice — 1

The Counseling Profession 1
Professional Practice 6
Consultation and Self-Assessment 14
Documentation 19
Ethics 25
Answer Key 33

2 Social and Cultural Diversity — 37

Multicultural Counseling 37
Culture, Religion, and Spirituality 45
Answer Key 53

3 Human Growth and Development — 55

Elements of Developmental Psychology ... 55
Cognitive and Language Development 60
Lifespan Developmental Theory 64
Personality 70
Motivation and Stress 72
Answer Key 76

4 Career Development — 79

Career and Finances 79
Career Assessment 86
Answer Key 88

5 Counseling and Helping Relationships — 91

Core Counseling Attributes 91
Working with the Client 97
Counseling Interventions 102
Conflict and Confrontation 105
Answer Key 109

6 Group Counseling and Group Work — 111

Working with a Group 111
Attributes in a Group Counseling Context ... 119
Conflict in Groups 122
Answer Key 124

7 Assessment and Testing — 125

Intake and Interview 125
Assessing the Client 131
Assessment Instruments 135
Diagnosis 148
Answer Key 153

8 Research and Program Evaluation — 157

Research in Counseling 157
Statistical Concepts and Methods Used in Research 159

v

Developing and
Evaluating Counseling Programs.................. 161
Evidence-Based Practice 163
Answer Key 164

8 CPCE Practice Test   **165**
    ANSWER KEY 191

Online Resources   **207**

Online Resources

Trivium Test Prep includes online resources with the purchase of this study guide to help you fully prepare for your CPCE exam.

Practice Tests

In addition to the practice test included in this book, we also offer an online exam. Since many exams today are computer based, practicing your test-taking skills on the computer is a great way to prepare.

Review Questions

Need more practice? Our review questions use a variety of formats to help you memorize key terms and concepts.

Flash Cards

Trivium Test Prep's flash cards allow you to review important terms easily on your computer or smartphone.

From Stress to Success

Watch "From Stress to Success," a brief but insightful YouTube video that offers the tips, tricks, and secrets experts use to score higher on the exam.

Reviews

Leave a review, send us helpful feedback, or sign up for Trivium promotions—including free books!

Access these materials at: www.triviumtestprep.com/cpce-online-resources

Introduction

Congratulations on choosing to take the Counselor Preparation Comprehensive Examination (CPCE)! By purchasing this book, you've taken the first step toward becoming a counselor.

This guide will provide you with a detailed overview of the CPCE, so you will know exactly what to expect on test day. We'll take you through all of the concepts covered on the exam and give you the opportunity to test your knowledge with practice questions. Even if it's been a while since you last took a major test, don't worry; we'll make sure you're more than ready!

What Is the CPCE?

The **Counselor Preparation Comprehensive Examination (CPCE)** is developed by the **National Board for Certified Counselors (NBCC)** as part of its certification program. The CPCE measures the skills necessary to safely practice as an entry-level counselor.

To qualify for the exam, you must have graduated from or be an advanced graduate student in a counseling program accredited by the **Council for Accreditation of Counseling and Related Educational Programs (CACREP)**. In some states, candidates with other related helping degrees may qualify to take the CPCE and earn licensure.

What's on the CPCE?

The CPCE consists of **160 questions**. Only 136 of these questions are scored; the remainder are unscored, or pretest questions. These questions are used to test their suitability for inclusion on future tests. You'll have no way of knowing which questions are unscored, so treat every question like it counts. Questions are aligned with the CACREP common core areas.

The questions on the CPCE are multiple-choice with four answer options. The CPCE has **no guess penalty**. That is, if you answer a question incorrectly, no points are deducted from your score; you simply do not get credit for that question. Therefore, you should always guess if you do not know the answer to a question. You will have **four hours** to complete the test.

WHAT'S on the CPCE?	
Subject	Number of Questions per Subject
Human Growth and Development	20
Social and Cultural Foundations	20
Helping Relationships	20
Group Work	20
Career and Lifestyle Development	20
Appraisal	20
Research and Program Evaluation	20
Professional Orientation and Ethics	20
Total: 4 hours	160 multiple-choice questions (136 scored)

How Is the CPCE Scored?

Once you have completed the test, you will receive your unofficial score from the proctor and may print a hard copy of your score to take with you. You will receive your official results electronically four weeks after the end of the testing window. Remember, you may not use your CPCE credentials until you have received your official results, even if you pass the test.

The CPCE is a pass/fail test. Of the 160 questions on the test, 136 are scored. Your raw score is how many of the 136 scored questions you answered correctly. That score is then scaled based on the level of difficulty of the questions you answered correctly. Different programs have different requirements for a passing score.

If you pass the test, the Center for Credentialing & Education (CCE) will report your official scores to your licensing organization within thirty days. If you do not pass the test, you may appeal, or you may retake the test after a three-month waiting period.

The number of correct answers needed to pass the exam will vary slightly depending on the questions included on your version of the test. (In other words, if you take a version of the test with harder questions, the passing score will be lower.) For security reasons, different versions of the test are administered during every testing window.

How Is the CPCE Administered?

To register for the exam, you must first apply through the **Center for Credentialing & Education (CCE)**. You must register online at http://www.cce-global.org under the "ProCounselor" tab. After your application is accepted, you will receive an exam eligibility email with instructions on how to register for the exam. If you wish to retake the exam, you may do so, but only after a three-month waiting period.

The CPCE is administered at Pearson VUE testing centers around the nation. Plan to arrive at least **thirty minutes before the exam** to complete biometric screening. Bring at least one form of **government-issued photo ID** and be prepared to be photographed and have your palms scanned. You may also be scanned with a metal detector wand before entering the test room. Your primary ID must be government issued, include a recent photograph and signature, and match the name under which you registered to take the test. If you do not have proper ID, you will not be allowed to take the test.

You will not be allowed to bring any personal items into the testing room, such as calculators or phones. You may not bring pens, pencils, or scratch paper. Other prohibited items include hats, scarves, and coats. You may, however, wear religious garments. Pearson VUE provides lockers for valuables; you can keep your ID and locker key with you.

About Trivium Test Prep

Trivium Test Prep uses industry professionals with decades' worth of knowledge in their fields—proven with degrees and honors in law, medicine, business, education, the military, and more—to produce high-quality test prep books for students.

Our study guides are specifically designed to increase any student's score. Since our books are shorter and more concise than typical study guides, you can increase your score while significantly decreasing your study time. We're pleased you've chosen Trivium to be a part of your professional journey.

1 Professional Counseling Orientation and Ethical Practice

The Counseling Profession

History and Philosophy of Counseling

Counseling emerged as a profession in the mid-twentieth century. Before that time, the term *counselor* referred to someone who acted as an advisor or mentor to another person, both formally and informally. In these early days, counselors held advisory roles, mostly in career or vocational counseling, where they helped people select the education or job that suited them best.

Psychologists began to develop psychotherapy as a client-led practice, and the asylum-based mental health system changed to community-based outpatient treatment. The need for the professionalization of mental health care became more apparent. With industrialization and urbanization, social changes led to an increased demand for services. Additionally, soldiers returning from World War II who needed care to deal with the trauma of the war were not being helped.

Many people called themselves counselors but had no real qualifications. False practitioners operated freely because there were no laws, rules, or standards that determined what qualifications a counselor should have. Sometimes, their actions harmed clients.

There was little agreement on the definition of a mental illness, without which clients could not depend on standardized research or interventions. Additionally, there was no way for clients to determine which counselors were legitimate.

The *Diagnostic and Statistical Manual of Mental Disorders* was published in 1952; in the 1960s and 1970s, laws and regulations were created to clarify the required education and qualifications to advertise as a professional counselor. The movement toward standardization was inspired in part by the Community Mental Health Act of 1963, which moved care from a hospital-based medicalized mental health system to community-based mental health centers.

To gain public trust, those providing services at the new community mental health centers needed to be qualified. As a result, professional organizations in various counseling specialties advocated for and influenced the standardization of educational programs and licensing requirements. Laws were created to protect the public from unethical or incompetent counselors. State licensing boards were formed to become governing and disciplinary bodies for professional counselors.

The philosophy of counseling in general is based on creating positive change in clients' lives by offering therapeutic interventions that treat or manage mental, emotional, or behavioral problems. Counselors do this by promoting wellness, resilience, and prevention in direct client care:

- **Wellness** is a state of being in which clients can thrive in their physical, mental, emotional, relational, and social lives.
  - Wellness is also informed by a strengths-based approach to clients rather than a focus on their problems.
- The philosophy of **resilience** suggests that counselors work with clients to build up protective factors in their lives so they have the tools, resources, and support to overcome any challenges.
- **Prevention** is a philosophy that gives clients tools to improve well-being, bolster resilience, and prevent mental illness through healthy lifestyle choices, coping skills, and support systems.
  - Prevention also helps people in clients' social support systems learn how to help them through challenges associated with their mental illness.

A central component of counseling philosophy is **client-centered care**. Early psychotherapists created methods of intervention that focused on empowering clients to lead their treatment by setting goals and choosing treatment methods. Client-centered care emphasizes that clients can recover from mental illness. Counselors must use interventions and basic counseling skills to help clients recognize their illness and implement new strategies to manage and overcome them.

PRACTICE QUESTION

1. Which piece of legislation inspired the creation of standards for education and qualifications for professional counselors?
   - A) Health Insurance Portability and Accountability Act
   - **B) Community Mental Health Act of 1963**
   - C) Affordable Care Act
   - D) Professional Counselors Licensure Act

Professional Roles of Counselors

Counselors work with a variety of behavioral health care and human service systems. Although they recognize the importance of client-centered care, they also understand that other issues significantly influence a client's mental health.

For example, primary health care providers increasingly screen for mental illnesses like depression, anxiety, and post-traumatic stress disorder (PTSD). Early intervention improves client outcomes, so more counselors work with health systems as referral sources.

In addition, grief counselors in hospitals, hospices, and palliative care centers assist the families of people diagnosed with a terminal illness. Counselors also work with these systems as consultants and in collaborative teams. In addition, they collaborate and consult with education, criminal justice, and other social systems, including

- school systems,
- the juvenile justice system,
- the child protective services system,
- vocational rehabilitation, and
- the prison system.

In those cases, the counselor is a member of a team working to assist clients in achieving their goals. The counselor helps other team members by sharing information to provide more appropriate services to clients.

<Helpful Hint: For counselors to share any client information with a collaborative team, they must have written permission from the client. Counselors must also discuss with clients what is appropriate to share with the team.>

Counselors are instrumental in interdisciplinary community outreach and emergency management response teams. For instance, counselors might teach community organizations about the signs and symptoms of child abuse to increase awareness and instruct people what to do if they suspect a child is being abused. **Community outreach** efforts include

- prevention,
- education,
- training, and
- advocacy.

As part of **emergency management response** teams, counselors deliver psychological first aid to people affected by and responding to an emergency. These services are available on a short-term or long-term basis for people dealing with delayed reactions to the emergency.

The demand for qualified counselors increases in tandem with the need for therapeutic services. Counselors can expect to advocate for increased access to treatment. Additionally, the demand for substance use treatment counselors is projected to increase. Finally, there is a particular need for counselors of diverse racial, religious, ethnic, and cultural backgrounds.

Professional organizations help counselors progress in their careers. Counselors are provided with information, networking opportunities, and advocacy opportunities.

TABLE 1.1. Benefits of Professional Organizations

Information	Networking	Advocacy
important trends developments in research training continuing education	counselors researchers educators policymakers conventions volunteer opportunities	establish appropriate legal and ethical policies ensure that members provide service according to the organizational mission, values, and ethics

Networking connections are important for consultation resources, referral sources, and job seeking. Conventions, volunteering, and continuing education provide a connection to a larger purpose. Professional organizations are the main advocacy arm, working on behalf of professionals and the public to ensure ethical standards and values.

Many specialties within the counseling profession have their own professional organizations that address research, best practices, education, and advocacy within those specialty fields. Some examples of notable organizations follow:

- The **American Counseling Association (ACA)** is the largest organization for counselors.
- The **American Mental Health Counselors Association (AMHCA)** supports clinical mental health counselors.
- The **American School Counselor Association (ASCA)** serves school counselors.
- The **Association for Addiction Professionals (NAADAC)** supports addiction counselors and other addiction professionals.
- The **American Association for Marriage and Family Therapy (AAMFT)** and the **International Family Therapy Association (IFTA)** support marriage and family counselors.
- The **International Association for Correctional and Forensic Psychology (IACFP)** is for counselors who work with people convicted of crimes.
- The **American Rehabilitation Counseling Association (ARCA)** supports counselors who work in rehabilitation and with clients with disabilities.
- The **American College Counseling Association (ACCA)** supports counselors who specialize in higher education.

PRACTICE QUESTION

2. Which ethical and legal principle must counselors adhere to when collaborating with other providers, professionals, or systems?
   A) beneficence
   B) justice
   C) confidentiality
   D) verity

Specialty Areas in Counseling

All counseling education and training programs prepare professionals in areas of assessment, diagnosis, treatment, research, evidence-based practice, and care coordination in a variety of settings; however, many choose to **specialize** in one area or to provide care to specific populations.

Some of these specialties, such as addiction and marriage, couple, and family counseling, offer separate licenses depending on the state in which one works. For example, a professional counselor may be a licensed professional counselor and also holds an addiction counselor license and a marriage and family therapist license.

License offerings vary by state, and each carries its own set of education and training requirements. Many educational institutions offer specialty tracks for one or more specializations; however, earning a degree with that specialization does not automatically qualify one for a license within that specialization. The **Council for Accreditation of Counseling and Related Educational Programs (CACREP)** recognizes counseling specialties described in Table 1.2.

TABLE 1.2. CACREP-Recognized Counseling Specialties

Counseling Specialty	Description
Addiction counseling	offers services to people with substance use issues or behavioral addictions (e.g., gambling, eating, shopping)
Career counseling	helps determine appropriate career paths for clients through assessments; discusses clients' goals, values, and available resources; and determines attainable paths for clients to achieve their goals
Clinical mental health counseling	formerly known as mental health counseling and community counseling; focuses on the treatment of mental illness in a community or outpatient setting
Clinical rehabilitation counseling	helps clients with emotional, mental, behavioral, or developmental disabilities to thrive, achieve their goals, and improve their quality of life
Marriage, couple, and family counseling	addresses people and their relationships, especially those in marriages or romantic relationships and/or their families; uses a systems perspective to focus on the relationship; often considers the relationship as the actual client

Rehabilitation counseling	supports people with disabilities to help them achieve independence; works with a person's family, support system, and uses other relevant processes to assist clients
School counseling	provides students with mental health intervention; work in the school system and may also be involved in prevention and education programs that focus on mental health
Student affairs/college counselors	offer counseling services to college students; usually provide short-term counseling and maintain a referral network that students are sent to if they require long-term care; provide on-campus prevention and education programs that focus on mental health
Gerontological counseling	focuses on working with older adults and their families; also work with older adults with neurocognitive decline (e.g., dementia and Alzheimer's disease)
Counselor education and supervision	focuses on the next generation of counselors; professionals who become administrators, educators, and clinical supervisors and teach other counselors how to implement evidence-based best practices in their fields

PRACTICE QUESTION

3. Which counseling specialty focuses on working with relationships?
    A) rehabilitation counseling
    B) gerontological counseling
    C) counselor education and supervision
    D) marriage, couple, and family counseling

Professional Practice

Counselor-Client Relationship

The counselor in a treatment setting should demonstrate empathy while maintaining a level of clinical detachment. This is the basis for a therapeutic relationship.

The **therapeutic relationship** exists to benefit the client, not the counselor. Within a therapeutic relationship, the counselor

- limits self-disclosure;
- establishes boundaries with clients;
- focuses sessions on the client's treatment goals.

Building trust with a client in the therapeutic relationship involves

- honesty;
- empathy;

- boundaries;
- communication;
- client-led care.

In **client-led care**, clients set the agenda guided by the counselor. The counselor does not engage in coercive behaviors, such as forcing a client to participate in a particular type of therapy. Instead, the counselor explains the recommended therapies for a particular issue and allows clients to choose what will work best for them.

When clients present for treatment, they enter the therapeutic relationship with less power than the counselor. The counselor must be aware of this and equalize the power dynamic by consistently **monitoring the therapeutic relationship** and building trust as needed.

The counselor can use these techniques to monitor the therapeutic relationship:

- Determine how the client feels about the relationship and the therapy process by asking what is working and what else is needed.

Based on the answers, it may be necessary to reestablish a rapport with the client.

- Observe and assess the client's behaviors and nonverbal communication in session.

A client who starts to close up and become quiet may be losing trust in the counselor, and the counselor must call attention to the change and switch gears to reestablish trust. This might mean stopping the work of therapy and establishing common ground again.

- Provide standardized assessments to the client before a session at various intervals whereby the client can rate his interaction with the counselor.

Client rights and responsibilities are often listed in the mental health regulations of the state in which the counselor practices. These rights and responsibilities generally fall into the categories of high-quality care, client-centered practice, informed consent, confidentiality, and right to records.

High-quality care ensures that the client can expect prompt service from adequately trained professionals in an environment of physical and psychological safety.

- If the client feels she is not receiving high-quality care, she has the right to complain and request a referral to another provider.
- The client will not be subject to unnecessary or unending treatment.

In **client-centered practice**, the counselor must inform the client of all treatment options and allow him to choose his goals and treatment methods.

- The client has the right to ask questions about treatment, including methods and finances.

Clients must provide **informed consent** for treatment. To obtain informed consent, counselors must

- disclose to the client their training and expertise;
- explain how the counseling process works and what the client can expect;
- describe the boundaries of the therapeutic relationship.

Counselors may not conduct treatment interventions they are not trained for.

Clients have the right to a level of **confidentiality**. The counselor will keep the client's personal information confidential according to state and federal laws and explain to the client under what circumstances confidentiality may be broken.

Confidentiality is discussed in depth later in this chapter.

Clients have the **right to records**. The counselor should explain

- how sessions are documented;
- why sessions are documented;
- how clients can access their records.

Since many clients may not understand their records, counselors can go over the records with them.

Although this is usually covered in the first session, the counselor should make a practice of reminding clients of their rights periodically throughout therapy. The first session is usually stressful, so it is irresponsible to expect the client to remember everything that was said.

PRACTICE QUESTION

4. Which of the following BEST describes client-centered practice?
    A) A counselor tells a client how many sessions she will have.
    B) A client wants to focus on anxiety, so the counselor recommends therapeutic interventions.
    C) A client with depression asks the counselor to disregard his history of self-harm.
    D) A client asks to have ninety-minute sessions instead of the usual sixty-minute sessions.

Group Practice

In **group practice**, the therapeutic relationship between counselor and client changes. The "client" is the group as a whole, rather than each individual member.

Different types of group therapy have their own best practices; however, the general rule is that the primary mode of therapy is the interaction among group members and the counselor as the facilitator. Ultimately, group work focuses on the members working together.

The counselor clarifies how groups work at the first session as well as when new members join (if the group is an open one). The counselor explains her role as facilitator and helps establish group rules with the full participation of members.

The **counselor-client role in group therapy** is a little different than it is in individual therapy. The counselor establishes group work **expectations** like attendance requirements and other administrative policies set forth by the organization and state laws.

In group work, the counselor is required to maintain the confidentiality of the group members, but individual members are not bound by confidentiality rules. Therefore, it is up to the members to create a confidentiality agreement among themselves when establishing group rules.

Group rules (in group counseling) are most effective when the members both set and agree to them. While there may be organizational policies and state laws that apply to group work, members should set a majority of the working rules. These may address

- confidentiality;
- how group members should treat each other;
- the extent to which the members want the facilitator involved;
- whether someone can be removed from the group for disrespectful behavior.

The group should also discuss and agree on the process for member removal. Once the rules are established, they are usually posted in the room and revisited each time someone joins the group.

Termination criteria depend largely on the type of group:

- In **open-ended groups**, members come and go as they please; termination is not necessary.
- Curriculum-based or **closed groups** have a start and an end point, so termination occurs when the group curriculum is finished.

Another criterion for termination is the violation of group rules. If a member violates rules after agreeing to comply with them, she will be asked to leave. These situations should be documented.

> **HELPFUL HINT**
>
> Some groups are open-ended but require clients to attend a certain number of sessions. In these situations, termination occurs once the requirements are met.

PRACTICE QUESTION

5. It is the first session of a closed group therapy meeting. There will be fifteen sessions focusing on dealing with childhood trauma. The facilitator should do which of the following FIRST?

   A) explain to group members that any confidentiality breaches will lead to removal from the group and could result in legal actions

   B) ask group members to share their childhood trauma stories

   C) explain the differences between group and individual therapy and guide the group in creating rules

   D) invite the organization's administrator to the first group to explain the rules members must abide by

Policies and Procedures

The counselor is obliged to explain agency policies at the first session and any time these issues arise during the therapeutic relationship. This is typically done during the informed consent discussion.

Policies generally address

- attendance and appointments;
- payment;
- how the organization documents the counseling process;
- how a client's records will be used, how requests for records will be handled;
- how the organization approaches confidentiality;
- threats to self and others.

Additionally, the organization may have policies regarding working with children and adolescents, including sharing information with parents.

During the first session, the counselor should also explain counseling processes, procedures, risks, and benefits.

Counseling **processes** define the parameters of the relationship and include

- how many sessions the client can expect to attend;
- what methods the counselor will likely use;
- assessment, diagnosis, and treatment planning methods.

Counseling **procedures** address specific issues such as

- what the client should do if he cannot make an appointment;
- what happens if the client does not show up for an appointment;
- under what circumstances the counselor will terminate the relationship;
- under what circumstances the counselor will refer the client;
- what to do in case of a mental health emergency.

Counseling comes with risks and benefits. These should be explained to the client as part of informed consent.

TABLE 1.3. Risks and Benefits of Counseling

Risks of Counseling	Benefits of Counseling
• The client's symptoms may get worse before they improve.	• The client can cope with mental health symptoms.
• Current relationships with family or friends may change or end.	• The frequency and severity of the client's symptoms decrease.
• Therapeutic intervention may not be effective for the client.	• The client's quality of life and daily functioning improve.
• The counselor may not be appropriate for the client.	• The client's relationships improve.

PRACTICE QUESTION

6. A counselor is meeting with a client for the first time. The client appears distraught, saying he feels quite awful. He denies he is in crisis but feels he needs mental health treatment. Which of the following is an appropriate counselor response?

    A) welcome the client and immediately address his problems and concerns to make him feel better faster

    B) call a supervisor to assist with crisis management based on the observed behavior

    C) obtain informed consent, including reviewing policies and procedures, before beginning counseling

    D) explain the counselor's credentials and plan for helping the client

Accommodations

Clients with disabilities should be accommodated. Most health care organizations have policies and procedures in place to accommodate clients with disabilities. For instance, clients who are deaf, hard of hearing, blind, or who have low vision should be offered interpretation services or other assistance as appropriate. Whenever possible, the counselor should ask the client what his preferred method of communication is.

Cognitive impairments can often result from trauma or injury, like a stroke. In these cases, clients may not be able to speak due to motor impairments. Or they may have neurological conditions that prevent them from processing communication. The counselor should ask the client or the client's representative which method of communication works best and remain aware of changes in the client's cognitive status.

The **Americans with Disabilities Act (ADA)** prohibits discrimination against individuals determined to be disabled. The ADA defines disabilities to establish which individuals need to be protected under the law. These individuals must have a mental or physical impairment that substantially limits one or more major life activities. The person may have a record or history of such impairments or may be perceived by others, such as an employer, as having such limiting impairments.

Most compliance with the ADA is initiated at the organizational level. Still, counselors must adhere to the ADA in their physical practice by providing

- sufficient space for wheelchairs or other assistive devices;
- ADA-compliant furniture (can accommodate people of various weights and body types);
- materials in alternative formats if requested (large-print forms, for example);
- frequent breaks to support cognitive challenges.

Part of the assessment process will include asking the client if she requires any accommodations.

Persons with disabilities may require **accommodations** adjustments in their job duties or environment. Employers must provide these accommodations as long as they are reasonable and do not cause "undue hardship" to the employer, such as high expense or difficult installation.

Counselors may be called on to provide documentation of a client's disability.

> **HELPFUL HINT**
>
> It is a good idea to review with the client what information will be disclosed.

First, the counselor must get the client's written permission to share the information. The counselor must then limit documentation to issues covered within the counseling relationship.

If the client has cognitive challenges and the counselor has assessed the client for that, then the counselor can provide supportive documentation for that issue. However, if the client is requesting accommodation for a physical disability, the counselor cannot provide supporting documentation for the client's physical condition. The counselor could, however, provide information about how the physical disability impacts the client's mental health.

Language barriers can occur when a counselor does not speak the client's primary language or speaks it as a second language. Counselors who do not speak the client's language have options:

- The client brings someone he trusts to act as an interpreter. The interpreter will have to sign confidentiality forms.
- The counselor can use professional interpreting services. Many health care organizations have relationships with professional interpreting services. Being under contract, interpreting services agree to abide by HIPAA and confidentiality rules.

> **HELPFUL HINT**
>
> The counselor must always communicate with the client, not with the interpreter.

It is important for the client to feel comfortable with the interpreter. The counselor is responsible for checking in about this and ensuring that the client understands that he can ask for someone else.

Conducting counseling sessions with an interpreter present can be challenging for both the client and the counselor, so counselors may wish to undergo additional training on providing these services with compassion and empathy.

Distance counseling and **telemental health** are becoming an important part of counseling services. Two of the most significant issues in providing services this way are confidentiality and security.

> **HELPFUL HINT**
>
> In the spirit of client-centered practice, the client should choose the translation option.

Organizations that permit this type of interaction with clients often create organizational policies for how counselors may provide services and what methods are allowed. Part of the reason for these policies is that insurance companies will not pay for services conducted via certain media. For example, an insurance company may pay for counseling services delivered via a licensed and secure video therapy service but will not cover services provided via a counselor's personal phone or online messaging.

Technology-based services that facilitate distance counseling and telemental health include

- telephone;
- video chat;

- online messaging;
- texting.

The technology used for therapy must be secure, and clients must be informed that even though the counselor, the organization, and the technology provider are legally obligated to provide secure services, there is always the chance that security will be breached.

Another concern with distance counseling and telemental health is the risk associated with a client in crisis. In an office environment, clients in crisis can receive immediate care and therapeutic intervention, whereas if a client tells a counselor over the phone that she is considering harming herself or someone else, the counselor's intervention options are limited. Therefore, organizations need to have policies in place for how to deal with these situations.

Benefits of distance counseling and telemental health include the following:
- Clients can obtain therapy services at their convenience without having to travel to an office, thereby increasing accessibility.
- There will be fewer cancellations and no-shows.
- Clients can participate in therapy more frequently.

Risks of distance counseling and telemental health include
- data security breach;
- difficulty observing nonverbal communication;
- confidentiality of the client if there are other people in the client's location;
- challenges establishing a therapeutic relationship.

Although there are many benefits to providing distance counseling and telemental health, technology creates an additional barrier between the counselor and the client. Potential problems include
- difficulty establishing a therapeutic relationship;
- interference with accurate assessment;
- difficulty interpreting nonverbal communication.

Counselors who want to offer distance counseling and telemental health should pursue continuing education and training that will help reduce these potential problems.

PRACTICE QUESTION

7. A client gave a counselor permission to disclose confidential information when filling out a disability accommodation request form for his employer. The human resources director left the counselor a message requesting more information. What should the counselor do?

    A) obtain written consent from the client to speak to the human resources director and agree on what information the client will allow the counselor to share

- B) return the call to human resources to provide the needed information as quickly as possible
- C) call the client and let him know the counselor will be returning the call to human resources to answer these questions
- D) ignore the voicemail message and do not mention the call to the client

Advocacy

Counselors are in a unique position to advocate for professional and client issues. Because counselors are privy to the needs, causes, and consequences of mental health issues, that knowledge can be useful for public policy, health care policy, and prevention programs.

Professional advocacy may occur in several forms:

- lobbying for laws that protect the liability of counselors in client safety situations
- advocating for changes in licensure requirements
- asking for credentialing requirements for joining insurance panels

Counselors should join professional organizations to stay informed about issues pertaining to the profession.

Counselors advocate on behalf of clients to help them secure services. Advocating for a client's needs may include connecting them to a vocational rehab organization to help them find a job.

Counselors also advocate for clients on a broader social level. For example, counselors can be instrumental in advocating for public policy that increases client access to mental health services.

While advocacy is an honorable endeavor, a counselor advocating on behalf of clients must consider whether that advocacy is appropriate and ethical. If advocacy might result in a breach of confidentiality or create a dual relationship, then it may not be appropriate.

PRACTICE QUESTION

8. Which ethical issue must a counselor consider before advocating for a client?
    - A) amount of time required
    - B) whether the client issue is important
    - C) breach of confidentiality
    - D) the counselor's qualifications

Consultation and Self-Assessment

Self-Assessment

Counselors must continually **assess their competency to work with a specific client** through a process of self-awareness and objective evaluation. Choosing to work with a client when not qualified to do so violates professional ethics and could potentially harm the client.

- Counselors must be honest about the education and training they have received.
- Counselors should pursue continuing education and additional training to keep up with best practices.
- When meeting a client for the first time, counselors must objectively evaluate whether they are qualified to work with the client based on the client's presenting problem.

Being forthcoming about training and education usually applies to certain interventions with clients. For example, if a counselor has not received training and certification to perform EMDR, she must disclose this to a client requesting EMDR and offer another method of therapy or refer the client to someone who is trained.

Self-evaluation about competency to work with clients is more complicated. For example, if a client presents with severe addiction and the counselor is not trained in working with addiction, he must disclose that to the client and refer the client to someone who is qualified. Finally, consultation with a supervisor can help the counselor evaluate her effectiveness and competencies, including creating plans for professional development.

A prominent adage among counselors is, "When in doubt, consult." Counselors who work in community mental health clinics or organizations have access to an on-site supervisor, clinic director, or someone who acts as the senior counseling professional. **Supervision and consultation** are not just for inexperienced counselors; they provide support to all levels.

A counselor should seek supervision or consultation in specific situations:

- difficulties with client assessment, diagnosis, and treatment planning
- when a client's progress appears to stagnate
- when a client is in crisis
- when presented with an ethical situation
- when faced with a court order or other legal issue

A significant benefit of seeking supervision and consulting with a colleague when dealing with a client issue or an ethical issue is documented evidence that additional help was requested with an incident. In legal situations, this can act as a level of protection and ensure that proper procedures are followed.

When consulting with a supervisor or colleague within the organization that employs a counselor, client confidentiality should be honored, but those consultations tend to fall under the confidentiality exception that clients agree to in informed consent. Counselors in private practice who establish a consultation relationship with another colleague should also disclose to clients the potential for consultation and explain how the counselor will keep the client's information confidential.

Consultation and supervision should be limited to issues pertaining to the counseling process, not gossip or disclosure of client information that is not relevant to treatment.

PRACTICE QUESTION

9. Why is it inappropriate for a counselor to provide treatment using methods she has not been fully trained for?

    A) The client will not know to ask about the therapy.

    B) An untrained counselor could harm a client.

    C) The client will not receive any benefit from it.

    D) The counselor could make money from referring the client elsewhere.

Referrals

Not every client is appropriate for every counselor, and vice versa. A counselor should **provide a referral** in certain situations:

- The counselor does not have adequate training to work with the client's issues.
- The counselor and client cannot establish a productive therapeutic relationship.
- An ethical issue such as dual relationships precludes a counselor from working with a client.
- The counselor experiences an issue that would disrupt the client's treatment.
- The counselor is quitting, retiring, or otherwise leaving the organization or the profession.

When providing referrals, there are several **best practices** recommended for counselors:

- Give the client plenty of notice, if possible.
- Provide the client with several choices for other providers and offer to facilitate the transfer.
- Ask the client if he wants a joint session or a phone introduction with the new provider.
- Ask the client if she wants the counselor to give the provider information about her; if so, discuss what information to share.

A counselor should **provide information to third parties** as required by law. These generally include

- insurance companies;
- health care professionals;
- legal guardians.

Information provided to insurance companies and other health care professionals is regulated under state law and HIPAA, with those policies outlined in the informed consent.

A counselor should share the minimum amount of information necessary to honor the confidentiality of the client. For example, to get reimbursement for services rendered, the counselor may need to disclose the diagnosis and treatment plan objectives to an insurance company. However, the counselor should not include process notes that include intimate details of the client's session. Those are not required to secure payment and should therefore remain confidential.

Within the comprehensive care model, organizations often encourage counselors to consult with a client's physician or case manager. This should be discussed with the client and included in the informed consent discussion. When the counselor shares information with other members of the care team, she should let the client know when and what information was disclosed. For example, for court-mandated clients, the court usually requests reports of the client's progress in treatment. This may include attendance records and progress toward goals, but it should be limited to required information only.

When the counselor provides services to a client with a legal guardian, he may be required to disclose some information to the guardian. Again, that information should be limited. The counselor should discuss disclosure of other information with the client and receive permission to disclose it; then the information can be shared in the client's presence.

For example, an adolescent client may not want the full extent of her substance use shared with her parents. The counselor is not required by law to tell them, but he feels it would be therapeutic for the client and the family. The counselor may rehearse the disclosure with the client and then facilitate a family session where the adolescent discloses the substance use to the parents. However, it is not the counselor's responsibility to tell the parents unless required to do so by law. Doing so without the client's consent could damage the therapeutic relationship and harm the client.

PRACTICE QUESTION

10. A counselor has been working with a client weekly for six months. The counselor is diagnosed with an illness that will require him to leave work for at least three months. Which action should the counselor take?
    A) assure the client that he can keep up with weekly sessions
    B) coordinate with the client and refer her to another counselor
    C) tell the client that the counselor will be out for three months and will contact the client when he returns
    D) have the receptionist cancel the client's appointments and schedule with another counselor

Self-Care

Being a counselor can be a challenging, stressful job. Counselors often work with clients who are dealing with illness, death, or financial hardship. The emotional toll of managing these clients can be immense.

At the same time, counselors may also have to navigate complex systems like hospitals, insurance companies, and government agencies. The impact of these stressful situations cannot be underestimated.

> **DID YOU KNOW?**
>
> Counselors cannot serve clients well if they are not taking good care of themselves. In fact, counselors who do not practice self-care become more at risk of harming their clients either through ignorance or negligence.

Because of these strains, counselors should not overlook their own **self-care**. The first step in practicing self-care is practicing **self-awareness**. Understanding one's limits and the signs of strain can let the counselor know when it's appropriate to engage in self-care.

Counselors who work with clients who have experienced traumatic events are subject to **secondary trauma**, a condition that mimics the symptoms of PSTD. Although less severe than PTSD, secondary trauma interferes with the counselor's ability to function. Furthermore, when stress is left unattended for too long, counselors can suffer from burnout. **Burnout** is one of the primary reasons counselors leave the profession.

Signs of exhaustion, stress, and burnout can include the following:

- increased anxiety
- worrying about clients after hours
- taking work home
- difficulty concentrating
- sleep disturbances
- emotional lability
- social isolation
- increased irritability

Counselors should develop proactive practices for self-care and self-awareness. This may include regularly scheduled activities to promote health and happiness. There are many ways a counselor can fulfill the goal of being healthy and happy:

- routine exercise
- eating a well-balanced diet
- getting adequate sleep
- enjoying hobbies
- relaxing
- spending time with friends and family
- refraining from overuse of alcohol or other substances

The counselor should also set physical and emotional boundaries with clients and be willing to ask for assistance when confronted with unmanageable tasks. A crucial boundary for counselors is the one between work and personal life. While counselors should check in with themselves, it is also recommended that counselors in an agency setting check in with each other. Counselors should also talk with spouses, partners, or family members about signs of stress and let them know how to point out those signs when they notice them. Sometimes others will notice the signs of stress before the counselor does.

PRACTICE QUESTION

11. A positive, proactive method for managing stress and burnout in counseling might include which of the following?

    A) scheduling lunch away from the office and leaving work right at closing time

    B) taking on as many clients as possible to keep busy

    C) talking to colleagues about stressful clients

    D) refusing to work with difficult or complex clients

Documentation

In counseling, if something is not documented, it did not happen. Therefore, counselors must create and maintain documentation appropriate for each aspect of the counseling process in compliance with state law, for insurance reimbursement, and to document client progress.

Creating and Maintaining Documentation

The counselor is responsible for maintaining accurate, objective documentation of the client's care. Accurate documentation has obvious benefits for the client's care, but it is also important for the counselor. Counselors can use accurate, timely documentation to prove they have complied with standards of care and practice, which is important for professional advancement and a possible legal defense. Counselors should

- only document facts; opinions do not belong in the official documentation;
- record details of the client visit as soon as possible after the visit;
- always record if the client agrees or refuses case management, interventions, or other types of care;
- record all communication with people or organizations involved in the client's care, including the client's family, medical providers, employer, and insurance companies;
- document the care plan, including assessments, interventions, evaluations, and the outcomes of each;
- document all instances of consultation about the client with supervisors and colleagues, including what was discussed and with whom, and recommendations;
- document modifications of the care plan, the rationale for the changes, and whether the client agreed;
- include all legal documents, including advance directives and informed consent forms;
- document discharge plans and client education.

Many organizations require documentation and regular review by the clinic director to ensure compliance with state law.

There are two types of notes taken by the counselor that are added to the client's documentation.

Progress notes are the official record of a session and tend to follow a **SOAP note** format:

- **S**ubjective information about the client and what she is experiencing
- **O**bjective findings from assessments or observation
- **A**ssessments that includes findings of the client's diagnosis or evaluations of how the client is progressing in the treatment plan
- **P**lans that includes next steps, both therapeutic and otherwise

Progress notes may be shared with others:

- Insurance companies receive progress notes when determining reimbursement.
- Progress notes may be included in client records requests from other providers.
- Progress notes are subject to inspection by agency quality control personnel and government regulators.

When clients request a copy of their records, these are the notes that are included. When the courts request records, these are the notes that are subject to a subpoena.

The second type of notes, **process notes**, are considered a counselor's private notes. Process notes are not required to be part of the client's official record. Process notes generally include

- hypotheses;
- theories;
- the counselor's thoughts regarding client treatment;
- questions to address during supervision.

Process notes are considered privileged and are not generally accessible to the client or other parties except in certain circumstances:

- If a client is involved in a legal action, it is possible that the counselor's records, notes, and documentation will be shared with the court.
- When a counselor leaves an agency, the documentation stays with the agency; the counselor's notes will influence how future providers interact with that client.

Not all counselors use process notes. Still, counselors should consider the impact of every piece of documentation on the client. There are certain times when the counselor should **review client records:**

HELPFUL HINT

When writing progress notes, keep them clinical and focused on the client's treatment plan.

- When starting with a new client, reviewing his records can provide relevant historical information about his issues. These can be requested as part of the intake process or by asking the client to bring the records to the first session.

- When taking a referral from another counselor, the client's records can be helpful for understanding which therapeutic interventions worked and which did not. These can be requested as part of the referral process.

- During a quarterly review process, often required by state law or for funding purposes, client records are subject to review. For example, many agencies that provide substance abuse treatment services must conduct client reviews every thirty or sixty days to determine the client's progress in treatment. It is also considered best practice to review client records quarterly to determine if the present course of treatment is appropriate, to evaluate client engagement, and to ensure that documentation is compliant with state law.

- Before discharging a client, the records must be reviewed to create a discharge summary.

PRACTICE QUESTION

12. A client with severe anxiety frequently talks about other people in session, especially his family members, because he believes his anxiety is all their fault. Which of the following would be included in a well-written progress note?

    A) the counselor's observations of the client's anxiety symptoms
    B) specific unpleasant remarks made by the client's mother to him
    C) actions the client's brother takes to bully him
    D) what the client said about his last counselor

Payment, Fees, and Insurance Benefits

Counselors should be aware of payment, fee, and insurance benefit issues. Agencies and clinics generally have staff or departments to address these issues. It is best practice to allow the administrative staff to handle billing and insurance so that any challenges do not infringe on the therapeutic relationship.

However, a counselor must be aware of the policies governing care to be able to answer questions and navigate the treatment process. For instance:

- Insurance providers decide how many sessions of therapy are appropriate for a particular diagnosis.
    - If therapy is going to take longer than originally planned, the counselor must request authorization for more sessions.
    - The counselor must submit documentation in support of that request.

- Payments, fees, and insurance benefits also determine session length, frequency, and mode of delivery.
  - Some insurance companies cover forty-five-minute sessions; others allow sixty-minute sessions.
  - Counselors should be aware that an insurance provider will only pay for the determined amount of time. This may affect how many clients they can see in a day as well as how long a session might be.
  - A counselor usually cannot bill an insurance company for services provided outside of established parameters.
- Insurance companies do not reimburse counselors for the time it takes to complete documentation.
- Some insurance companies will not provide reimbursement for therapies that are not evidence based; some even list which therapeutic interventions are acceptable.
  - During the credentialing process, counselors must disclose to the insurance company which methods of therapeutic intervention they have received training for.
- The insurance company may also dictate the mode of service delivery that is acceptable for reimbursement.
  - Some insurance companies will not reimburse counselors for unscheduled telephone sessions or home visits.
  - Counselors must know what they are allowed to do based on the client's insurance benefits.

 DID YOU KNOW?
If counselors provide therapy they are not trained to do, the insurance company can refuse to provide reimbursement.

PRACTICE QUESTION

13. What is a clinically relevant reason a counselor must pay attention to the client's insurance provider?
    A) to explain the client's health care benefits to them
    B) to determine whether the counselor wants to work with the client
    C) to understand how many sessions the company will pay for
    D) to act as intermediary between the insurance company and agency administration

Health Care Laws and Legislation

Counselors should be familiar with the important elements of several pieces of health care legislation.

The **Affordable Care Act (ACA)**, popularly known as "Obamacare," changed behavioral health care coverage. Key elements of the ACA include the following:

- Insurance companies cannot deny coverage due to a preexisting condition or charge more because of the condition or based on gender.
- Adults who cannot obtain health insurance through a job may remain on their parents' policies until the age of twenty-six.

- Essential health benefits must be covered. These include
  - mental health;
  - substance use disorders.

Congress passed the **Health Insurance Portability and Accountability Act (HIPAA)** in 1996. HIPAA allows workers to continue or transfer health coverage when they change or lose a job. HIPAA also focuses on how health care information is handled.

The HIPAA Privacy Rule and the Security Rule, developed by the Department of Health and Human Services, protects the privacy and security of certain health care information. This **protected health information (PHI)** includes

- demographic information, such as name, address, phone numbers, SSN;
- information included in the medical record;
- payment history.

The counselor must follow HIPAA privacy and security policies. PHI must be safeguarded, released, and disposed of in the manner described by HIPAA. Only personnel who require clients' PHI should have access to that information for treatment or administrative purposes, such as billing and scheduling.

When medical records are no longer needed (a period usually specified by state regulations), they must be destroyed so the information cannot be retrieved.

PHI can only be released under specific circumstances:

- A **Privacy Rule Authorization form** must be signed by the client.
  - This form allows the provider to release information to the parties included in the form.
- Clients may also authorize the provider to release their PHI to others, usually family members.
- PHI can be shared within the health care team only when it is considered relevant to treatment.
  - PHI should not be shared with anyone not directly involved in the client's care.

Counselors may also need to share PHI with outside government agencies:

- State law specifies that the practitioner must warn authorities if harm (exploitation or abuse, for example) to the client is suspected.
- If counselors are aware of HIPAA violations and do not report them, they and the organization at fault can be held liable.

Annual HIPAA training is a component of most mental health providers. This ensures that faxing, internet communications, and phone delivery of clients' health care records, including personal notes and billing, are properly handled.

The **Mental Health Parity and Addiction Equity Act (MHPAEA)** was enacted in 2008 to fill in the gaps in the Mental Health Parity Act of 1996 (MHPA). According to the MHPAEA:

HELPFUL HINT

HIPAA's Security Rule establishes rules pertaining to the transfer of electronic records. The Privacy Rule sets national standards for the protection of health care information.

- Insurance plans that offer mental health care benefits must manage them as they manage medical/surgical benefits.
  - The insurance company cannot place limits on mental health benefits that it does not place on medical/surgical benefits.
  - These rules also apply to substance use disorders.
- The MHPAEA specifies limitations on how insurance companies can cover mental health and substance use disorder benefits.

Agencies or counselors who provide services to clients with substance abuse issues must also abide by **42 CFR Part 2,** a federal law that offers strict confidentiality rules for clients with substance use disorders. It was originally written for agencies that receive federal funding to provide substance abuse treatment only, and those organizations and providers are not allowed to acknowledge that a person is a client at the organization.

In agencies and organizations that provide both mental health and substance abuse treatment, it is best practice to include the privacy provisions of 42 CFR Part 2 as part of the confidentiality policies.

DID YOU KNOW?

Not every health insurance plan was required to offer mental health benefits under the MHPAEA. However, the ACA has greatly extended insurance plan coverage and lists mental health care as an essential health benefit.

PRACTICE QUESTION

14. Which of the following is MOST likely a violation of HIPAA?
    A) using a password to log onto a shared computer
    B) shredding records when they are expired
    C) accessing the mental health record of a client's parents
    D) faxing the results of an assessment to a client's primary care provider

Electronic Health Records

The **Health Information Technology for Economic and Clinical Health (HITECH) Act** was written to encourage the use of electronic health records (EHRs) and related technology. The Centers for Medicare and Medicaid Services (CMS) have several objectives for using EHRs:

- Electronic exchanges of summary of care: An **exchange of summary of care** (also referred to as a discharge summary) refers to the movement of a client from one setting to another. For example, the exchange of summary of care is used when a client is discharged from an inpatient to an outpatient facility.
- There is greater ease of sharing records with supervisors and other members of a client's care team.
- Documentation compliance is improved.
- Clients can access an online portal to check on appointments and reminders.

PRACTICE QUESTION

15. A provider wishes to use electronic health records. Which objective BEST helps to eliminate gaps in care?

- A) reporting specific cases
- B) structured electronic transmission of laboratory test results
- C) use of electronic prescriptions
- D) electronic exchanges of summary of care

Ethics

Ethics and the Counselor

Ethics are moral principles, values, and duties. Whereas laws are enforceable regulations set forth by the government, ethics are moral guidelines established and formally or informally enforced by peers, the community, and professional organizations. Ethics include norms and duties.

Norm is short for *normal*, a term used for a behavior or conduct that is valued and usually expected. Norms are also often described as aspirational ethical principles because they are not enforceable by law, but counselors aspire to the highest ethical standards to maintain trust between the public and their profession.

Duties are commitments or obligations to act in an ethical and moral manner. These fall under the minimum ethical standards and are usually part of the state regulations. Counselors can be held legally accountable for violating ethical standards.

Core ethical principles include autonomy, beneficence, nonmaleficence, justice, veracity, and fidelity:

- **Autonomy** is acknowledging that a client is a unique individual with the right to her own opinions, values, beliefs, and perspectives.
- **Beneficence** describes acting with the intent of doing the right thing or the most good. The counselor has an obligation to act in the best interest of the client, regardless of other competing interests.
- **Nonmaleficence** describes the intent to do no harm. This principle addresses the counselor's responsibility to keep the client from harm in the care setting.
- **Justice** can be considered fairness. The counselor should be fair to clients in counseling matters and regarding administrative issues.
- **Veracity** is the practice of complete truthfulness with clients and families.
- **Fidelity** concerns honoring promises or commitments made to a client.

The National Board for Certified Counselors (NBCC) has a Code of Ethics. A **code of ethics** is a statement of the expected behaviors of its members. This code may also set standards and disciplinary actions for violations, including suspension, censure, fines, or expulsion.

Some key elements of the NBCC Code of Ethics follow:

- Counselors must take appropriate action to prevent harm.
- Counselors may only provide services they are qualified for.
- Counselors should promote the welfare of clients, students, and those individuals they supervise or provide services to.
- Counselors must communicate truthfully.
- Counselors should recognize that their behavior reflects on the counseling profession, and avoid damaging actions accordingly.
- Counselors should encourage the participation of clients, students, or supervisees, and recognize the importance of supervision.
- Counselors are accountable for their actions and should adhere to professional standards and practices.

If a counselor has an ethical concern, she is encouraged to contact the NBCC for advice.[1]

When addressing ethical concerns with a client case, the counselor should consult with a supervisor or colleague and document the ethical decision-making process in the client's record.

> **DID YOU KNOW?**
> Counselors are expected to hold each other accountable for professional ethics and are obligated to report violations.

PRACTICE QUESTION

16. A client tells the counselor that he wants to try EMDR to work on anxiety. The counselor is not trained in EMDR. What should the counselor do?

   A) refer the client to a qualified practitioner
   B) suggest avoiding EMDR and instead focus on techniques the counselor is trained in
   C) explain that EMDR will be discussed later in treatment
   D) ask her supervisor for guidance

Nonmaleficence

Nonmaleficence is the principle of not doing harm. It requires counselors to consider the impact of their actions (and inaction).

The potential for nonmaleficence in counseling includes referrals. A counselor should refer a client to another provider if

- the client's treatment progress seems stagnant;
- the counselor does not have the expertise to treat the client's particular condition.

A counselor might have good intentions in wanting to continue working with the client, but by not referring the client, he is harming her: another counselor might be able to help the client progress through her issues more quickly.

1. NBCC Code of Ethics, https://www.nbcc.org/Assets/Ethics/NBCCCodeofEthics.pdf

Another example of nonmaleficence application in clinical practice is hospitalization, especially **mandatory psychiatric treatment**. Some states have a provision that stipulates a person can be committed to a psychiatric facility against his will for a minimum period, often seventy-two hours, if he presents a danger to himself or others. While this may sound like a positive action to save someone's life, it must be considered whether that forced commitment will harm the client.

If a client shows signs of suicidality, proactive measures such as developing a crisis plan can be instrumental in providing the client with the help she needs without resorting to a potentially traumatic experience.

In any type of ethical dilemma, a counselor needs to balance state laws and agency policies with the principles of beneficence and nonmaleficence. Consultation and documentation are vital in these situations for reasons noted previously.

PRACTICE QUESTION

17. A client presents for therapy with a medium risk for suicide. Although a crisis situation is not imminent, the client may experience a crisis at some point. A counselor practicing nonmaleficence would do which of the following?

- **A)** work with the client to develop a crisis plan that includes family and friends for social support
- **B)** explain to the client that any crisis situation will land him in the psychiatric hospital
- **C)** avoid discussing the problem until the client actually experiences a crisis
- **D)** continue with therapy interventions and do not discuss suicide any further

Dual Relationships

The clinical therapeutic relationship requires the counselor to refrain from any type of **dual relationship** with clients. A dual relationship is when the counselor has both a counseling relationship with the client and a relationship outside the clinical setting.

Avoiding dual relationships reduces the chance of a counselor exploiting a client or conveying the perception of power and authority. For example, if a counselor has any type of personal relationship with a client outside of the treatment setting, it is unethical for her to provide services to that client. In general, counselors should avoid

- any sexual or romantic relationship with former or current clients;
- a counseling relationship with someone with whom the counselor had a previous sexual or romantic relationship.

Any counselor who becomes aware of another counselor engaged in dual relationships or of sexual harassment or exploitation is obligated to follow procedures for reporting the legal and ethical violation.

A dual relationship can also apply to business relationships. In some states, business relationships are permissible with clients; however, these relationships

HELPFUL HINT

The NBCC Code of Ethics states that a counselor cannot engage in a dual relationship with a client for two years following the termination of a counseling relationship. However, state laws and regulations may have longer timelines. It is the counselor's responsibility to know and follow those laws.

are still unethical. For example, if a client is a carpenter and the counselor needs work done on her home, it is unethical to hire that client as a carpenter. Business relationships such as these have the potential for exploitation and the expectation of favors.

PRACTICE QUESTION

18. A client comes to therapy but explains that he does not have the money to pay for therapy. He has a house-cleaning business and offers to trade services by cleaning the counselor's house and office in exchange for therapy. How should an ethical counselor respond?

    A) accept the offer of trading services

    B) accept the offer but limit the trade to cleaning the office

    C) decline the offer

    D) explain the law to the client and refer them to a clinic that offers free mental health services

Privacy

In the age of social media, privacy is of particular concern for counselors and clients. Clients may share personal information in a public forum, but it is unethical for a counselor to use social media, technology, or other resources to find information about clients without their written permission.

Social media privacy is also appropriate to address in group therapy. Group members may have access to information about other members. Group rules should stress not only the importance of confidentiality but also of privacy.

Counselors consulting with supervisors or other care team members about the client should consider the client's privacy and only provide information relevant to his treatment plan.

Counselors should also avoid accepting gifts from clients except in cases of cultural significance or therapeutic significance. Gift exchanges can create confusion about the nature of the therapeutic relationship, and the counselor needs to consider that as well as the impact that nonacceptance could have on the client's well-being.

HELPFUL HINT

If the counselor decides it is appropriate to accept a gift, the reasoning should be documented.

PRACTICE QUESTION

19. When is it acceptable for a counselor to look up a client's social media presence?

    A) when a client is mandated to treatment by the judicial system

    B) not acceptable; constitutes an invasion of privacy

    C) before the first session so the counselor can get to know the client

    D) if a client makes comments in session that make the counselor uncomfortable

Consent

Client **consent** is required for treatment. A client must provide **informed consent** for a counselor to perform a treatment or procedure, or if she is going to take part in a research study.

For informed consent to be valid, the counselor must cover key elements:
- description of procedures
- risks
- benefits
- alternatives

The counselor must also assess **client competency** to provide informed consent. A competent client understands
- the procedure or practice;
- the risk and benefits involved;
- possible consequences.

Finally, the client must acknowledge having provided consent. Most states have regulations for practices that include having a signed informed consent form for each client.

State regulations vary regarding the age of consent. The age of consent to sign informed consent forms ranges from fourteen to sixteen. Regardless of the legal age of consent, a good way to establish trust with adolescent clients or with clients unable to provide legal consent for themselves is to gain the client's assent for treatment. Obtaining **assent** means
- going through the entire informed consent process with the client;
- explaining the role of the counselor;
- making sure the client understands the therapeutic process
- ensuring that the client agrees to participate freely.

Obtaining assent helps establish trust with clients and engages them in the therapeutic process. This can be especially powerful for those who may feel they are being coerced into treatment.

 DID YOU KNOW?
Informed consent forms may need to be updated once per year to remain valid.

PRACTICE QUESTION

20. While obtaining informed consent is required by law, obtaining assent is not. Why is it a good idea to obtain assent anyway?

   A) Clinic administrators want documentation that everyone involved in therapy has signed the proper forms.

   B) Parents will probably not tell their children what the process of therapy will include.

   C) Even if clients are not of legal age to consent, it is important to the therapeutic relationship that they understand the process and agree to participate.

   D) It protects the counselor from future legal action.

 HELPFUL HINT
To obtain assent, many counselors use a form similar to the informed consent form.

Confidentiality

Confidentiality means that the counselor will keep the client's personal information confidential according to state and federal law. The counselor must also explain to the client when and under what circumstances confidentiality may be broken. In general, confidentiality requires that counselors must not disclose client information to anyone not authorized by the client.

Confidentiality is a vital aspect of the counseling relationship and is protected not only by professional ethics but also by law.

There are several **limits to confidentiality** that are usually explained in writing in the informed consent process:

- Client information will be shared with clinic personnel for record-keeping and billing purposes.
- Client information may be shared with a clinical supervisor or colleague for the purposes of consultation for the benefit of the client.
- Client records may need to be included in state or federal auditing procedures.
- Client information may be shared if the client expresses a desire to hurt themselves or someone else.
- Client records may be shared in the case of a medical emergency.
- Records may be shared if the client discloses that she has experienced abuse or that she perpetrated abuse that falls under the requirements of mandated reporting.
- If the client brings someone else to the session and grants the counselor permission to waive confidentiality, client information may be shared.
- A court order may require a counselor to break confidentiality.

Counselors should abide by the principle of sharing the least amount of information needed to get the job done. Furthermore, it is best practice that any breaches of confidentiality be shared with the client either before or immediately after the breach, including what information was shared. Also, the counselor should document the incident, along with the personal information disclosed, in the client's records.

Social media and electronic communication should be considered risks for confidentiality breaches. Information posted on social media is not private, as the platform owners can access a person's data at any time. Therefore, counselors should be careful what they post about themselves on social media.

Some counselors use social media as a professional referral opportunity that includes a business page with how to contact them. However, connecting with clients as friends on social media is unethical. Also, communication with clients via social media is not recommended due to the confidentiality risks.

It is not ethical for counselors to look up clients on social media to learn more about them. Electronic communication may be used for setting appointments, but it is recommended to only use electronic communications for therapeutic purposes if that is part of an agency's protocols for conducting telehealth or distance counseling.

Communicating with clients on social media outside of the counseling relationship would ethically be considered a dual relationship unless it is conducted outside of the legal time allotted. States set the rules about this period; in some cases, a counselor may have to wait two to five years before engaging in a dual relationship with a client, and that includes social media friendships.

PRACTICE QUESTION

21. A client collapses during a therapy session, and the counselor needs to call an ambulance. Since this is an emergency, what can the counselor reveal to the emergency medical personnel?

- **A)** the client's history of childhood sexual abuse and how it causes significant distress
- **B)** the reasons why the client is in therapy
- **C)** no information because he does not have permission from the client
- **D)** the client's name, how the client collapsed in session, and any physical conditions that may have contributed to the collapse

Legal Aspects of Counseling

Counselors are vulnerable to legal action. There are multiple situations that may result in legal system involvement, including

- disability evaluations;
- workers' compensation evaluations;
- workplace accommodations;
- school accommodations for children;
- custody disputes;
- divorce disputes;
- abuse and neglect cases of children, adults, people with disabilities, or older adults;
- use of therapeutic interventions that are not evidence-based or are unlawful;
- criminal cases involving mental illness or substance abuse;
- duty to warn cases;
- complaints against a counselor to the licensing board.

Counselors must be aware of and understand

- state laws;
- regulations;
- standards of care;
- agency policies;
- the differences between subpoenas and court orders in their state;
- the procedure for responding to subpoenas and court orders.

Consistent supervision and consultation on client cases and thorough documentation of this help protect the counselor by showing that she followed policy and regulations. Counselors should seek advice from a supervisor or legal representative in these cases. Agencies usually have policies for handling these situations, but legal requirements will determine how a counselor must respond to requests for information by attorneys.

Not every state requires a counselor to provide records to a subpoena. Furthermore, when presented with a request for client records by someone within the legal system, it is important to discuss this with the client and document what and how the information was shared.

Therefore, two rules of best practice apply to protect counselors in legal situations:

1. If it is not documented, it never happened.
2. Consult, consult, consult.

Many clients are referred for treatment by courts or systems affiliated with the courts. For example, child protective services may require that families or individuals engage in services. Also, mental health courts and drug court programs are becoming more widespread as incarceration diversion efforts. In these cases, there are special considerations for documentation requirements and sharing information with the courts and the rest of the client's care team.

Counselors should take extra care during the informed consent process to not only meet the needs of the referring system but also protect the privacy and confidentiality of the client to preserve the therapeutic relationship.

DID YOU KNOW?

Complaints against a counselor can be made against both the agency and the individual counselor, including HIPAA violations. Therefore, counselors should carry professional liability insurance to protect their interests. They should not rely on their employer to do so.

PRACTICE QUESTION

22. A counselor has been working with an adult client for several months. Without warning, the counselor receives a letter from an attorney working on behalf of the client's spouse, requesting the client's mental health records. What should the counselor do?

    A) send the attorney a letter clarifying which records are being requested

    B) consult with a supervisor or legal representative to determine the next steps

    C) ask the client what the attorney's purpose is in requesting the records

    D) fax a copy of the client's records to the attorney

Answer Key

1. B

    To gain public trust, the Community Mental Health Act of 1963 moved care for mental health from a hospital-based medicalized mental health system to community-based mental health centers and required professionals to be qualified and competent.

2. C

    If counselors are sharing information, they must obtain written permission from clients and maintain client confidentiality.

3. D

    While all specialties of counseling work with relationships to some degree, the marriage, couple, and family therapy specialty specifically focuses on relationships from a family systems perspective.

4. B

    In client-led care, counselors provide guidance, but clients determine the agenda.

5. C

    The counselor's role is group facilitator—the group is the client. Therefore, the counselor needs to guide the group in establishing rules of conduct not otherwise covered.

6. C

    Although the client demands immediate help, he is not in crisis. The counselor can offer the client empathy and understanding about his needs, but before offering help, the counselor is obligated to obtain informed consent. Part of that informed consent is explaining policies and procedures so the client can make an informed decision about whether he wants to proceed.

7. A

    The counselor may only speak or disclose information to other parties after receiving written permission from the client; otherwise, it is a breach of both confidentiality and the Health Insurance Portability and Accountability Act (HIPAA). If the client only provided written permission for the counselor to fill out a form, the counselor must receive written permission to talk to the human resources director, as it is a separate instance of sharing the client's personal information. Some states and organizations also require counselors to discuss with their clients what information will be disclosed and why. Even when it is not required, this is considered best practice to maintain trust between the client and the counselor.

8. C

    Advocating on behalf of a client might risk breaching the client's confidentiality.

9. B

    Without proper training in a given technique, there is a significant risk that the counselor will inadvertently harm a client.

10. B

    When a counselor will be unavailable for any length of time, it is best practice to refer the client to another provider to continue the same level of care.

11. A

    Proactive boundaries and time away from clients can help counselors balance work stress and life.

12. A

    Progress notes include objective observations of the client's symptoms and progress through treatment. While the other items may influence the client's symptoms, the details are not relevant to the treatment progress. Instead, a counselor might note "client's anxiety increases due to mom's verbal taunts."

13. C

    Insurance companies often dictate the number of sessions they will cover.

14. C

    Under the Health Insurance Portability and Accountability Act (HIPAA), counselors are not allowed to access the medical records of people they are not providing care for.

15. D

    Electronic exchanges of summary of care improve coordination of care.

16. A

    The counselor is not trained in the technique the client wants to try, so she should offer to refer him to a qualified practitioner. Practicing EMDR with the client would violate the NBCC's Code of Ethics, which says that counselors may only provide services they are qualified for. It also violates the principles of veracity, nonmaleficence, and justice. Postponing the conversation (Option C) could also cause harm by preventing the client from accessing the treatment sooner. The counselor should not need to ask her supervisor for advice; she should understand these ethical principles.

17. A

   Counselors understand the risk associated with suicidality and the potential for a traumatic experience in mandatory psychiatric treatment. So, a counselor practicing nonmaleficence will work with the client to create a crisis plan that will help mitigate a crisis without requiring mandatory hospitalization.

18. D

   While the counselor should decline the offer, an ethical counselor would explain the conflict related to dual relationships and refer the client to a clinic that offers free services.

19. B

   It is unethical for a counselor to use social media, technology, or other resources to find information about a client without his written permission.

20. C

   Obtaining assent from underage clients makes them feel part of the process, helps them understand the counselor's role and how therapy will work, and establishes trust with the counselor.

21. D

   In a medical emergency, the counselor may reveal confidential information about the client, but only enough to help the emergency medical personnel do their job. Therefore, the client's name, a description of how she collapsed, and any known physical conditions that could impact her medical treatment are appropriate to disclose. Following the incident, the counselor should document the incident, including what was disclosed in the client's record, and share this information when the client is stabilized.

22. B

   The client's confidentiality and privacy are paramount. Depending on state law and agency policy, the counselor may not be required to turn over any records. Counselors should always consult with a supervisor or legal representative and document the consultation before taking action.

2 Social and Cultural Diversity

Multicultural Counseling

Multicultural Issues

Culture refers to the collective behaviors and beliefs that are characteristic of a particular group, be they ethnic, social, or religious. Culture includes the shared values, language, and religion of the people living in a location or region. It also includes how people feed, clothe, and shelter themselves. Shared traits include

- norms of behavior (greetings and interactions on a day-to-day level);
- values (the moral beliefs and codes that guide a culture's textual and subtextual behavior);
- language (cultural communication, including through formal language, slang, and colloquialisms).

Some cultures view the rest of the world through the lens of **ethnocentrism**, the belief that one's culture is superior to others, and those other cultures are judged by the former's values and assumptions. **Cultural bias** is a phenomenon whereby a person's worldview is informed by his own culture, and he therefore perceives the rest of the world through that lens.

Cultural bias impacts interpersonal relationships, including therapeutic relationships, especially when it comes to practicing nonjudgment and empathy. Competent counselors will practice self-awareness regarding their cultural biases and take steps to reduce these so they do not interfere with the therapeutic relationships they have with clients. Additionally, cultural bias can influence a counselor's diagnosis of a client because it provides a lens through which the counselor views a client's behavior, thereby preventing the counselor from seeing the client's concerns through her own unique experiences.

Multicultural issues play a significant role in mental health and can affect

- the way people think about mental health issues;
- the causes for mental health issues;
- seeking treatment;

 HELPFUL HINT

Cultural bias is evident in research: most psychological research has been conducted using White, middle-class participants. Therefore, the results do not reflect or apply to the experiences of people of other populations.

- appropriate diagnosis and treatment;
- recovery;
- a client's preferences for and expectations of a counselor.

Culture can impact internal and external stigma related to mental health. Cultural issues also influence family relationships, friendships, and social support networks, and define what constitutes socially acceptable behavior. Counselors must educate themselves about the potential multicultural issues they may encounter with clients. A culturally competent counselor asks clients about their own cultural perspectives and understands how important cultural perspectives are to them.

HELPFUL HINT

In some cases, a counselor must be prepared to acknowledge that a client would be better served by working with another counselor who is more able to meet the client's cultural needs.

PRACTICE QUESTION

1. Self-reflection and seeking knowledge about multicultural issues can help counselors reduce which of the following?
    A) anxiety
    B) cultural bias
    C) conflict
    D) empathy

What Is Multicultural Counseling?

In **multicultural counseling**, issues of culture and identity are openly addressed as concerns how they impact a client's functioning. When clients present for therapy, they often focus on the symptoms they experience in an effort to fix them. However, in multicultural counseling, a counselor will redirect to further explore issues such as

- race,
- ethnicity,
- family,
- religion,
- socioeconomic status,
- environment, and
- identity.

Multicultural counseling explores how those factors contribute to a client's symptoms. It also considers how those cultural factors function as risk or protective factors. Multicultural counselors might also discuss with clients how they view therapy and what their expectations are for the therapeutic process.

Culture impacts the way people experience mental health issues. It is therefore also appropriate, for example, to ask a client who says she is depressed how she experiences depression and how the cultural factors that impact her most play a role in what she experiences.

For example, a client might report that he experiences depression as sadness, fatigue, loss of appetite, and a desire to socially isolate. Perhaps he feels as though his family expects him to stop feeling depressed because he comes from a culture that does not believe depression is a mental health issue or that it requires treatment. The family's invalidation of the client's depressive symptoms may be a contributing factor to his treatment plan in addition to addressing the symptoms of depression.

Multicultural competence is demonstrated by counselors who

- regularly practice self-awareness regarding their own cultural bias;
- pursue knowledge of other cultures;
- can interact with people of different cultural backgrounds effectively and respectfully.

Counselors must continually pursue multicultural competence. For example, a non-Native counselor might live in a state with a significant Native American client population. That counselor should network with counselors in the Native American community to learn about available resources and how to integrate appropriate Native American concepts or ideas in treatment.

Multicultural competence also requires a degree of cultural humility, especially when the counselor is not immersed in the client's culture. Using the Native American population as an example, a White counselor might ask a Native American client about his tribal affiliations and how important that connection is to him. The counselor might also ask the client how he feels about discussing his personal issues with a non-Native counselor. A multicultural counselor will be able to have that conversation respectfully and honestly while inviting the client to discuss cultural issues of importance to him.

The **emic perspective** is a way of learning about and perceiving culture by becoming a part of that culture. Taking this perspective can lead to a more in-depth understanding of the values and beliefs inherent to a culture in a way that an outsider cannot perceive.

The **etic perspective** is a way of learning about and perceiving culture from the outside of that culture. This perspective enables a person to acquire knowledge and to answer questions about a culture but often does not go deeper than a superficial understanding.

The **transcultural perspective** is an approach to counseling that references five dimensions:

1. culture knowledge
2. understanding power, privilege, and oppression
3. positionality and self-reflexivity
4. partnership
5. cultural competence
    - A counselor understands that a client may already experience hardship due to cultural issues and seeks to understand the client's cultural perspectives on issues related to counseling.
    - A counselor using a transcultural perspective will explore the client's culture on his terms and discuss what it means for the counseling process. Counselors understand that the client is the expert on his own life, experiences, and struggles.

The **Association for Multicultural Counseling and Development (AMCD)** is a professional counseling organization dedicated to providing professional development for counselors to improve cultural competence. The AMCD also advocates for human rights and policies to enhance cultural diversity within the counseling profession.

PRACTICE QUESTION

2. What is the BEST way for counselors to demonstrate cultural competence with clients?

    A) avoid talking about their own culture

    B) match the client with a counselor who has the same cultural background

    C) discuss cultural issues with clients of other cultural backgrounds respectfully

    D) read a book about multicultural counseling

Considerations in Multicultural Counseling

A multicultural counselor practices the basic skills and core attributes of counseling (genuineness, congruence, nonjudgmental stance, positive regard) and keeps sessions focused on clients and their needs. Additionally, counselors pursue knowledge of cultural issues by learning about the populations within their community that they may encounter in a therapeutic setting. This means that they learn about the general values, beliefs, and behavioral norms of each group. Acquisition of knowledge leads to awareness of

- the counselor's own cultural biases;
- the counselor's attitudes toward people of different cultural groups;
- the attitudes of various cultural groups toward each other.

Acquiring knowledge enables the counselor to put knowledge and awareness into practice with clients by

- asking about cultural issues during the assessment process;
- creating a safe environment for the client to discuss cultural issues.

The counselor can further demonstrate knowledge about cultural differences by drawing attention to the differences between the counselor and the client and seeking understanding about how culture influences a client's mental health.

Psychologist Gilbert Wrenn drew attention to the culturally encapsulated counselor. **Culturally encapsulated counselors** are counselors who

- look at the world and other people only through their own cultural lens;
- do not venture outside that lens;
- ignore anything contrary to that lens;
- treat clients as if they can all be treated the same way;
- views themselves as free of bias and are therefore not open to learning.

To avoid becoming culturally encapsulated, the counselor must practice and demonstrate respect for and acceptance of diversity. The first way to do this is to recognize the various aspects of diversity that affect people.

The **RESPECTFUL counseling** acronym provides a useful framework for counselors to approach multicultural issues. Each of the letters represents areas of diversity within people. This model can serve as a template for discussing issues during assessment or throughout the counseling process:

- **R**eligious/spiritual issues
    - Does the client hold religious or spiritual beliefs? Why or why not?
    - How do those beliefs or lack thereof influence the client? Are they important to the client?
- **E**conomic class issues
    - What is the client's experience with socioeconomic class?
    - How has the client's socioeconomic experience affected his life, worldview, and choices?
- **S**exual identity issues
    - How does the client identify sexually? Is this important to her?
    - How has the client's sexual identity affected her life, relationships, and family?
- **P**sychological developmental issues
    - Did the client have any developmental or psychological issues during his childhood that impacted him either positively or negatively?
    - Did he get treatment for any of these issues?
    - How did the experience impact the client?
- **E**thnic/racial identity issues
    - How does the client identify ethnically/racially?
    - How has her identification shaped her values and beliefs?
    - Has she encountered discrimination? How has that impacted her life?
- **C**hronological issues
    - How old is the client? What is the client's developmental stage?
    - How were previous developmental stages resolved?
    - How does the client's age impact him now?
- **T**rauma/threats to well-being
    - Does the client have a history of trauma?
    - What does the client experience in terms of the effects of trauma?
    - How does that trauma influence her perception of herself and others?
    - How does it impact her relationships?

- **F**amily issues
  - How does the client define family?
  - How does the client describe his family of origin?
  - How are those relationships now?
  - How does family influence the client's choices and identity?
- **U**nique physical issues
  - Does the client have different or limited physical abilities?
  - Are those differences something the client was born with or acquired?
  - How do the client's unique physical issues impact her life, functioning, and relationships?
- **L**anguage/location of residence issues
  - Is the client a native of the location in which he lives, or did he immigrate there from another city, state, or country?
  - Does the client have a non-Native immigration status?
  - Does the client speak a second language?
  - Is English the client's first or second language?
  - How do these issues and experiences impact the client?

PRACTICE QUESTION

3. A counselor who refuses to acknowledge cultural differences and claims she has no cultural bias could be characterized as what?

   A) culturally encapsulated

   B) stuck in her ways

   C) conservative

   D) liberal

Specific Cultural Groups

Every client who presents for therapy is a unique individual, and each session with that client will be unique. Counselors should check their assumptions about clients—whether based on cultural bias or any other preconceived ideas—at the counseling office door. By maintaining a client-focused approach to therapy and adopting the core attributes of a counselor, one can approach each session with each client with an open, nonjudgmental mind.

Counselor self-examination is a practice of consistent self-reflection whereby counselors examine their own cultural diversity, attitudes, beliefs, and values, and how those influence how they interact with clients. Several concepts aid in self-examination and working with clients from different cultural backgrounds:

- **White privilege** refers to the unearned social status and advantages held by White people.

- For example, White characters and figures generally have more widespread positive representation in the media than do people of other races. Perhaps a White child sees more characters or toys that look like him than would a Black, Latino, or Asian child.
- This disparity can be harmful to individuals who are not White, as they will not grow up and live with similar experiences.
- **Racial microaggressions** are small behaviors and messages that occur in everyday situations and are characterized by a bias toward a marginalized group.
    - They include questions, comments, and actions.
    - They can be both intentional and unintentional.
    - One example would be to presume that an individual is dangerous because of her race, ethnicity, or gender; for instance, a pedestrian crosses the street to avoid a person of a different race.
- The term *model minority* describes myths that are commonly associated with Americans of Asian descent.
    - This can include the idea that children of Asian descent are smarter than other children, more musically inclined than others, and pushed harder by their parents than are other children.
    - These seemingly positive stereotypes might be downplayed or considered less offensive or harmful than negative stereotypes about education or ability.
    - Stereotypes associated with positive attributes can be just as harmful to the individual as negative stereotypes.
- **Unconscious bias** refers to the attitudes and stereotypes people do not consciously realize they have about others.
    - Unconscious bias results in behaviors that can be interpreted as offensive.
    - Education and self-reflection can help bring unconscious bias into the conscious mind so the counselor can reduce it.

Counselors should also be aware of **historical hostility and minority racial identity development (MRID)**. According to MRID, trauma is passed from one generation to the next. The following are all vehicles for historical trauma:

- how a group of people feels about themselves
- how a group views others
- how the group perceives systems
- how the group interacts with other people and systems

These attitudes, values, beliefs, and behaviors can be passed through generations. Groups of people who have been subjected to hostility, oppression, and discrimination throughout history carry the trauma of those experiences throughout the subsequent generations within their families.

The MRID model is a framework that explains the various stages minority groups go through to develop their cultural identities. It includes four stages that range from devaluing their minority identities to developing confident identities as minorities within the majority population.

Cultural groups often contain more **within-group differences** than **between-group** differences. For example, there are distinct differences between collectivist and individualist cultures; however, within the collectivist culture, there will be even more differences.

Within-group differences are even visible within families. Therefore, even if a counselor knows someone from a particular cultural group, that does not mean the next person she meets from that group will hold the same values, beliefs, and behaviors.

PRACTICE QUESTION

4. A family who has immigrated to the US from Haiti comes to therapy for help with adjustment issues. The parents are devout Christians and value traditional family and gender roles. The three teenagers are rejecting the family's religious preferences and are strongly influenced by US popular culture. What is this an example of?

    A) unconscious bias

    B) within-group differences

    C) between-group differences

    D) model minority

Gender Issues

Culturally competent counselors also recognize diversity regarding gender. They must demonstrate knowledge of and sensitivity to gender orientation and issues pertaining to gender. Congruence, unconditional positive regard, and empathy are important during sessions with lesbian, gay, bisexual, transgender, queer, intersex, and agender (LGBTQIA+) clients:

- **Gender** refers to a person's subjective experience of gender, which may or may not be congruent with the gender assigned to that person at birth.
  - Gender characteristics may fall within a range of masculinity and femininity. A person's identified gender will impact that person's gender roles and gender identity.
- **Gender issues** can refer to a variety of experiences, including
  - gender orientation,
  - gender identity,
  - gender dysphoria,
  - how to talk to family about gender,
  - discrimination at school or work, and
  - navigating intimate/romantic relationships.

Gender socialization is the process individuals undergo when learning and conditioning themselves to the societal expectations and attitudes of their gender. Gender socialization is a lifelong process that can impact a person's beliefs, thoughts, feelings, and behaviors. Early socialization is most often shaped by parents, caregivers, and others within the family of origin. As a child grows up, socialization is further shaped by friends, school, the media, and the community.

Gender role conflict occurs when people are in a rigid or restrictive environment that leads them to devalue themselves or restrict how they express themselves. These individuals are unable to live as their true selves in their environment, which is harmful and distressing. Gender role conflict can be assessed by using the **gender role conflict scale**, a thirty-seven-item assessment that can be self-administered and explores four domains:

1. success, power, and competition
2. restrictive emotionality
3. restrictive affectionate behavior between men
4. conflicts between work and family relations

PRACTICE QUESTION

5. A person who grows up being told that a woman should aspire to be a wife and mother has experienced which of the following regarding the idea of femaleness?

    A) therapy
    B) gender socialization
    C) gender orientation
    D) diversity

Culture, Religion, and Spirituality

Culture and Oppression

Cultural competence is key to providing excellent counseling care. **Cultural competence** means treating clients as experts in their own lives and personal stories.

To be culturally competent is more than simply knowing basic facts about a person's culture or being aware of certain norms. Developing cultural competence is an ongoing process that involves seeking guidance from the client, from supervisors, and doing external research on cultural norms for clients in treatment. Understanding cultural norms is an important starting place for any counselor, but it is not the end of the conversation.

Additional factors are important to consider when approaching client care in a culturally competent manner. **Level of acculturation** refers to how comfortable clients feel in the dominant culture as opposed to their culture of origin. For example, a client from Mexico who has only been in the US for two years is going to have very different life experiences and cultural norms than a client born in Mexico who has lived in the US for most of her life. A client's level of acculturation and how he interacts with the dominant culture is impacted by

- the level of acculturation of the client's family;
- the primary language spoken in the home;
- the culture of the client's partner or spouse.

Research shows that genuine cultural competence can lead to high-quality therapeutic care. Counselors can exhibit cultural competence in several ways:

- demonstrating a warm and open attitude
- showing genuine interest and curiosity about the client's culture
- using humor to engage with mistakes or misunderstandings to ease any tension that may arise
- asking good-natured and humble questions to show care and a willingness to learn

HELPFUL HINT

Acculturation is different from **assimilation**, a negative process of forcing people from nondominant cultures to abandon or suppress their culture. Acculturation is a natural process that happens over time and does not necessarily involve abandonment of one's values or cultural norms.

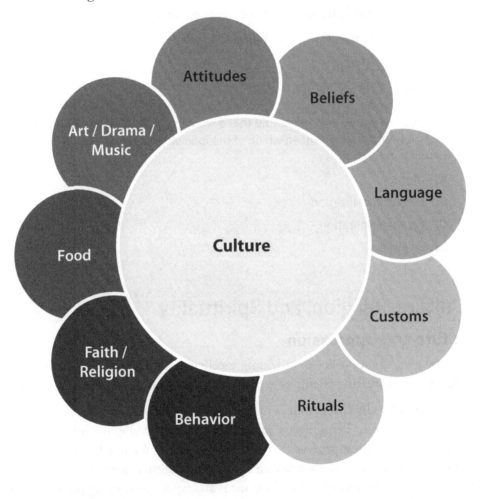

Figure 2.1. Cultural Competence

Counselors must be particularly mindful of issues related to culture and oppression:

- **Racism** is the belief that certain races are superior to others.

46 Elissa Simon | CPCE EXAM PREP

- **Discrimination** occurs when someone or a group of people are treated unfairly based on immutable characteristics, such as race, ethnicity, age, gender, sexual orientation or gender identity, or religion.
- **Oppression** is a situation in which people are governed or controlled unfairly or in a cruel or harsh way, often based on immutable characteristics.

Current events often make their way into the counselor's office. It is likely that clients, especially clients who are people of color, are experiencing distress due to racism, police brutality, microaggressions, and more. Witnessing people being targeted by racist attacks can cause individuals to remember their own experiences of racial discrimination. Racially motivated attacks—whether physical or verbal—are degrading and humiliating experiences for the survivors. A counselor must be present and practice active listening when navigating these sensitive topics with clients.

Counselors are called on to be anti-racist in their practice and overall work. Providing quality care to individuals from all walks of life with particular attention to those who are most vulnerable is essential to that practice. Competent counseling for individuals from diverse backgrounds in particular requires the counselor to educate herself on the role of systems and their impacts on clients' lives.

Furthermore, counselors can enact anti-racist counseling by practicing cultural respect and curiosity, maintaining a learning attitude, and advocating for increased access to quality mental health resources for people of all races, ethnicities, ages, sexualities, and abilities.

HELPFUL HINT

Some counselors may have personally experienced racism and discrimination; others may have never endured racial attacks or microaggressions. Self-disclosure should be used with discretion in these situations: keeping the focus on the client's experiences is the top priority.

PRACTICE QUESTION

6. Which of the following is an example of cultural competence in a therapy session?
    A) explaining to a client that her religion is oppressing her because of her gender
    B) asking a client to explain why immigrants come from their country to the United States
    C) expressing surprise or shock at a client's English proficiency
    D) inviting a client to discuss family expectations surrounding his bar mitzvah

Cultural Adjustment

Cultural adjustment issues are most common when people move to very new cultures, for instance when moving to a new country or using a new language. However, even moving to a new city in one's home country can trigger a cultural adjustment period. Navigating the norms, expectations, and ways of life can be both exciting and challenging, and many people may seek out counseling for their experiences if they need additional support. Cultural adjustment occurs over four stages as described in Table. 2.1.

TABLE 2.1. Four Stages of Cultural Adjustment
Stage 1: Honeymoon/Tourist Stage
When someone first moves to a new location, everything can seem exciting and new. There are new foods to try, places to see, and people to meet. It is common for people to feel excited and hopeful during this stage, envisioning what their new life will be like. This stage can last from a few days to several weeks.
Stage 2: Distress/Crisis Stage
Problems begin here. Learning the language may be difficult, adjusting to different cultural norms and expectations can be an issue, and challenges start cropping up. In this stage, homesickness may take over, and it is common for people to compare their new lives with their previous circumstances. Challenges such as language barriers, gender relations, deference for authority, social norms such as tipping, use of curse words, food availability from one's home location, and many other issues can compound and create significant stress and homesickness in individuals. This phase typically starts a few weeks or months into the move and can last several months.
Stage 3: Reintegration Stage
Several months to a year after the move, feelings of crisis may start to subside. As people become more used to the norms and expectations in their new home, they can relax and navigate more situations with ease. They begin to reintegrate aspects of their old lives into their new lives (such as cooking favorite childhood meals) and can laugh off minor cultural frictions. Their new location still feels "new," but thoughts of being an outsider or feelings of loneliness or intense homesickness begin to subside.
Stage 4: "Home" Stage
People have fully integrated themselves into their new environment and culture. Language barriers have eased, and their understanding of cultural norms in the new environment has heightened. They can bring aspects of their old home and environment into their new location. Problems or challenges in the new location are not perceived as negatively as before and are instead accepted as part of the way of life. The new location begins to feel like home.

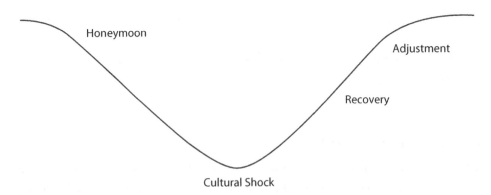

Figure 2.2. Cultural Adjustment

Not every person goes through all four stages of cultural adjustment. Some people remain at Stage 2, Distress/Crisis, for extended periods. This phenomenon, known as **culture shock**, was originally described by anthropologist Kalervo Oberg. People experiencing culture shock may display

- heightened negative emotions about their new location;
- anger and annoyance at various aspects of their new environment;
- a lack of interest in integrating into the new environment;
- a strong preference for norms from their home environment.

If left untreated, these negative emotions can lead to anxiety and depression, self-isolation, and physical symptoms such as upset stomach, poor sleep, and aches and pains. Counselors with clients experiencing significant culture shock should help them determine what specific triggers are causing their difficulties. It could be that they have not made friends yet, or perhaps there are specific norms in their new environment that are particularly challenging for them compared with their home environment. For example, someone coming from a more conservative country might struggle to adapt to the more open dating culture in the United States.

Counselors should work to understand the client's home culture to validate the difficulties of the transition. It is important to monitor symptoms to ensure that the cultural adjustment does not develop into more significant mental health concerns, like anxiety and depression.

Some clients may feel insecure about making mistakes when practicing their new language. If this worry is significant enough, it can prevent them from socializing in their new location. For these clients, working on building self-esteem and confidence can help improve their ability to practice the local language more often, which will help immensely with adjustment issues. Connecting with fellow expats can also be an important way to ease into the transition. Finally, psychoeducation on the norms of cultural adjustment can be a reassuring conversation for people who have not traveled before and may be unfamiliar with the concept of cultural adjustment.

PRACTICE QUESTION

7. Which of the following is the first stage of cultural adjustment?
   A) "Home" stage
   B) Honeymoon/Tourist stage
   C) Reintegration stage
   D) Distress/Crisis stage

Religion and Spirituality

Religion and spirituality can be very important parts of some clients' lives. **Spirituality** can include formal religious practices, such as prayer and worship, but can also encompass broader concepts, such as sense of self and purpose, values, community, forgiveness, and mental well-being.

Spirituality has been found to have positive impacts on people's lives: It can offer a framework or set of values for how to live one's life and foster self-esteem and self-worth. It can also encourage positive outlooks and ways of interacting in the world, such as expressing compassion, generosity, forgiveness, and inner peace. Clients who are experiencing spiritual difficulties might report issues such as

- a feeling of emptiness or a lack of purpose in the world;
- negative outlook on life;
- excessive judgment of themselves or others;
- excessive anxiety;
- loneliness and isolation.

In the past, it was considered inappropriate to discuss spirituality with clients. Practitioners felt it was unprofessional, were concerned about differences in beliefs, or wanted to avoid controversy in the counseling room. However, research has found that incorporating religious or spiritual practices that align with the client's values can have a positive impact on the therapeutic process.

Counselors can encourage clients to incorporate religion and spirituality into therapy sessions and to continue beneficial practices outside the session. Depending on the client, these may include

- meditation;
- mindfulness techniques (like deep breathing);
- values exploration (such as mood boards);
- developing personal rituals or practices;
- complementary health approaches (for example, yoga);
- prayer and reading spiritual texts (religious or otherwise) related to their faith practice.

A counselor should ensure that religious or faith-based practices are client-led. The counselor should also have a high level of cultural competency. For example, counselors who are not qualified to perform a certain service (like teaching yoga) should not do so; however, they may encourage their clients to try a yoga class if the clients are medically capable. A nonreligious counselor can still encourage a religious client to refer to comforting religious texts when he is feeling anxiety and can even have him read them in session, allowing him to take the lead.

When using spiritual practices with clients, the counselor needs to separate her personal spiritual or religious beliefs from those of the client. It is inappropriate to proselytize or push one's personal beliefs onto clients; however, encouraging clients to explore their own spiritual beliefs, practices, and values can be an enriching and rewarding tool in a holistic therapeutic practice. Again, any spiritual or religious exploration should be client-led.

Values exploration may be neutral or centered in religious and spiritual beliefs. Everyone has values and beliefs about what is important in life, how the world works, and what it means to be a good person. For people who are experiencing a big change in life, revisiting or clarifying their values in a therapeutic environment can encourage them to make decisions based on what is most important to them.

HELPFUL HINT

Approaches to spirituality can vary widely. While some people find spiritual benefits from tarot cards, doing creative activities, or listening to music, others are more traditional and attend services or practice a faith. Exploring areas that have been spiritually meaningful to you as a counselor can help prepare you for spiritual discussions with clients.

Navigating Religious Values Conflicts

Some clients seek counseling because they are experiencing values conflicts regarding religious norms and expectations. These **values conflicts** may be external and causing discord with family members (for example, a person who is no longer religious and is being pressured to continue attending church by family members) or within themselves (for example, a gay person who belongs to a faith practice that does not accept the LGBTQ community). Whatever the source of the conflict, the approach will be similar.

First, it is important to approach the issue with an open and non-judgmental attitude. The goal is to help the client explore his own values, not impose the counselor's values on the client. Developing a strong rapport that allows room for open communication and trust between the client and counselor is essential for values conflict work.

Second, the counselor must understand what the exact conflict is, the source of the conflict, and how the client feels about it. For example, a married couple comes from different religious backgrounds. One wants their children to be baptized in the local church; the other wants the children to come to their own decisions. To navigate the conflict, the counselor and client must be able to identify these different desires and understand any outside pressure (like family or cultural expectations) that may influence decision-making.

Finally, the counselor and client can explore different options for how to proceed. Consider the example of the married couple:

- What will the outcome be if the client insists on the baptism?
- How will it impact the client's life?
- How will the client feel about the decision?
- What about waiting and letting the child decide?

Are there options that haven't been considered, such as baptism in a different church, an alternate religious ceremony, or waiting for a year or two before conducting the baptism?

The counselor's role is to help clients explore the various options and help them decide for themselves what choice to make to resolve the conflict.

While religion and spirituality can have many positive impacts on one's life, spiritual abuse can occur as well and create negative impacts. **Spiritual abuse** is a broad term that encompasses religious and spiritual beliefs to control, coerce, shame, humiliate, or terrorize people.

The use of shame and guilt is one of the most common tools of spiritual abuse. It can be used against people to pressure them into giving money, control their behavior (such as who they socialize with or marry), or dictate how they should dress. It can even influence the career they choose. Spiritual abuse can be used to manipulate someone's emotions or silence their questions. Appeals to authority may be used to enact spiritual abuse as well (for example, a faith leader who has to personally give permission before people are allowed to date or marry).

Spiritual abuse can include insulting people's spiritual beliefs, forcing people to act in ways that violate their spiritual beliefs, or, in the case of parents, not allowing their children to make their own spiritual decisions.

People who have experienced spiritual abuse need support and a safe space where they can explore the pain of their experiences and take the time to realign their spiritual values free of coercion or guilt. The validation counselors can provide regarding the pain associated with spiritual abuse can be an important step in the healing process for these clients. Working from a trauma-informed perspective can be a key part of providing competent care for clients who have experienced spiritual abuse.

PRACTICE QUESTION

8. Ethan is a new client who has just moved out of his parents' home to attend college. Ethan was raised Catholic and is still a devout believer. Now that he is in college though, he has begun having sex with his new girlfriend. Ethan is very anxious about this because he believes it is a sin. What is Ethan experiencing?

    A) spiritual abuse
    B) a values conflict
    C) spiritual growth
    D) an existential crisis

Answer Key

1. **B**

   Self-reflection and knowledge can reduce a counselor's reliance on his own worldview and thereby reduce cultural bias.

2. **C**

   A significant aspect of multicultural counseling is applying the knowledge and skills learned within relationships with people of different cultures, which can be facilitated through respectful discussions about cultural issues.

3. **A**

   Culturally encapsulated counselors look at the world and other people only through their own cultural lens, do not venture outside that viewpoint, ignore anything contrary to that lens, and treat clients as if everyone can be treated the same way. They also view themselves as free of bias and are not open to learning.

4. **B**

   The group is the Haitian family. Within the family, there are differences among individuals even though they are all part of one family unit, which is an example of within-group differences.

5. **B**

   Gender socialization is the process individuals undergo when learning and conditioning themselves to the societal expectations and attitudes of their own genders.

6. **D**

   Cultural competence means letting the client be the expert of his culture and experiences. Asking a client to describe a cultural experience in his own words shows cultural competence.

7. **B**

   The Honeymoon/Tourist Stage is the first stage of cultural adjustment. For many people, it can feel similar to being on vacation or a honeymoon.

8. **B**

   A values conflict is when a person is acting in a way that conflicts with his values, has conflict with other people in his life because of differences in values, or is feeling personal distress over the lack of alignment between his behavior and his beliefs.

3 Human Growth and Development

An understanding of human growth and development is essential for any counselor. This chapter reviews theories of human growth and development.

Elements of Developmental Psychology

Lifespan Development and Behaviorism

Development begins at conception and continues throughout a person's lifetime. **Developmental psychology** studies the ways in which people change over time. Because most developmental change occurs during childhood, that is the emphasis of this field.

- **Cephalocaudal development** refers to the concept that human development and growth start at the head and move down. The head is the first to grow, and then the body grows to fit the size of the head.
- **Heredity** is the passing on of genetic traits from parents to their offspring through genes, chromosomes, and DNA.
- **Hereditability** refers to the possibility that a trait or condition can be passed from parents to offspring and to the portion of a trait that can be explained via genetic factors.

There are several significant debates in developmental psychology. Does biology or environment have a greater impact on human development? Psychologists have determined that both play a significant role.

Every person has certain biological traits that shape their personality traits. For example, research has found that some people have neurons that are sensitive to over-stimulation. These people tend to be introverts (in fact, as a general rule, introverts have these neurons).

However, some of these people are raised in ways that help them overcome this sensitivity to an extent—perhaps their parents required them to engage in lengthy conversations with other adults frequently—leading them to become extroverts.

The concept of **power of the environment** centers around the fact that humans do not live in a vacuum. Rather, they are influenced by people, places, ideas, and conditions in the world around them.

Empiricism is the theory that all data comes from the senses or through measurable observations or quantifiable data. Empiricism is a forerunner of behaviorism, which theorizes that developmental changes are quantitative, and experience creates knowledge.

> **DID YOU KNOW?**
> John B. Watson coined the term *behaviorism* in 1913.

Behaviorism is the psychological theory that all human behavior is learned through the various forms of conditioning that people encounter from experience. It can be measured and changed by modifying behaviors. The psychologist **B. F. Skinner** was often referred to as the "father" of behaviorism. He believed that all behavior is learned and therefore all behavior can be shaped through operant conditioning.

Applied behavior analysis (ABA) is a method of behavioral therapy. Most often used with children with autism spectrum disorders, ABA can also be applied to a variety of issues that require a purely behavioral intervention. The therapy uses the principles of conditioning to gradually change behaviors.

Organismic theorists look at human development and personality as a total experience where developmental changes are qualitative and require a holistic perspective.

PRACTICE QUESTION

1. A sixteen-year-old male presents for therapy with symptoms of schizophrenia. During the intake, the counselor learns that his grandfather and paternal uncle had similar symptoms, though they were never officially diagnosed. This indicates that schizophrenia is what?

   A) heritable
   B) cephalocaudal
   C) empirical
   D) organismic

Motor Sensory Development

The greatest changes in sensory, motor, and perceptual development happen in the first two years of life. When babies are first born, most of their senses operate in a similar way to those of adults. For example, babies are able to hear before they are born; studies show that babies turn toward the sound of their mother's voice just minutes after being born, indicating they recognize the mother's voice from their time in the womb.

The exception to this rule is vision. A baby's vision changes significantly in its first year of life; initially it has a range of vision of only eight to twelve inches and no depth perception. As a result, infants rely primarily on hearing; vision does not become the dominant sense until around the age of twelve months. Babies also prefer faces to other objects. This preference, along with their limited vision range, means that their sight is initially focused on their caregiver.

While babies' senses might be similar to those of adults, their ability to interpret sensory inputs is very different. They must learn to **perceive** or interpret the sensory information they receive. This occurs as they interact with their environment and their caregivers, and as they age.

Eleanor Gibson conducted an experiment in which she created a "visual cliff" by extending a Plexiglass ledge off a wooden table. All babies looked to their mothers for guidance when they approached the cliff; older babies refused to cross it regardless of their mothers' expressions. Gibson posited that while all babies could see the cliff, the older babies had a more complex perception of it because of their more advanced development and their experiences with crawling (and falling).

Figure 3.1. Gibson's Visual Cliff

In early psychology, babies were not believed to have any innate motor skills; the brain was considered to be **tabula rasa**, or a blank slate. However, later research revealed that all humans are actually born with certain reflexes which then later disappear. These include **rooting**, turning the head and opening the mouth in search of food when the cheek is touched; **sucking**, moving the mouth to draw milk from a nipple; **grasping**, the tight clenching of anything placed on a baby's palm; the **Moro reflex**, a startle reflex in which a baby throws its arms out and pulls them back in; and the **Babinski reflex**, when a baby's extends its big toe when the bottom of the foot is touched.

These reflexes fade through the process of **maturation,** the biological process of aging. Maturation is also a key component of other motor development: a baby cannot perform certain skills until its body has properly matured. For example, no matter what a parent tries to do, a six-month-old baby cannot run or jump.

PRACTICE QUESTION

2. Which of the following senses is most different at birth as compared to adulthood?
   A) sight
   B) smell
   C) hearing
   D) taste

Attachment Theory

In 1953, psychologist **John Bowlby** posited his attachment theory to explain the nature of the relationship between caregiver and child. Bowlby argued that in infancy, babies form an **attachment**, an enduring emotional bond to a particular figure, usually the primary caregiver.

Whereas psychologists previously attributed attachment to the association between being fed and the caregiver, Bowlby noticed that babies often maintained a strong attachment to their mothers, even when they were not the ones doing the feeding. So he theorized that attachment is actually evolutionary in nature, developed for an infant's survival.

Having someone who will provide that care allows babies to then use them as a base to explore their world, returning to them when they feel threatened. Attachment is not about food, but about care and responsiveness to needs. Thus, attachment is essential to development as a prototype for future relationships; disruption of attachment leads to difficulties in adulthood. He identified the ages of 0 – 5 as a critical period for the development of attachment.

In the early 1970s, **Mary Ainsworth** empirically proved Bowlby's attachment theory through her experiment titled "the Strange Situation." Ainsworth conducted an experiment where she first had mother and baby in a room, then introduced a stranger. The mother then left, leaving the baby alone with the stranger for a few minutes. After this, the mother returned and the stranger left. Then the mother left the baby alone in the room, after which the stranger returned, followed shortly thereafter by the mother (and the stranger left again). Ainsworth concluded that babies exhibited three types of attachment, related to the care provided by the attachment figure:

1. **Secure Attachment**: In this case, the baby is very secure in its relationship to the attachment figure. The baby uses this figure as a base for exploration and is soothed easily by them when upset. The baby is unhappy to see them go but calms quickly when they return. Ainsworth found that secure attachment resulted from a caring and attuned caregiver.

2. **Ambivalent Attachment**: In this case, the baby exhibited extreme fussiness and clinginess. The baby was unhappy when left alone with the stranger but was not easily soothed by the caregiver. This resulted from an inconsistent level of responsiveness from the caregiver.

3. **Avoidant Attachment**: In this case, the baby was completely detached from the caregiver. The baby explored the room without any orientation toward the attachment figure and responded equally to the caregiver and the stranger.

PRACTICE QUESTION

3. A baby who cries when approached by a stranger, but who calms quickly when held by her primary giver, is exhibiting which of the following?

    A) conditioned response
    B) ambivalent attachment
    C) avoidant attachment
    D) secure attachment

Baumrind's Parenting Styles

Diana Baumrind developed the theory of parenting styles based on her interactions with children and their parents. Underlying Baumrind's theory is the idea that children need both structure and warmth. Baumrind theorized three main parenting styles, which are described in Table 3.1.

TABLE 3.1. Baumrind's Parenting Styles

Style	Definition
Authoritarian	• focused on structure • parents often described as strict • limited freedom, warmth, or love toward children • no explanations provided to help children make choices
Permissive	• little structure • children allowed to do what they want • offers children more warmth and love • few boundaries • indulges children
Authoritative	• balanced version of the authoritarian and permissive • considered the ideal mode of parenting • boundaries, limits, and structure balanced with warmth and love • rules and the consequences for breaking them understood by children • children's knowledge that they are loved even when making bad choices

PRACTICE QUESTION

4. Michelle is fifteen and in therapy for anxiety. When asked to describe her parents, she calls them "drill sergeants." Which parenting style does this indicate?

    A) authoritative
    B) authoritarian
    C) permissive
    D) involved

Harlow's Maternal Deprivation Theory

Harry Harlow is most known for his experiments with **rhesus monkeys**, which explored the effects of maternal deprivation and attachment. His theory was that the bonding process between mother and infant requires not only attachment but also **contact comfort**, or the tactile sensation of comfort. In the experiment, he separated baby monkeys from their mothers at birth and put them in cages with two different artificial "mothers."

- One of the fake mothers was made of wire and provided the monkeys with food.
- The other mother was wrapped in soft cloth but did not offer food.
- Harlow found that the baby monkeys spent most of their time with the soft mother.

In a variation of this experiment, Harlow introduced a frightening stimulus. Again, the babies sought comfort from the soft mother. Finally, when the monkeys developed into adults, those with artificial mothers had more social problems with other monkeys compared to the ones who grew up with their real mothers.

PRACTICE QUESTION

5. What did Harry Harlow's experiments with monkeys reveal about mother-infant attachments?

    A) Baby monkeys need food to grow strong.

    B) Baby monkeys need contact comfort for healthy development.

    C) Having a mother makes no difference to development.

    D) Contact comfort is not necessary for monkeys.

Cognitive and Language Development

The study of cognitive development looks at the ways in which people—mostly children—think about and evaluate the world, and how that changes over time. The most significant figure in cognitive development is **Jean Piaget**.

Piaget theorized that children view the world through **schemata**, cognitive rules for interpreting the world which are developed based on their experiences. When they encounter new information or have a new experience, they either incorporate it into their existing schemata, called **assimilation**, or—if the new information is contradictory or does not fit—they adjust their schemata based on the new information, called **accommodation**. The balance between assimilation and accommodation is called **equilibration**.

For example, all of the men in a girl's life may have short hair. She then believes that all men have short hair. If she encounters a young boy with short hair, she will assimilate the information into the existing schema: all males have short hair. If, however, she encounters a man with long hair, her first reaction might be surprise, confusion, or even amusement. She will then accommodate the information by adjusting her schema: most men have short hair, but some have long hair.

Piaget's Stages of Cognitive Development

Piaget identified four stages of cognitive development:

Sensorimotor Stage (Birth – Age 2): In this stage, a baby's behavior is governed by its senses, and its schemata are based on its reflexes. Most significantly, during this time babies develop **object permanence**, the understanding that, even if an object is outside of their perceptual range, it still exists. If a four-month-old baby is fussing for his father's keys, the father need only put the keys away, and the baby will forget they exist.

Preoperational Stage (Ages 2 – 7): The most important development during this stage is **language**. Children learn to use symbolic schema—through speech, drawing, letters, and numbers—to represent real-world objects. Their memories are developing and there are able to use their imaginations. However, they still cannot understand more complex ideas like cause and effect, time and comparison. A three-year-old pours her milk over her dinner plate in an attempt to understand cause and effect. During this stage, children are also completely **egocentric**; they cannot think beyond their own worldview. Children in this stage demonstrate **centration**, focusing on a singular aspect of a situation or object without noticing other elements of it.

S
P
C
F

Concrete Operations (Ages 8 – 12): During this stage, children begin to develop logical thinking. They understand the passage of time and can comprehend that an action causes a certain reaction. Piaget identified **conservation** as the biggest developmental leap during this stage. Children in this stage can understand that the properties of an object stay the same even when its shape changes. For example, they understand that a rope is still a rope whether it is stretched out long or wrapped into an intricate knot. Another important step is developing the **concept of reversibility**, the idea that an action can be undone.

Formal Operations (Age 12 – Adulthood): In this final stage, humans develop abstract reasoning and consider ideas and objects in their mind without physically seeing them. For example, they are able to formulate a hypothesis about what will happen in an experiment before ever running the experiment. People are also able to engage in **metacognition**, thinking about *how* they think. While this is the final stage, Piaget argued that not everyone reaches this stage; some remain at the concrete operations stage.

In recent years, critiques of Piaget's theory have emerged. For one, Piaget's primary research subjects were his own children; he lacked a diverse group of research subjects, and his judgment may have been clouded. Furthermore, psychologists believe that many children go through Piaget's stages more quickly than he posited.

Other psychologists question the validity of stages in general. These psychologists support the **information-processing model**, which follows the same development path as Piaget but in a continuous manner, rather than in stages.

 HELPFUL HINT

Remember, *conservation*, *concept of reversibility*, and *Concrete Operations* all start with the letter "C."

PRACTICE QUESTION

6. A group of students are discussing the best ways to study for an upcoming exam. This is an example of which of Piaget's stages of development?

    A) Concrete Operations stage
    (B) Formal Operations stage
    C) Preoperational stage
    D) Sensorimotor stage

Vygotsky's Cultural-Historical Theory

An alternative theory, the **Cultural-Historical Theory** of cognitive development, was posited by **Lev Vygotsky**. Vygotsky believed that society and culture were critical in a child's cognitive development. Vygotsky's work is based on the assumption that children learn about their culture—and how it interprets and responds to the world—through their formal and informal interactions with adults.

For example, a child is reading a book with her mother about animals that live in the forest. The mother points out the squirrels in the trees and the deer munching grass. In this way, the child learns how her culture classifies and talks about animals.

He also assumes that for cognitive growth to take place, children need both challenging tasks and room to play. Challenging tasks force children to stretch cognitively, making new connections and furthering their understanding. However, in order for this to be most effective, they need an adult—or anyone with more knowledge and experience than them—to **scaffold** their learning, by helping them through the process of acquiring the new skills.

Returning to the mother and child, the child is now trying to complete an animal puzzle. The mother scaffolds this process by encouraging her work, asking guiding questions, and helping her place a few pieces until she is able to do it on her own. Vygotsky called this learning area—the area between what a child can do without help and what she can do with help—the **zone of proximal development (ZPD)**.

PRACTICE QUESTION

7. The term *scaffolding*—providing a student guidance and support from an adult or peer, as appropriate, and eventually fading away from the support—came from which of the following theories?

    (A) Lev Vygotsky's zone of proximal development
    B) Howard Gardner's multiple intelligences theory
    C) Albert Bandura's social learning theory
    D) Erik Erikson's theory of psychosocial development

Language Development

Adults—and even children—cannot remember a time when language and thinking were separate. Once language is acquired, the two processes are completely intertwined.

But how does language develop? Researchers have found that, regardless of the language a baby is learning, all babies go through the same stages of acquisition. Around four months, babies begin to babble, practicing the sounds of the language (or languages) that they hear regularly. Around their first birthday, the babbling turns into single words, like "book." By eighteen months, babies begin to bring together their single words into two-word phrases with clear meaning but no syntax. So "book!" becomes "Mommy book!"

Syntax begins to develop as the child advances into forming three- and four-word phrases. At first, young children often misapply or overuse grammatical rules, a process called **overgeneralization**.

For example, knowing that one uses the suffix "-ed" to create the past tense, a child in the **telegraphic** phase might say, "Daddy throwed the ball," not understanding that it does not apply to every word. This is corrected through modeling: when adults or older children use correct grammar so that the younger child can model their mode of speaking.

There is debate over the actual process of language acquisition. Psychologists who study behavior have argued that language is acquired through a process called conditioning. Essentially, this means that when children properly use language, they receive praise and positive feedback (which may even be just receiving an item they request) from their parents or caregivers. This then encourages them to use the language in the same way again.

Cognitive psychologists argue, however, that people deprived of this kind of parental conditioning are still able to develop language. **Noam Chomsky** put forward the **nativist theory of language** which states that each person is born with a language acquisition device inside of them. This device allows for language acquisition unless it is interrupted or damaged during a critical period. Current researchers have concluded that language is acquired both through behavior modification and through natural development in that critical period.

PRACTICE QUESTION

8. Which of the following is an example of overgeneralization in language development?
   - **A)** "Mommy, I eated all of my vegetables!"
   - B) "Mommy, monkey."
   - C) "Baby cracker eat."
   - D) "Book!"

Lifespan Developmental Theory

Piaget, Vygotsky, Bowlby, and Ainsworth focused primarily on infancy and early childhood in their theories, as this is where the majority of developmental change happens. Other psychologists, however, developed theories examining development across the entire lifespan of a human.

Erikson's Psychosocial Development Theory

The most well-known lifespan developmental theory is **Erik Erikson's psychosocial development theory**. Erikson was trained in the psychoanalytic school of psychology, so his theory is based in that rather than in evidence-based research. However, it has still heavily impacted psychology as a whole, particularly the treatment and schooling of children.

Erikson theorized that development occurs in eight stages with each stage centered on a specific social conflict. The manner in which the conflict is resolved impacts who the person ultimately becomes.

- Stage 1 (age 0 – 1): Trust versus Mistrust

Babies determine if they can trust their caregivers. If they can, as adults, they will appreciate the value of relationships and interdependence. If they cannot, they will remain untrusting and disconnected.

- Stage 2 (age 1 – 3): Autonomy versus Shame and Doubt

Toddlers attempt to exert their will over their own bodies. This manifests itself through activities like potty-training and learning to dress themselves. If toddlers are able to develop a level of independence, as adults they will have a strong sense of autonomy. If not, they will be plagued by feelings of shame and self-doubt.

- Stage 3 (age 3 – 5): Initiative versus Guilt

This is also known as the "why?" stage. Children develop curiosity and a desire to exert control over their environment as well (because they feel they have some control over themselves and trust in the adults around them). If this initiative is encouraged, they will have a strong sense of curiosity and purpose going forward. If not, they feel guilt and avoid future curiosity.

- Stage 4 (age 6 – 11): Industry versus Inferiority

This is the beginning of a child's formal education. If they feel that they are as good academically and socially as their peers, they will develop confidence. If not, they will develop an **inferiority complex**, a generalized feeling of incompetence and performance anxiety.

- Stage 5 (age 12 – 18): Identity versus Role Confusion

During adolescence, the primary social task is to discover one's most comfortable social identity. All teenagers, then, try on different roles. If they find their identity, they will have a stable sense of self. If not, they will encounter an **identity crisis**, a period of profound identity confusion.

- Stage 6 (age 19 – 40): Intimacy versus Isolation

Young adults must develop loving relationships with others while balancing their work needs. Success leads to strong, lasting relationships; failure leads to isolation and loneliness.

- Stage 7 (40 – 65): Generativity versus Stagnation

Individuals in middle adulthood strive to create something that will outlast them—through raising children or engaging in meaningful work. Those who succeed feel fulfilled and accomplished. Those who do not, endure a **midlife crisis**, becoming disengaged with the world or trying to change the direction of their lives. They may change their identities or attempt to exert more control over those around them. The fear of death is greatest in this period.

- Stage 8 (65 – death): Integrity versus Despair

As individuals near the end of life, they will reflect to determine whether they are satisfied with their life choices. If they are, they will develop wisdom. If not, they will experience despair.

PRACTICE QUESTION

9. According to Erikson, toddlers who develop a sense of control over their own bodies will experience which of the following as adults?

    A) trust
    B) industry
    C) autonomy
    D) identity

Theories of Moral Development: Kohlberg and Gilligan

Lawrence Kohlberg took another perspective in examining human development, developing **Kohlberg's theory of moral development**. He became interested in the question, "How does the ability to reason in ethical situations change?"

To answer this question, he posed several dilemmas to people of varying ages. The most well-known of these is the **Heinz dilemma**: A man must decide if he should steal a drug that he cannot afford in order to save his wife's life. Based on the responses he collected, Kohlberg articulated three levels of moral development, each composed of two stages.

TABLE 3.2. Kohlberg's Three Levels of Moral Development

Stage	Age Range	Description
Pre-Conventional Level		
1: Obedience/Punishment	Preschool	Focus on avoiding punishment: Heinz should not steal the drug because he might get caught and put in jail.
2: Self-Interest/Reward	Elementary School	Focus on rewards instead of punishment; goal is to maximize benefits to oneself: Heinz should steal the drug because having his wife live would make him happy.

		Conventional Level
3: Interpersonal Accord	Middle School	Focus on being perceived as a "good" person and being liked: Heinz should steal the drug because he will be seen as a hero.
4: Law and Order	High School	Reliance on perceived fixed rules of conduct (e.g., learned from parents, peers): Heinz should not steal the drug because stealing is wrong.
		Post-Conventional Level
5: Social Contract	High School/ Young Adulthood	Understand that legally right and morally right are not always the same; laws are for majority benefit and may conflict with best interest of the individual: Heinz should steal the drug because, while theft is illegal, the protection of life is more important than the protection of property.
6: Universal Principles (only achieved by some)	Adulthood	Self-defined and protected ethical principles: Heinz should steal the drug because life must be preserved at all costs.

There are many critiques of Kohlberg's research. The primary criticisms are that the situations were fictional and unfamiliar for many of the participants. The participants ranged in age from 10 to 16, and so had no frame of reference for making a decision about saving a dying wife.

Carol Gilligan critiqued Kohlberg for his bias. All of the participants in the original study were male, and when girls were tested later, they demonstrated slower moral development. However, Gilligan argued that there is a difference in moral development based on gender, and Kohlberg's stages only articulate the development of male morality.

In her 1982 book *A Different Voice*, Gilligan posited that male morality is based on absolute abstract ideas, with justice being the fundamental moral principle. Female morality is based on specific, individual situations with caring for others being the fundamental moral principle. Later researchers have also questioned Gilligan's gender distinctions, and this debate continues.

PRACTICE QUESTION

10. Which of the following is NOT a critique of Kohlberg's moral development theory?

    A) He chose to examine a cross-section of participants rather than complete a longitudinal study.

    B) The study articulated a gender difference in moral reasoning that does not exist.

    C) His ethical dilemmas were artificial.

    D) Ethical decision-making can differ significantly in real-world versus hypothetical situations.

Daniel Levinson's Four Major Eras Theory

Daniel Levinson posited theories of adult development and divided them into four eras, or stages. He wrote about his ideas in two well-known books:

- *The Seasons of a Man's Life* focused on the life span that men experience.
- *The Seasons of a Woman's Life* chronicled the life span unique to women's experiences.

Both books expanded on the four major eras theory:

- Preadulthood (childhood and adolescence) is a stage of development characterized by dependence on adults.
- Early adulthood occurs after age twenty-two, but the transition period takes place between seventeen and twenty-two.
  - This stage is characterized by solidifying one's identity; understanding how one fits into the world; and changing family relationships, culminating in pursuing a career and family.
- Middle adulthood occurs after age forty, but the transition period takes place between forty and forty-five, which is when most people experience the midlife crisis.
  - The **midlife crisis** is a period when people question the trajectory of their lives.
  - Levinson considered it a positive event that inspires change if it is needed; without it, a person can feel stagnation toward the end of life.
  - The midlife crisis occurs regardless of class.
- Later adulthood occurs after age sixty-five, with the transition period between sixty and sixty-five. This is the stage of life when people transition out of their careers, into retirement, and often look back on their lives.

PRACTICE QUESTION

11. Tamara is forty-two and comes to therapy to discuss her anxiety and depression. During the interview, she reveals that her children are grown, and she does not know what to do with herself. She spent most of her time as a stay-at-home mom homeschooling her children, and now she has nothing to do, no purpose, and she feels lost. What might Tamara be experiencing?

    A) midlife crisis
    B) major depressive episode
    C) separation anxiety
    D) stress

William Perry's Four-Stage Theory of Intellectual and Ethical Development in Adults

William Perry developed a four-stage theory of intellectual and ethical development in adults. Perry's theory focuses on the cognitive and moral development of college students as they engage in higher learning and become more independent. He believed that students needed to go through each stage (described in Table 3.3.) to become effective at critical thinking skills.

TABLE 3.3. Perry's Four-Stage Theory of Intellectual and Ethical Development in Adults

Stage	Definition
Dualism	There is one right answer; a student just needs to find it.
Multiplicity	There is no right answer, but someone in authority must figure out the answer.
Relativism	One can prove any answer with enough evidence.
Commitment	One is open to independently learning and exploring for answers.

PRACTICE QUESTION

12. A college student who defers to the experts on a subject might be in which stage?

    A) dualism
    B) multiplicity
    C) relativism
    D) commitment

James W. Fowler's Theory of Faith and Spiritual Development

James W. Fowler was a theologian, minister, and human development professor who established the stages of faith development throughout the life span.

- **Stage 0: undifferentiated (primal) faith (0 – 4 years, infancy):** A baby does not feel faith, per se, but experiences feelings of trust and assurance that can grow into faith or neglect, the latter of which will lead to lack of faith.
- **Stage 1: intuitive-projective faith (two – seven years, early childhood):** A child develops the sense of right and wrong and learns faith stories without true understanding.
- **Stage 2: mythic-literal faith (childhood):** A child develops the sense of fairness associated with religious beliefs. The schema is simple: doing good deeds results in good things, and doing bad deeds results in bad things.
- **Stage 3: synthetic-conventional faith (adolescence):** An adolescent begins to identify with a belief system and form a sense of faith.

- **Stage 4: individuative-reflective faith (young adulthood)**: Young adults explore faith further, often encountering conflict in their beliefs or developing a greater appreciation for them.
- **Stage 5: conjunctive faith (mid-thirties)**: An adult comes to understand that faith is beyond basic religious beliefs.
- **Stage 6: universalizing faith (midlife)**: Adults live out the tenets of their faith and are not bothered by differences in religious traditions.

PRACTICE QUESTION

13. Which stage of faith is associated with fairness and justice in its simplest forms?
    A) stage 0: undifferentiated
    B) stage 1: intuitive-projective faith
    C) stage 2: mythic-literal faith —
    D) stage 3: synthetic-conventional faith

Robert Kegan's Six Stages of Life Span Development

Robert Kegan expanded on the work of Jean Piaget and theorized six stages of development based on how people create meaning, which grows throughout the life span. In counseling, **meaning-making** is the process of evaluating life events for their existential value. In particular, it means processing an event to find the good that comes from it that may not be readily apparent.

TABLE 3.4. Kegan's Six Stages of Life Span Development

Stage	Age Range	Definition
Incorporative	infancy – 2	A child is completely dependent on the mother or primary caregiver.
Impulsive	2 – 6	A child is guided by pursuing what she wants and giving in to impulses. Behavior is guided by rules and consequences.
Imperial	6 – adolescence	A child is more influenced by his relationships and whether others approve of him or not. Empathy develops, but much of how a child thinks of himself comes from the opinions of others.
Interpersonal	adulthood	Adults create mutual, interdependent relationships.
Institutional	adulthood	Adults exhibit autonomy and self-expression.
Interindividual	adulthood	Adults focus on intimacy and genuine relationships that contribute to identity.

In counseling, the *holding environment* refers to the space that a counselor creates for a client that includes safety and nonjudgment. It is an attitude and approach that allows clients to express what they need to. Thus, the counselor "holds" the space for clients, so they feel safe in the relationship.

PRACTICE QUESTION

14. Robert Kegan's life span development stages focus on which aspect of human development?

    A) physical growth

    B) spiritual development

    C) relationships

    D) meaning-making

Personality

The study of personality is essentially the study of what makes a person who they are. This is a complicated question, but one that is fundamental to psychology.

There are four general approaches to answering this question: psychoanalytic, trait, social-cognitive, and humanistic.

Freud's Psychoanalytic Theories and Criticism

The most well-known **psychoanalytic** psychologist is **Sigmund Freud**. Freud believed that personality was set in early childhood. According to Freud, the stages of development were:

1. oral
2. anal
3. phallic (Oedipal/Electra complex)
4. latency
5. genital

If a child progressed through the stages of development without a problem, they would be well-adjusted. If, instead, the child experienced an unresolved conflict at a certain stage, they would develop a **fixation**, or become stuck at that stage; this conflict would affect their adult personality.

For example, if an individual experienced a conflict in the first stage—the oral stage—he may develop an oral fixation and need to constantly have something in his mouth.

In addition to his developmental theories, Freud theorized that the personality was composed of three parts:

- **Id**: The unconscious or unknown mind that operates on instinct. Emotions reside here as these are instinctive and not actively created by the individual.
- **Ego**: Existing partly in the unconscious mind and partly in the conscious mind, the ego follows the **reality principle**, and it negotiates between the id and the limitations of the environment.
- **Superego**: The superego is a person's conscience, determining right from wrong. It can influence the ego to account for moral considerations.

While extremely popular, Freud's theories face significant criticism. They are not based upon empirical evidence, and the nature of many of his structures (e.g., the id) make them unprovable. His theories also have no predictive power. While they can be used to explain why someone acted the way that they did, they cannot predict how someone will act in the future. Freud is also criticized for overemphasizing early childhood and sex and for being offensive to women (e.g., he claimed all women have penis envy).

On the opposite side of Freud is Alfred Adler's **individual psychology**. Diverging from Freud's pessimistic view of humanity, Adler had an inherently optimistic view, arguing that people are all ultimately striving for success or superiority. If a person enjoys success—meaning that they contribute to the community benefit while maintaining their personal identity—their personality is unified. If not, or if the person strives for superiority (personal gain without real regard for others), they will be ultimately unfulfilled.

PRACTICE QUESTION

15. When accidentally rear-ended by another car, Mark becomes enraged and attacks the other driver. How would Freud explain Mark's actions?
    A) Mark's id was determining his actions.
    B) Mark's super-ego was determining his actions.
    C) Mark's ego was determining his actions.
    D) Mark's actions were the result of negotiations between his ego, his id and his superego.

Trait, Social-Cognitive, and Humanistic Theories

Trait theories describe personalities by identifying main traits or characteristics. Characteristics of an individual's personality are considered stable and motivate their behavior. **Nomothetic theorists** argue that the same set of traits can be used to describe all personalities. For example, Hans Eyesenck posited that a transection of an introversion-extraversion scale (essentially how shy or outgoing one is) originally created by **Carl Jung** and a neuroticism scale (how anxious or fearful one is) could classify all personalities.

Idiographic theorists, on the other hand, argue that one set of traits cannot be used to describe everybody. Instead, people should be defined by the few traits that best define them, which can vary from person to person.

The primary criticism of trait theory is that it assumes that personalities are stable, when in fact people might behave very differently depending on the situation. For example, someone might be extremely talkative and social among their family, but shy and reserved in public.

According to social-cognitive theories, personality is the result of a combination of environment and patterns of thought. **Albert Bandura**'s theory of **reciprocal determinism** posits that personality results from the interaction between the person (their traits), the environment, and the person's behavior. For example, a person might be naturally optimistic, but become less so after a series of disappointments and failures.

Julian Rotter's **locus of control theory** posits that personality is determined by whether one feels in control of what happens to them. Those who have an internal locus of control—those who feel in control of their lives—tend to be healthier and more engaged, while those with an external locus of control—those who feel luck or destiny controls their lives—tend to be less successful.

Humanistic theorists challenge the **determinism**—the idea that personality is determined by past events—innate in other personality theories. Instead, they argue that people are able to exercise free will to determine their own destinies.

According to humanistic theory, an individual's personality is determined by their overall feeling about themselves (called **self-concept**) and the level of confidence they have in their own abilities (called **self-esteem**).

- **Abraham Maslow** argued that people strive to reach **self-actualization**, the maximizing of their own potential. (See below for more on Maslow.)
- **Carl Rogers** posited that people need blanket acceptance, which he called **unconditional positive regard**, from other people in order to self-actualize.

Humanistic theory is criticized for being overly optimistic and vague. For example, it is difficult to measure if someone has reached their full potential.

 HELPFUL HINT

See chapter 1 for more on unconditional positive regard in counseling.

PRACTICE QUESTION

16. Bandura's theory of reciprocal determinism—that personality is the result of the interaction between the individual, their behavior and their environment—is part of which school of personality theory?

    A) humanistic
    B) psychoanalytical
    C) social-Cognitive
    D) trait

Motivation and Stress

The reason for an individual's behavior is called **motivation**. Motivations can be either conscious and obvious, or unconscious and subtle. Much of motivation theory is based on research in learning and personality.

Maslow's Hierarchy of Needs

Abraham Maslow theorized that motivation was based on need, but all needs are not equal. He identifies five levels of need from basic biological needs for safety and survival to the need to fulfill life goals and self-actualization.

According to Maslow, each level of need must be fulfilled before the next can be addressed. However, there are examples that contradict this model. For example, Buddhist monks who practice self-immolation (lighting themselves on fire) during the Vietnam War prioritized the need of self-actualization over the need for survival.

Self-Actualization
morality, creativity, spontaneity, acceptance

Self-Esteem
confidence, achievement, respect of others

Love and Belonging
family, friendship, intimacy, sense of connection

Safety and Security
health, employment, property, family and social stability

Physiological Needs
breathing, food, water, shelter, clothing, sleep

3.2. Maslow's Hierarchy of Needs

PRACTICE QUESTION

17. Which of the following is true of Maslow's hierarchy of needs?
  A) All needs ultimately relate to survival and safety.
  B) All needs must be met simultaneously.
  C) A level of need cannot be addressed until the previous level is met.
  D) Personal relationships are the ultimate need.

Sources of Motivation

Motivation comes from a variety of sources: internal, external, and environmental. The individual attitudes and goals of those people in an individual's life, as well as broader societal attitudes and goals, may serve as motivation for an individual. An example of this **social motivation** would be a student who works hard in school to gain admission to college because of the value society places on a college education.

If, however, that same student sought admission to college in order to master high level skills and to better understand the world, they would be propelled by **achievement motivation**. People who are motivated by achievement continually seek greater challenges.

All motivators can be classified as either **extrinsic motivators**—coming from outside of one's self—or **intrinsic motivators**—coming from within. For example, the person motivated to gain admission to college to get a good job or to be held in high esteem by others is extrinsically motivated. The student who seeks admission to college in order feel a sense of accomplishment or achieve mastery in a particular discipline is intrinsically motivated.

Both types of motivation are effective in encouraging desired behaviors; however, once extrinsic motivators end, so does the behavior. Once the student looking for peer approval gains admission to college, he is more likely than his intrinsically motivated counterpart to perform poorly. Therefore, extrinsic motivators are suitable for short-term behavior goals, while intrinsic motivators are better at encouraging long-term positive behaviors.

PRACTICE QUESTION

18. When Amy fails her math test, she decides it is because the questions were too confusing. This is an example of which of the following types of attribution?

    A) person-stable attribution
    B) person-unstable attribution
    C) situation-stable attribution
    D) situation-unstable attribution

Stress

Any situation that taxes one's coping abilities by threatening—or seeming to threaten—a person's wellbeing is considered **stress**. Common stressors include life changes, external and internal pressure, environmental factors, frustration, and conflict.

Acute stressors are relatively short in duration and have a clear endpoint, whereas chronic stressors are relatively long in duration and have no apparent time limit. Acute stressors have little negative impact and can even be beneficial at times. For example, short-term frustration, the thwarting of the pursuit of a goal, can act as a motivator for further achievement. **Chronic stressors**, on the other hand, have significant physiological and psychological consequences. Hans Selye detailed the body's stress response in his **General Adaptation Syndrome (GAS)** as it applies to all animals:

- **Alarm reaction:** The heart rate increases; blood is diverted away from other body functions to prepare the animal for action. This is also known as the **fight-or-flight response**, as the animal is prepared to either attack or flee.

- **Resistance**: Hormones are released to maintain the state of readiness. In chronic stress, this state is maintained for too long, depleting the body's resources.
- **Exhaustion**: The body returns to a normal state. If the resistance state lasted too long, the body will be more vulnerable to disease and sustain long-term damage. This is why chronic stress is associated with health problems like arthritis, ulcers, asthma, migraine headaches, heart disease, and depression.

Maintaining a resistance state resulting from some kind of stressful event—either acute or long-term (e.g., war, sexual assault, watching someone die, or almost dying themselves) can also lead to **post-traumatic stress disorder (PTSD)**. People with PTSD experience disturbed behavior—including nightmares, jumpiness, and temper flares.

Chronic stress also disrupts attention and inhibits memory. Chronic, or **toxic stress**, related to poverty can even change the chemical makeup of a child's brain, disrupting and weakening its circuits.

The best way to deal with stress is to use **constructive coping mechanisms** like confronting a problem directly, breaking it down into manageable pieces, maintaining flexibility, and remaining aware of one's coping and stress resources. Studies have also shown that maintaining **perceived control**, or the feeling that one is in control of a stressor, reduces the overall stress level. For example, the patient who is given control of his own pain control medication reports a lower overall pain level than the patient who is prescribed doses, even when the amount of medicine received is the same.

PRACTICE QUESTION

19. Hans Selye developed his general adaptation syndrome to describe which of the following?

    A) personality traits

    B) reactions to stress

    C) memory processes

    D) problem-solving processes

Answer Key

1. A

    The client's symptoms and history indicate that the disorder was passed on through the generations of his family.

2. A

    At birth, babies can only see 8 – 12 inches in front of their faces. They do not gain full sight until they are one year old.

3. D

    The baby's actions demonstrate a strong attachment to the caregiver.

4. B

    Authoritarian parents impose rules and structure with very little explanation or warmth, similar to how a drill sergeant might enforce order.

5. B

    The baby monkeys preferred the soft fake mothers even when they did not offer food.

6. B

    The Formal Operations stage is the final stage. Individuals develop the ability to engage in metacognition, thinking about how they think.

7. A

    Vygotsky's zone of proximal development describes tasks students can perform with help and gradually learn to do on their own.

8. A

    Overgeneralization describes the tendency of young children to misapply grammatical rules by assuming that the rules apply universally.

9. C

    According to Erikson, autonomy emerges when a toddler develops a sense of independence. This occurs in the second stage.

10. B

    Carol Gilligan critiqued Kohlberg for having a strong male bias in his theory, pointing to the fact that all the original participants were male and his own male perspective on moral reasoning impacted how he evaluated various types of reasoning. Gilligan herself articulated different types of moral reasoning based on gender, which has since been called into question.

11. A

    A midlife crisis occurs when people question their life's purpose.

12. B

    The multiplicity stage puts the burden of answers on authority figures.

13. C

    Children at the mythic-literal faith stage associate good deeds with good outcomes and vice versa.

14. D

    Kegan's developmental stages consider how people in each stage develop their social understanding, identities, and create meaning in their lives.

15. A

    The id governs all emotion and impulsive behavior. When attacking the other driver, Mark was being driven solely by his emotions.

16. C

    Social cognitive theory looks at the ways in which individual thought and overall environment impact personality. Bandura was a prominent social-cognitive theorist.

17. C

    According to Maslow, the ability to fulfill a need is dependent on the fulfillment of needs lower in the hierarchy.

18. D

    Amy attributes her failure to the situation of the particular test, making it an unstable attribution and a situational one.

19. B

    The general adaptation syndrome describes the physiological reaction all animals have to stress.

4 Career Development

Career and Finances

Career trajectories influence lifestyle, income, life satisfaction, work-life balance, and retirement and can therefore be a driving force in encouraging individuals to seek counseling. Counselors should be prepared to support people in developing career goals and helping them find the best career fit. Several theories of career development are useful in counseling.

Career Development Theories

Social cognitive career theory (SCCT) is based on Albert Bandura's research on social learning theory, which emphasizes self-cognition and social processes. This theory addresses the learning aspects of career development and how goals can shift and adjust over time based on positive or negative feedback from the environment. There are three main components of SCCT:

- self-efficacy
- outcome expectations
- personal goals

Self-efficacy refers to an individual's perception of her ability to complete tasks or execute certain behaviors. People can demonstrate high or low self-efficacy in different areas. For example, a person might feel that he is very good at communicating with people but struggles with complex math and analysis. Personal success is seen as the biggest factor in developing self-efficacy. According to SCCT, self-efficacy is driven by the following:

- personal accomplishments
- social persuasion (others telling a person that she is good at a particular task)
- vicarious experiences (seeing other people perform those same tasks)
- an individual's physical state (not being anxious when performing the task)

Outcome expectations are what a person believes will happen when a task is completed. As with self-efficacy, outcome expectations are typically built through experience and the observation of others. People with high self-efficacy about their job performance would expect certain positive outcomes, such as

- approval from others;
- tangible benefits (a raise or promotion);
- better working conditions.

Finally, **personal goals** are the decisions an individual makes to pursue specific activities to achieve future outcomes. Personal goals can help propel people forward in their careers even when there are long gaps between external benefits, like promotions or raises. In SCCT there are two types of personal goals:

1. **Choice goals** are related to decision-making, such as choosing a new career path or field of study.
2. **Performance goals** tend to be more concrete and measurable, such as pursuing an A in a class or a promotion at work.

According to SCCT, personal goals are related to outcome expectations and self-efficacy. This is because the level of a person's talent in her field will shape the kinds of goals she pursues, and her success or failure in achieving those goals will likely influence future self-efficacy and expected outcomes.

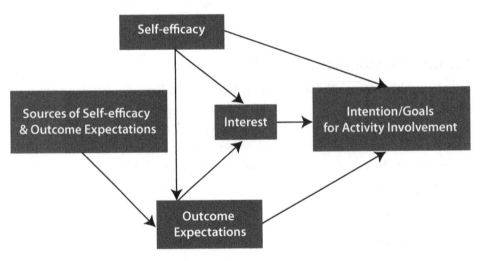

Figure 4.1. Social Cognitive Career Theory

Trait-factor theory is based on the idea that careers are best matched to people's individual traits and skills. This theory is particularly useful because the process of career development between client and counselor is broken down into stages. Educator Frank Parsons believed that three components were essential for successful career development:

1. accurate self-assessment of one's talents or proclivities and interests
2. accurate understanding of the current labor and job markets
3. fair judgment of the relationship between one's skill set and the need for it in the labor market

Individuals who are capable of accurately assessing their skills, interests, and the needs of the current labor market would find a job that leverages their skills. Parsons believed that workers who focus on tasks for which they have the highest aptitude would be the most successful.

Parsons developed a seven-stage counseling system to help people determine the best career path. This system can be used by counselors in guiding clients through career development and choice-making.

DID YOU KNOW?

Trait-factor theory was developed by **Frank Parsons**, who many consider to be the father of the career counseling movement. His theories are still used today to help people discover their ideal career paths.

TABLE 4.1. Parson's Seven-Stage Counseling System	
Personal data	The client and counselor together generate a list of traits and characteristics about the client, especially as they relate to career development.
Self-analysis	The client individually reflects on traits and tendencies that might impact his career. These can be positive, negative, or neutral. Some examples are being goal-oriented, task-oriented, results-driven; working better in groups or autonomously, etc.
The client's own choice and decision	Successful career development must ultimately be client-led. While the counselor can offer ideas, guidance, and feedback, the focus must always be on client goals.
Counselor's analysis	The counselor's role is to help clients both reflect on their stated choices and determine if they are in line with their other stated goals. For example, clients who say they want to be in a leadership position but don't want to work more than thirty hours a week might need to reflect on which goal is more important to them.
Outlook on the vocational field	Career counselors should understand current career trends, expectations, and skill norms to help clients match their skills and goals with available jobs.
Induction and advice	Both counselor and client will work best if the focus is objective and goal-directed, with a clear eye on the possibilities and limitations in the field and within the client's skills and abilities.
General helpfulness	The counselor helps clients adjust to their chosen positions, reflect on these, and make any needed adjustments.

Psychologist John Holland developed a theory of personality and occupation, known as **RIASEC**, to help people determine their best career fit. According to RIASEC, people are best suited to career environments that match their personalities. He theorized that there are six main personality types that correlate to career types:

- **R**ealistic
- **I**nvestigative
- **A**rtistic
- **S**ocial
- **E**nterprising
- **C**onventional

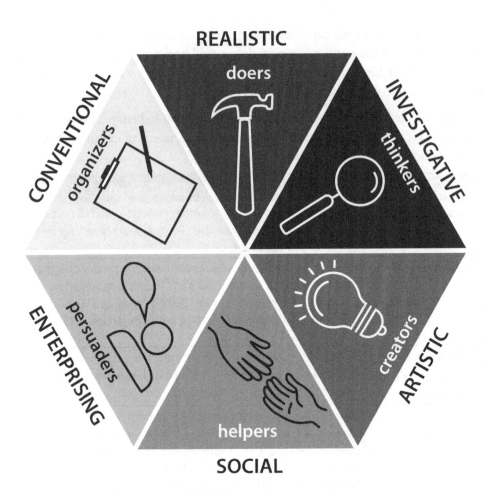

Figure 4.2. The Holland Hexagon (RIASEC)

TABLE 4.2. RIASEC Traits, Values, and Typical Careers			
Category	**Traits**	**Preferences/ Values**	**Typical Careers**
Realistic	pragmatic, concrete	• animals, tools, machines • appreciate practical things they can observe in their environment, such as plants and animals, equipment, or tools	trades such as plumbing, electrical work, and carpentry, or environmental work such as agriculture, wildlife preservation, veterinary care, etc.
Investigative	academic, cerebral	• math, science, logic, reasoning • avoid sales and jobs requiring persuasion	academia (especially STEM careers), engineering, research

Artistic	creative	• acting, dance, music, writing, art • independent, expressive • value creative output in themselves and others	fine arts, graphic design, writing, film/media
Social	personal, service-oriented	• outgoing, amiable, extroverted • value relationships	teacher, counselor, health care professional, sales
Enterprising	persuasive/leaders	• skilled at convincing others of the value of their ideas, products, or plans • perceive themselves as ambitious and high-energy with good people skills • may shy away from analytical or scientific thinking, preferring to think "big picture"	business, politics, leadership positions
Conventional	organized, reliable	• enjoy working with numbers, records, or machines; thrive on order, set tasks, and do not mind repetition • rely on external plans to set their work into motion	bookkeeping, CPAs, data analytics, secretarial work, project management, and other task-oriented and highly organization-reliant positions

PRACTICE QUESTION

1. Which of the following elements is a key component of Bandura's social cognitive career theory?

   A) personality assessments
   B) job market analysis
   C) self-analysis
   D) self-efficacy

Financial Concerns

Many clients seek out counseling to address financial stress and even seek guidance on improving financial habits. Some of the main financial concerns include

- managing debt;
- loss of income;
- increased expenses due to life events, such as injury, children, or retirement.

While money management is unlikely to be the primary focus of counseling sessions, understanding the most common financial stressors and accompanying mental health concerns is essential to best support clients who are facing financial difficulties.

A counselor must understand the origin of a client's debt to effectively discuss the issue. Does the client have student loan debt that she is slowly chipping away at? Or are there spending issues, such as charging bills to credit cards? In some cases, the spending issues might be more significant and related to addiction, such as shopping, gambling, or drug addictions. These may require more serious intervention with a referral to an addiction clinic.

Some clients may benefit from referrals to debt counseling. Others may benefit more from exploring coping mechanisms. Counselors can work with clients to

- avoid excess spending;
- shift existing habits;
- reevaluate their life priorities.

Income loss is another significant financial stressor and can occur in different ways:

- job loss
- cutbacks in hours
- being furloughed
- inability to work due to illness or disability
- a partner's job loss
- loss of benefits (for example, EBT benefits, social security, or child support)

These losses in income streams often coincide with stressful life events. Illness, injury, job loss, and other life changes can be significant stressors that clients may need help navigating and processing emotionally. Counseling may target

- coping and self-care skills;
- building up or relying on existing safety nets;
- working on finding ways to increase the income stream.

DID YOU KNOW?

About 80 percent of Americans have some kind of **debt**; the median debt amount carried is nearly $90,000. The likelihood that counselors will encounter clients with debt is very high.

Counselors are not typically equipped to handle all the nuances of navigating social welfare systems, so referring clients to an agency skilled in assisting with financial issues may be helpful in these cases.

Certain common **life events** can also have stressful financial implications:
- having a baby
- getting married
- becoming injured or disabled
- preparing for retirement

Some life changes might be expected (for example, retirement), whereas others might be unexpected. The counselor should create space to help clients express the emotions that arise with these life changes. Equally important, the counselor should collaborate with clients to develop concrete solutions to their financial challenges.

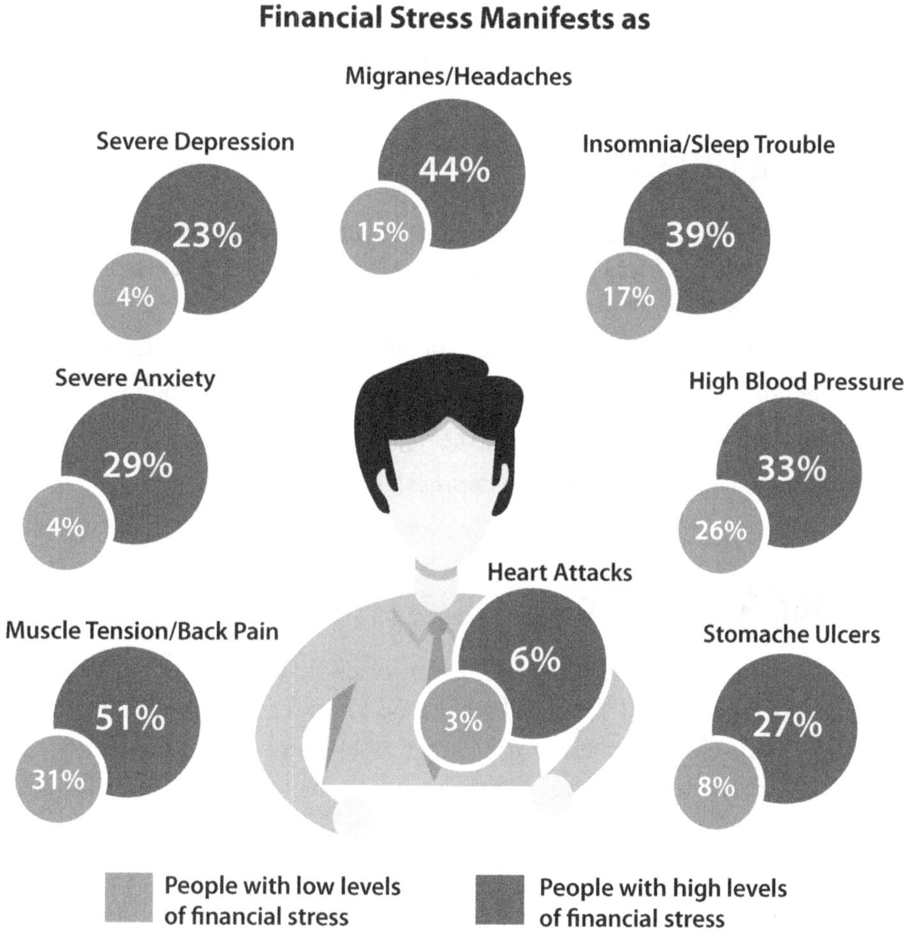

Financial Stress Manifests as

Migranes/Headaches: 44% / 15%
Severe Depression: 23% / 4%
Insomnia/Sleep Trouble: 39% / 17%
Severe Anxiety: 29% / 4%
High Blood Pressure: 33% / 26%
Heart Attacks: 6% / 3%
Muscle Tension/Back Pain: 51% / 31%
Stomache Ulcers: 27% / 8%

Legend: People with low levels of financial stress | People with high levels of financial stress

Figure 4.3. Physical Impacts of Financial Stress

Financial stressors can trigger a variety of mental health symptoms and exacerbate existing stress. Exploring these concerns with clients is essential to successfully navigate life's stressors. Counselors should screen for certain concerns, including

- grief;
- relationship problems;
- anxiety;
- depression;
- eating problems (too much or too little);
- physical complaints (for example, upset stomach, headaches, muscle tension);
- sleep difficulties (too much or too little).

Poverty can have a significant impact on mental well-being. Individuals living in poverty are twice as likely to report symptoms of depression as those who are not living in poverty. The constant stressors of not having enough money can impact sleep, overall well-being, and financial decision-making.

The impacts of living in chronic poverty are often not fully alleviated even when a person gains upward mobility. Many people who grew up in poverty continue to struggle in adulthood with feeling secure and stable in their finances, which may drive them to make emotion-based financial decision-making.

PRACTICE QUESTION

2. Linda is a thirty-two-year-old single mother with significant credit card debt. She comes to counseling seeking support for managing life stressors related to her financial difficulties. How should the counselor begin treatment?

    A) refer out to a professional who is qualified to provide financial counseling
    B) conduct a review of Linda's spending habits and debt-to-income ratio
    C) explore which stressors are of the highest concern for Linda
    D) screen Linda for anxiety and depression

Career Assessment

Career assessments are standardized inventories that allow people to explore their areas of interest and skills and what type of work environment they would thrive in. Counselors frequently use career assessments with high school and college students who are unsure of the career path they want to take, or for adults who want to revisit their current career choices. The following are some of the most common career assessment tools.

The **Strong Interest Inventory (SII)** is used for high school and college students as well as adults who are seeking guidance for a career path. It involves 291 questions across six domains in areas such as occupations and activities interests. It does not measure personality or aptitude. It is a reliable and valid assessment that counselors can use for clients who are unsure of what career path they are most interested in.

Psychologist John Holland developed a theory of career development known as **RIASEC** (realistic, investigative, artistic, social, enterprising, conventional). He theorizes that people fall into one of these six categories, which determines which work environment they are best suited for. Clients who would like to understand more about their personality and what type of environment they have the potential to thrive in would benefit from this assessment. Please see chapter 9 for more details.

The **Self-Directed Search (SDS)** is a formalized assessment based on Holland's career development theory. It is a self-directed assessment, making it ideal for independent clients who prefer to explore career possibilities on their own.

The **Kuder Occupational Interest Survey (KOIS)** is a normed survey that compares client scores of areas of interest compared to the scores of people currently in those fields. Known as "the Kuder," it is self-administered and can be interpreted at home. For clients who are concerned about personality and interest fit within certain fields, the Kuder can help illuminate how similarly a client may feel compared to others in that field.

The **Career Beliefs Inventory (CBI)** is a counselor-administered assessment that is designed to help counselors explore areas of mental blockage, assumptions, generalizations, and beliefs about themselves and others that may be preventing them from exploring their full potential. It is ideal to use as an initial assessment for a client experiencing career difficulties, as it can provide important information for the counselor to explore with the client.

Finally, the **DiSC Assessment** groups people into four main personality profiles:

1. dominance (results-oriented, confident)
2. influence (relationship-focused, persuasive)
3. steadiness (cooperative, sincere, dependable)
4. conscientiousness (competence, clarity, accuracy)

The DiSC assessment can be used in the workplace, especially to analyze candidates and leadership qualities.

PRACTICE QUESTION

3. A client comes in concerned that he would not fit in well in his preferred career choice. Which assessment would BEST help the counselor determine the validity of that concern?
    A) Career Beliefs Inventory
    B) Kuder Occupational Interest Survey
    C) Strong Interest Inventory
    D) Self-Directed Search

Answer Key

1. D

   Self-efficacy, outcome expectations, and personal goals are the three main components of Bandura's social cognitive career theory (SCCT).

2. C

   Therapy is always focused on what the client sees as her presenting problem and the area on which she would like to work. By asking Linda what her biggest concerns are, the counselor prioritizes the client's perspective on her life and encourages engagement with the therapeutic process.

3. B

   The Kuder Occupational Interest Survey (KOIS, or "the Kuder") is normed against scores of people across ten respective fields, which is ideal for helping a client who wants to know if he has similar thoughts and feelings as other people in his chosen field.

5 Counseling and Helping Relationships

Core Counseling Attributes

Counseling Attributes

Many basic counseling attributes form the foundation of the therapeutic relationship with a client and distinguish the professional counseling relationship from other interpersonal relationships:

1. **Genuineness** is a counseling attribute that refers to authenticity.
   - Counselors should say what they mean and mean what they say.
   - Counselors should be authentic in sessions with clients and not put on a false front.
   - For example, if a counselor smiles when greeting a client, the smile should be authentic and not forced.

2. **Congruence** is similar to genuineness. The psychologist Carl Rogers defined congruence as the genuineness necessary for a counselor to provide unconditional positive regard and empathy. Rogers believed that when counselors show congruence in their sessions, they appear more trustworthy, which strengthens the therapeutic alliance.
   - Counselors should be fully attentive to both their clients and themselves while practicing transparency.
   - Counselors' insides should match their outsides.
   - Counselors should be completely honest with clients about what the counselors experience.
   - For example, if a counselor cringes in response to a client's remark, a congruent counselor will explain that reaction to the client.

3. **Nonjudgmental stance** requires counselors to remain open-minded to the client's experience and refrain from evaluating the clients, their issues, or their behaviors.
   - This attribute emphasizes the benefits of practicing self-awareness and self-reflection.

- Judgment can be communicated both verbally and nonverbally, so counselors must learn to remain neutral in words and body language during sessions with clients.
- A counselor can exhibit a nonjudgmental stance with a client by
  - keeping facial expressions pleasant and neutral;
  - staying in a relaxed body posture;
  - maintaining eye contact regardless of what the client says.

4. **Positive regard** expands on the nonjudgmental stance. A counselor practicing positive regard
- projects an attitude of acceptance of the client as a person;
- adopts a worldview and philosophy of seeing all people as worthy of dignity and respect regardless of their thoughts, emotions, or behaviors, which are separate from people's inherent worth.
- A counselor exhibits positive regard by
  - verbally affirming that the client is worthy of dignity and respect no matter what;
  - treating the client with dignity and respect in sessions;
  - reinforcing the idea that clients are not defined by their thoughts, feelings, or behaviors;
  - clarifying that even if counselors disapprove of a client's behavior, they accept the client as a person.

PRACTICE QUESTION

1. A client discloses to the counselor that he uses illicit substances at night when his kids are in bed. The counselor believes this behavior is risky and could endanger the children. Which of the following statements would BEST reflect the implementation of counseling attributes?

   A) "You need to stop using immediately, as it could put yourself and your children in danger. What if there is an emergency and you're unable to respond?"

   B) "The potential of something bad happening concerns me, and I don't agree with your choices, but I am here to help you if you would like to make better ones. I know you can do it."

   C) "If this continues, I will have to report you to child welfare for putting your children at risk. You could be facing serious charges."

   D) "What kind of parent does something like that? You should reconsider your choices and think about your kids from now on."

Self-Awareness

As an objective participant guiding a therapeutic process with clients, a counselor must practice clinical detachment while conveying empathy. This requires awareness of self. **Awareness of self** is a practice of reflection and observation both in and outside of the moment.

Awareness of self in the moment is a skill whereby the counselor notices his own thoughts, beliefs, emotions, and behaviors without judgment and recognizes how these impact the client. By noticing and evaluating, the counselor can adjust based on the client's reactions. For example, a counselor may find himself reacting emotionally to a client:

- The client may react with surprise.
- The counselor can then choose how to handle the situation without judging his own emotional reaction.
- Sharing an emotional reaction with a client may increase trust.
- The counselor may react negatively to a client's disclosure.
- In practicing self-awareness, the counselor can recognize a negative reaction, evaluate it, and put it aside so the client does not feel judged.
- The counselor may choose to share the process of self-awareness and invite the client to do the same.

Another aspect of self-awareness is the practice of self-reflection on one's own or in consultation with others. Before meeting a client of a significantly different cultural background, for example, the counselor might reflect on her values and beliefs about the client's culture and how those beliefs could impact the client in the session. By practicing self-reflection beforehand, counselors can

- check whatever bias they may have;
- educate themselves about the culture;
- meet the client without bringing that bias into the session.

The counselor's verbal and nonverbal communication impact clients in both positive and negative ways. Clients can tell if something is not right with the counselor, and that may interfere with building a therapeutic relationship. Therefore, the counselor needs to remain self-aware in sessions and must read the client's cues to understand the client's reaction and make adjustments as needed.

 HELPFUL HINT

Counselors can also practice self-reflection with a supervisor or other colleague to help bring awareness to any bias or prejudice that could adversely affect the client relationship.

PRACTICE QUESTION

2. During a session with a client, a counselor makes a statement and notices the client flinch. What is one thing the counselor can do in the session to demonstrate self-awareness?
   A) continue the session as if nothing happened
   B) ask the client what he got out of the session when it is over
   C) point out the client's reaction and seek understanding from the client
   D) discuss the situation with a supervisor at the next supervision meeting

Communication and Active Listening

The basic elements of communication and active listening form the foundation of a counselor's rapport and relationship with the client. To build a strong rapport with a client, the counselor must

- be engaging;

- be an active listener;
- avoid interrupting the client.

Clients will trust that the counselor cares about their issues and advocates for their well-being. A counselor who actively listens will deliver on guarantees, establish and maintain boundaries, and build trust with the client. Building trust can take time, but doing so makes managing the client's condition easier for all involved.

The theory of basic communication is made up of several components:

- **sender**: the individual or thing sending the message
- **channel**: the method by which the sender transmits the message
- **receiver**: the individual or thing translating the message
- **destination**: the individual or thing for whom the message is targeted
- **message**: the information transferred from the sender to the recipient

People use these elements in everyday conversations without even realizing it. The sender will transfer information through the channel to the receiver, who interprets or translates the message to the destination. In recent times, oral conversation has given way to texting, emailing, and using social media; sometimes, the intended tone of the message can be lost without aural cues.

Active listening means paying attention to the speaker, not just hearing his words. The listener makes eye contact with the speaker to indicate interest in what is being said. An active listener repeats important points the speaker has made to ensure understanding, asks follow-up questions, and does not interrupt. The goal is threefold: to convey to the speaker that the listener understands the message, to show the speaker that the listener cares about what the speaker is saying, and to let the speaker know that the listener empathizes with the speaker.

TABLE 5.1. Dos and Don'ts of Client Communication

Do...	Don't...
• make eye contact with the client	• use medical jargon
• introduce yourself and use the client's name	• threaten or intimidate the client
• speak directly to the client when possible	• lie or provide false hope
• ask open-ended questions	• interrupt the client
• speak slowly and clearly	• show frustration or anger
• show empathy for the client	• make judgmental statements
• be silent when appropriate to allow the client time to think and process emotions	• make accusations
• use person-first language	• tell the client what to do
• maintain pleasant facial expressions	• force clients to answer questions
• use relaxed body language	

In addition to active listening, a variety of techniques are used for therapeutic communication:

- **Sharing observations** may open up the conversation to how the client is feeling.
- **Using touch**, such as a gentle hand on the shoulder or arm, when appropriate or welcome, can offer comfort. However, this may not be appropriate in mixed-gender relationships, with those who have experienced trauma, or with those with other relational differences.
- **Silence** allows the client a moment to absorb or process information and sit with emotions to experience them fully.
- **Summarizing and paraphrasing** information back to a client helps ensure or confirm understanding and convey empathy.
- **Asking relevant questions** that pertain to the situation helps the counselor gather information for decision-making and can lead to insight for the client.
- **Reframing** is a technique that counselors use to offer the client another way to consider a situation. It offers an alternative perspective while demonstrating that the counselor understands the client.

Communication includes both verbal and nonverbal components:

- **Verbal communication** uses language to convey information. Characteristics of verbal communication include tone, volume, and word choice.
- **Nonverbal communication** includes behavior, gestures, posture, and other nonlanguage elements of communication that transmit information or meaning.

Finally, attending and reflecting are foundational skills for counselors:

- **Attending** is a basic skill whereby the counselor communicates to the client that she is present and listening.
  - Attending is a vital skill for establishing rapport with clients because it lets them know that the counselor's attention is solely on the client.
  - A counselor can practice attending verbally through greetings, showing interest in the client's life, and asking questions, when necessary, to clarify what the client said.
  - A counselor can convey attending to a client nonverbally through eye contact, facial expressions, and gestures that encourage a client to keep talking.
- **Reflecting** is a skill that demonstrates attention, understanding, and empathy. Just as a mirror shows a reflection, reflecting in the therapeutic setting is a way of repeating what the client says.
  - Reflecting shows that the counselor is listening.
  - A counselor uses this skill to increase the connection with the client.
    - When clients feel that they are truly heard, they feel valued, which increases positive feelings toward the counselor.

- A counselor demonstrates reflecting by repeating what the client just said.
  - For example, a client tells a story about a family conflict and says, "I just wanted to hit someone, but I didn't."
  - The counselor might say, "You wanted to hit someone, but you didn't."
  - This shows the client that the counselor heard what he said and invites him to say more without asking a direct question.

PRACTICE QUESTION

3. Which of the following scenarios demonstrates attending behaviors by the counselor?
    A) maintaining eye contact with the client and smiling to encourage the client to keep talking
    B) using a laptop to type notes while the client talks
    C) fidgeting and looking at the clock many times throughout the session
    D) sitting tensely and still with a neutral facial expression

Empathy

Empathy is the ability to understand and accurately perceive the feelings and experiences of clients from their perspective. Carl Rogers viewed empathy as a state of being for counselors that facilitates being non-judgmental and accepting.

Empathy differs significantly from sympathy. Although both involve emotions, empathy does not involve the counselor's personal experience, nor does it involve judgment. Sympathy, on the other hand, is the process of pitying or feeling bad for someone without really understanding that person's perspective; this means it includes judgment.

Sympathy is a surface-level intellectual understanding based on personal experience. Empathy is a deeper understanding and sharing of emotions based on the other person's perspective. Empathy builds connection; sympathy does not.

- **Empathetic attunement** combines empathy with attending skills. When using empathetic attunement, the counselor is aware of the client's emotions as well as his own.
  - The counselor communicates verbally and nonverbally that he recognizes the client's emotions.
  - For example, if a client starts to cry in a session, the counselor can demonstrate empathetic attunement by staying silent and relaxed, being present with the client, and allowing her to experience that emotion without judgment or comment.
- **Empathetic responding** is a verbal response from the counselor that tells the client she understands what the client is feeling and why he feels that way.

- This skill shows the client that the counselor respects and understands his emotions and the reasons for them.
- Using the example of the client who feels like hitting someone during a family conflict, the counselor might empathetically respond by saying, "You feel intense anger because you feel that person is not listening to you."

PRACTICE QUESTION

4. A client tells the counselor that her spouse just gave notice of divorce. The client is in shock and asks questions in rapid succession, wondering what she missed, what is wrong with her, and what will she do now. She is taking short, shallow breaths and talking fast. How can the counselor demonstrate empathetic attunement in this situation?

   A) try to answer the client's questions or help her answer her own questions

   B) tell the client to calm down and speak more slowly so the situation can be discussed productively

   C) help the client identify the cognitive distortions forming in her mind that contribute to her feelings

   D) allow the client to continue to express her frustration without judging her

Working with the Client

Establishing the Counseling Relationship

Individual counseling follows a template:

- Assess client issues.
- Determine diagnosis.
- Set goals based on the diagnosis.
- Design an evidence-based plan of treatment for the diagnosis.

Everything flows together and relates back to the diagnosis. Even as new information emerges over the course of treatment, any changes to the treatment plan must still directly relate to the client's diagnosis. For clients to be correctly diagnosed, they must

- feel safe enough with the counselor to truthfully disclose information needed to form a correct diagnosis;
- feel like the counselor is not judging them; embarrassment and shame often accompany mental health issues.

The importance of the **therapeutic relationship** can therefore not be understated. The counseling relationship is the most important factor that predicts treatment outcomes. For clients to accept the proposed treatments, they must first trust the counselor enough to be honest about their experiences and issues:

- Without trust, the client may not feel comfortable sharing everything with the counselor.

- If the client does not share openly, it can lead to the wrong diagnosis and the wrong plan of treatment.

For example, a person with depression who does not trust the counselor might not disclose a serious trauma, like childhood sexual abuse. Without that information, the counselor may make the wrong recommendations for treatment. While the client may experience some relief, he will not truly benefit from the treatment plan if therapy does not address the underlying issues.

The foundation of the counseling relationship is the therapeutic alliance. The **therapeutic alliance** is an unwritten agreement between the client and the counselor based on trust, boundaries, and mutual respect. It is not a friendship but rather a formal treatment relationship.

In the therapeutic alliance, clients feel safe to explore issues and be vulnerable with the counselor. At the same time, they know that the counselor will hold them accountable and maintain professional boundaries. Clients need assurance that the counselor will not judge them.

The therapeutic alliance is also an equalization of power between the client and the counselor. Often, clients enter into counseling viewing the counselor as a person of authority, much like many people view physicians. In that type of relationship, clients may expect the counselor to tell them what to do to get better. Unlike the client-physician relationship, however, the counselor in the therapeutic alliance

- makes it clear that clients lead the way and establish their own goals;
- uses therapeutic techniques, not force or coercion, to help clients achieve their goals.

PRACTICE QUESTION

5. At her first appointment, a client asks the counselor for help with sleep difficulties that interfere with functioning. After talking about the sleep issues, the client says, "Okay, that's my problem, tell me how to fix it." Which aspect of the relationship should the counselor address to create a therapeutic alliance?

    A) explain that counseling is client-focused and not counselor-focused

    B) establish the counselor's position as an expert and tell the client what to do

    C) question the client's experience and tell her there is nothing wrong with her

    D) explain to the client that the problem is all in her head and the issue is not really about sleep

Motivation to Change

Motivation is the driving force behind people's actions. Counselors should assess clients' sources of motivation in the context of managing their mental health to better educate, encourage, and advocate for them:

- **Intrinsic motivation** is the desire to achieve a goal, seek challenges, or complete a task that is driven by enjoyment and personal satisfaction (for example, exercising because it is enjoyable). Motivation comes from within the client.
  - People who are intrinsically motivated to pursue change are more likely to follow through with counseling.
  - For example, a woman who struggles with depression and irritability and who is intrinsically motivated may come to counseling because she wants to be a happier person.
- **Extrinsic motivation** is the desire to accomplish a goal that is driven by external rewards or punishment (for example, exercising to prevent anxiety). Extrinsic motivation comes from forces outside the client.
  - People who are extrinsically motivated may follow through with counseling, but they are less likely to do so than those who are intrinsically motivated.
  - For example, an adolescent forced into therapy by his parents may only come to counseling to avoid punishment. This will impact the level at which he engages in the process.
  - Another example is a client referred to therapy by a drug court proceeding whereby her success in therapy will determine whether or not she goes to jail for a drug offense. In this case, extrinsic motivation may positively influence the client.

Counselors should also consider a client's motivation for change as it pertains to the stated problem. In other words, a client may have intrinsic motivation to feel better but may not be ready to make the behavioral changes necessary to do so.

In these cases, the counselor should help clients discover and tap into their motivations to change. This will move them from the stages of change talk to change action. The **transtheoretical model** allows counselors to identify which stage of change clients are in and how to guide them to a stage of change where they are motivated to engage in change behavior.

Clients with an **external locus of control** will attribute their successes or failures to outside forces. These clients tend to blame others for what they experience and feel there is little to nothing they can do to change these experiences. Some of these clients will feel helpless and hopeless that anything can change, while others recognize that even if those outside forces impact their success or failure, there are options to counter them.

Clients with an **internal locus of control** will attribute their success or failure to themselves. Some of these clients will unrealistically take the blame and responsibility for everything that happens to them; others use their strengths to overcome adversity.

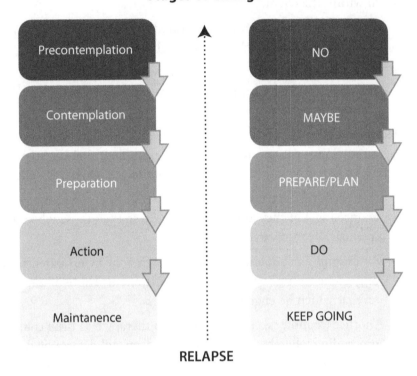

Figure 5.1. Transtheoretical Model

PRACTICE QUESTION

6. A college student comes to therapy seeking help for depression. The client says he is doing poorly in school and wants to quit. During the assessment, he says school is too hard, the professors are unfair graders, and his peers sabotage his work. What do the client's statements indicate?

    A) The client has an internal locus of control.

    B) The client is depressed.

    C) The client has an external locus of control.

    D) The client is motivated to change.

Client Education

Counselors should provide educational resources on relevant topics (for example, stress management, assertiveness training, divorce adjustment). This type of education in the context of mental health is often referred to as **psychoeducation**, or education focused on sharing evidence-based information about a mental health issue and how to cope with it.

Psychoeducation is valuable because it helps clients understand the what, how, and why of what they are experiencing. For example, a counselor who diagnoses a client with generalized anxiety disorder would teach her about the diagnostic criteria for the condition, evidence-based causes for the disorder, what options are available to her for treatment, evidence-based means of coping with the disorder, and the potential prognosis for the disorder based on research. Often this education can help clients understand that they are not alone in this experience, that their experiences are valid, and that there is hope for treatment. When seeking social support, it can also help when clients explain to other people in their lives what they are experiencing. Strategies for teaching include the following:

- **Lectures** (groups or one-on-one) are effective for conveying cognitive knowledge, particularly to auditory learners. A counselor uses this strategy to convey information on a specific subject to a client individually or to a group.
- **Group discussions** in which clients can ask questions and share information are effective for social learners and can help with affective learning (for example, changing attitudes) and practicing skills in a safe environment.
- **Role-playing** is a good way to teach affective skills (like responding to peer pressure) and to practice relational and communication skills in a safe environment.
- **Instructional materials**, like films or pamphlets, may be used as part of a larger education plan; however, they may be ineffective if clients are disengaged or the materials do not match the client's needs and learning abilities.
  - Counselors may provide instructional materials to clients within the context of treatment to support additional learning. For example, during a session, the client learns about healthy coping skills and discusses coping skills to try during the next week.
  - A counselor might give the client a pamphlet that defines healthy coping skills and provides a list of healthy coping skills to try, including ones that were discussed in the session. This serves as a reminder for the client and reinforces what happened in the session.

Some specific strategies to engage clients in the learning process include the following:

- Link new information to current behavior; new learning is better received when it focuses on what the client already knows.
- Be clear, explicit, and specific.
- Suggest alternatives or adaptations that apply directly to clients and their situations.
- Be transparent about the goals of the learning process and why these are important.
- Involve other health providers (like dieticians) to engage clients and reinforce learning.
- Invite people from the client's social support network to participate in the learning process.

Finally, technology can engage clients and connect them to providers and support communities. **Webinars** or **live events** are often available in the community and geared toward specific client populations (for example, parents). When recommending these resources, the counselor should verify the credentials of presenters as well as the validity and quality of the information presented.

PRACTICE QUESTION

7. A mother brings her teenager to therapy because of significant mood changes and increased social isolation. During the assessment, the counselor diagnoses the teenager with PTSD due to recent bullying at school. How can the counselor use psychoeducation in a session with the mother and teenager?
   A) explain the symptoms of PTSD and ways to manage the symptoms during treatment
   B) refer the client to a psychiatrist for medication
   C) bring in another counselor to work with the mother
   D) tell the mother to keep the teenager home from school until symptoms subside

 **DID YOU KNOW?**
In some cases, third-party payers will not reimburse counselors for interventions unless they can provide documentation of authorized training.

Counseling Interventions

Counselors must be able to apply evidence-based counseling interventions. Ethical and competent counselors receive proper education and training before using these interventions with clients. Counselors must take care to use therapeutic techniques properly; the improper application of evidence-based interventions could harm the client.

Cognitive Behavioral Therapy

Cognitive behavioral therapy (CBT) is based on the theory that thoughts and feelings influence behaviors. The theory further suggests that many of the thoughts that influence behaviors occur without a person's conscious knowledge.

The point of using CBT as therapy is to guide clients to become aware of those thoughts and identify the unhealthy ones. Clients can then learn to take control of their thoughts and separate the thoughts from their behaviors. Because several mental health issues are associated with negative thoughts and beliefs, the counselor can use this theory-based counseling intervention with clients who have a variety of diagnoses. The counselor's role in CBT is to

- help clients explore their thoughts and beliefs;
- analyze where thoughts and beliefs originated;
- evaluate the truth or effectiveness of thoughts and beliefs;
- revise or create new thoughts and beliefs that help clients achieve their therapeutic goals.

Dialectical Behavior Therapy

Dialectical behavior therapy (DBT) uses concepts from CBT but also considers the significant impact of strong emotions on thinking and behavior. As implied by the name, DBT suggests that opposing forces exist in a state of tension. For example, a person practicing DBT understands that he may feel very strong negative emotions, but his whole life is not ruined. Someone using DBT would understand that he might perform badly on an exam, but that does not mean he is unintelligent or that he has no future. The goal of DBT is to help clients learn to balance between extremes and choose constructive or positive behaviors despite strong emotions. The therapy itself focuses on helping clients

- learn mindfulness;
- learn to regulate their emotions and tolerate distress;
- identify dysfunctional thinking patterns;
- choose healthy coping skills.

Another characteristic of DBT is establishing and maintaining boundaries with clients to teach them how to do the same in their lives. Implementation of DBT interventions requires the counselor to engage in additional education and training.

DID YOU KNOW?

Dialectical behavior therapy was originally created to treat women with borderline personality disorder and high rates of suicidality.

Eye Movement Desensitization and Reprocessing

Eye movement desensitization and reprocessing (EMDR) is considered an evidence-based treatment intervention for clients with post-traumatic stress disorder (PTSD) and other diagnoses. This treatment is based on the theory of information processing. According to this theory, memories associated with traumatic events are not stored properly. The techniques used in EMDR employ bilateral stimulation while recalling a memory to store it properly in the brain and reduce the strong emotions attached to it.

To apply bilateral stimulation, a counselor may ask a client to hold two joysticks that vibrate alternatingly or to wear a headset that plays tones or clicks in one ear, then the other. This therapy can be very effective for clients with the following diagnoses:

- PTSD
- phobias
- bipolar disorder

HELPFUL HINT

Counselors should not use EMDR with clients until they are properly educated and trained by a qualified EMDR trainer.

Acceptance and Commitment Therapy

Acceptance and commitment therapy (ACT) is based on the theory that people can choose positive behavior even if their thoughts and feelings are negative. In other words, negative thoughts or feelings do not have to dictate a person's behavior. This therapy uses techniques such as

- mindfulness;
- changing the way a client thinks and behaves regarding strong feelings;

- establishing values;
- encouraging clients to take action consistent with those values.

This therapeutic intervention can be used for clients with a variety of mental health issues. One example of its use is to help clients manage the discomfort of withdrawing from substance use or to manage the cravings involved in substance use recovery. The client may feel she needs the substance, and her thoughts tell her she needs it to curb the discomfort. The client can choose to exercise instead because she has the goal of remaining abstinent. Although there is no requirement to receive education and training to use ACT as an intervention, it is recommended.

Solution-Focused Brief Therapy

Solution-focused brief therapy (SFBT) involves bringing attention to clients' internally held strengths and developing these into skills to solve their problem behaviors. SFBT it is effective in three to ten sessions. SFBT is used for clients working on

- substance use disorders;
- depression;
- eating disorders;
- anger management.

SFBT interventions include

- the miracle question (asking clients to envision an alternate reality where their problem does not exist);
- exception questions (focusing on when the client is not experiencing their problem);
- presupposing change questions (helping clients recognize change that has occurred in their lives);
- scaling questions (having clients rate their experience or feelings on a scale of worst to best);
- coping questions (reviewing times clients have used coping mechanisms and shown resiliency).

PRACTICE QUESTION

8. A client comes to therapy with social anxiety that prevents him from having a social life because he thinks people are judging him. Which type of therapy would benefit this client?

    A) acceptance and commitment therapy (ACT)

    B) dialectical behavior therapy (DBT)

    C) eye movement desensitization and reprocessing (EMDR)

    D) cognitive behavioral therapy (CBT)

Conflict and Confrontation

Conflict and Crisis

Conflict in the therapeutic relationship can generate insight and provide beneficial therapeutic moments. **Transference** describes a situation in which the client interacts with the counselor as if the counselor were someone else in the client's life. These interactions can be positive or negative, but either way, they are unhealthy:

- A positive example of transference might be treating the counselor as if she were a friend.
- A negative example might be directing anger at the counselor when the client is angry at his spouse.

In either case, the counselor's skill at bringing awareness to the interaction and processing it with the client can be a constructive therapeutic moment. For example, if the client behaves toward the counselor in anger, the counselor can direct the client's attention to the emotion of anger. The counselor could ask the client to describe what she is feeling in the moment and determine the cause and object of that anger. Also, the counselor might invite the client to engage in a dialogue in which she imagines the counselor is the object of her anger, which allows her to process the emotion through role-play.

When discussing transference, it is also appropriate to bring attention to **countertransference**, which is the counselor's transference toward the client transference. For example, a client treats the counselor as if he is a friend, perhaps telling him that he reminds her of her friend, and then discloses a painful experience. The counselor reacts to the client's transference by sharing a similar painful experience instead of simply listening to the client. That disclosure is countertransference and often happens without the counselor realizing it, which is another reason counselor self-awareness and self-reflection are important:

- Countertransference can shift the focus from the client's therapeutic needs and toward the counselor.
- It also compromises the counselor's objectivity because the professional boundary has been blurred by the disclosure of personal information.

Defense mechanisms are another source of conflict within a therapeutic relationship. These are techniques clients use to protect themselves from feelings of anxiety or hurt. There are a number of defense mechanisms that people use. Some of the more common ones appear in Table 5.2.

TABLE 5.2. Defense Mechanisms

Mechanism	Definition	Example
Denial	ignoring reality	A parent denies that his child is misusing substances despite obvious signs.
Repression	deciding to avoid thinking about something distressing	A client pushes away memories of an ex-partner who treated her badly.

Regression	engaging in childlike behavior or emotions	A woman speaks in baby talk when someone gets angry with her.
Intellectualizing	focusing on rationalizing an issue rather than the emotions	A client's loved one dies; he only talks about the person's illness, the course of treatment, and the inevitability of death without acknowledging the sad emotions.
Compartmentalizing	keeping a part of one's life separate from the others to reduce distress	A client works a very dangerous job but keeps it completely separate from her home life.

Constructive confrontation is a helpful therapeutic tool counselors use to call attention to the client's behaviors and feelings in the present moment, especially when there is incongruity. This method is useful to confront transference and defense mechanisms.

For example, if a client is talking about something distressing but is smiling or laughing, the counselor might stop the client and share his observation about her behavior. By confronting the client about the difference between the painful experience she is discussing and the outward emotional expression, the counselor can guide her to increased self-awareness and, possibly, some insight.

Risk assessments for **crisis** situations should be part of every assessment counselors conduct with clients. It is also necessary to ask clients how they define a crisis and what a crisis might look like for them. Everyone's interpretation of a crisis is different. Counselors cannot rely solely on their own judgment. Potential crisis situations can include

- suicide risk;
- self-harm;
- danger to self;
- danger to others;
- interpersonal violence;
- situational violence;
- a health emergency for self or loved ones;
- sudden changes in education, employment, or housing;
- natural disasters;
- accidents;
- sudden change in relationship status;
- psychotic episodes;
- substance use lapse;
- sudden strong mood changes, such as mania or depression.

Safety planning is a client-led process whereby the counselor and the client discuss

- what determines a crisis;

HELPFUL HINT

Risk assessment should occur at intake and periodically throughout the counseling relationship.

- what the client will do in a crisis;
- whom the client will reach out to in a crisis;
- under what conditions outside help will be sought.

Depending on the client's situation, a safety plan will be put in writing so that the client and counselor can each keep a copy and the client can share the plan with others who will be involved in the plan. As clients progress through treatment, their needs will change, so safety plans should be revisited and revised over the course of treatment. Safety plans include the following information:

- how to tell if the client is in crisis
- whom to call when the client is in crisis
- whom not to call when the client is in crisis
- what supporters should do
- what supporters should not do
- under what circumstances to call for outside help
- which outside help to call
- how to tell when the client is no longer in crisis

Counselors need to keep boundaries with clients and ensure that they understand when it is appropriate to contact the counselor when in crisis and when to call others. Most counties in the United States have a crisis hotline; some have hotlines specific to sexual assault and domestic violence. If a counselor works for a community mental health agency, the organization will likely have emergency and crisis policies in place for clients.

> **DID YOU KNOW?**
> Counselors must establish boundaries in crisis planning: some clients use crisis situations to seek attention from counselors.

PRACTICE QUESTION

9. During a session, a client has tears in her eyes while discussing her mother. She screams at the counselor, "I don't care what my mother thinks!" What therapeutic tool can the counselor use to help the client process her outburst?

   A) summary reflection
   B) positive reframing
   C) constructive confrontation
   D) empathetic attunement

Conflict Resolution Strategies

Conflict resolution is important in both the counseling relationship and the group counseling context. Some strategies to resolve conflict include conflict avoidance, giving in, standing one's ground, compromising, and collaborating.

Conflict avoidance involves not acknowledging the conflict. **Giving in** means acquiescing to the other party, thereby giving her what she wants or letting her have her way. **Standing one's ground** is a way of competing with the opposing party in the hopes that he does not win the battle. **Compromising** involves seeking out common ground as a stepping-stone to negotiating and resolving the conflict. **Collaborating** consists of actively listening to the opposing party's perspective, discussing areas of like-mindedness and common objectives, and confirming that both parties understand each other's viewpoints. This strategy is sometimes difficult, but it can be rewarding when it is effective.

PRACTICE QUESTION

10. Jolie manages a department in a mental health clinic. Mary, one of her employees, is constantly at odds with Nicole, another employee. Mary has seniority over Nicole but is not her direct supervisor. Mary wants Jolie to write Nicole up for disrespecting her. Jolie listens to both sides but takes no action and goes about her work as if no conflict has occurred. What type of conflict resolution strategy is Jolie employing?

    A) compromising
    B) conflict avoidance
    C) giving in
    D) collaboration

Answer Key

1. **B**

   The counselor demonstrates genuineness and congruence by stating that she does not agree with the client's choices, shows nonjudgment by keeping the behavior separate from the person, and expresses positive regard by encouraging the client to work toward better choices.

2. **C**

   A self-aware counselor will read the client's nonverbal feedback immediately, recognize something is wrong, and address it in the session as soon as possible to maintain a good therapeutic relationship with the client.

3. **A**

   Attending behaviors, like eye contact and other nonverbal signals, communicate that the counselor is present and paying attention to the client.

4. **D**

   The client is in shock, not thinking straight, and needs to express these emotions. The counselor can demonstrate empathetic attunement by giving her time and space to feel what she needs to feel without judgment.

5. **A**

   This client expects the counselor to be the expert professional and give direction, but the therapeutic alliance relies on equal power and trust between client and counselor.

6. **C**

   The client's statements suggest that he blames his failure on the school, professors, and peers—not himself; this demonstrates external locus of control.

7. **A**

   Psychoeducation can help the teenager and the mother understand what the teenager is experiencing.

8. **D**

   Cognitive behavioral therapy would focus on identifying and addressing the client's thoughts and beliefs related to how others view him.

9. **C**

   The counselor can use constructive confrontation to draw the client's attention to the discrepancy between the words she is speaking and the visible emotion she is displaying.

10. **B**

    Jolie is practicing conflict avoidance by pretending that no conflict has happened.

6 | Group Counseling and Group Work

Working with a Group

Group counseling is significantly different from individual counseling because the client is the entire group, not just one person. Therefore, the focus of intervention is on the interactions among group members. This shift requires a purposeful approach from the group counselor when determining the type, size, and duration of the group.

Group type, size, and duration depend on the goal of the group. Some groups focus on a specific purpose and benefit from interaction among members; others offer support for members with minimal interaction among them. The following section discusses the different types of groups and their characteristics.

Types of Groups

Open groups, or **open-ended groups**, have no set beginning or ending; members can come and go as they please. Open-ended groups might teach members a set of coping skills for substance use or follow a psychoeducational curriculum that starts again once one cycle of the program ends:

- Some open-ended groups follow a **manualized program**, which provides a curriculum for the group counselor and includes instruction techniques and exercises to use for practice.
- Manualized programs can run in cycles, allowing members to start at any time and finish when the cycle is complete.
- Examples of manualized programs include anger management and court-ordered driver education and counseling (for DUI clients).
- Other open-ended groups function as support groups, like mutual aid groups, where members receive support from each other.
- Examples of support groups include open groups for people dealing with depression or grief.
- The level of interaction among group members is superficial.

- The size of the group depends on factors such as
  - the number of group counselors;
  - room size;
  - program capabilities;
  - state rules regarding group sizes.

Open-ended groups can last as long as necessary. Some run continually; others have a start and end date. **Closed groups** are the opposite of open groups:

- New members are not allowed to join once the group begins.
- Closed groups tend to have a specific purpose as well as a start and end date.

Closed groups are effective for especially delicate matters. For example, closed groups for people who have experienced sexual assault are appropriate due to the level of trust required among group members and the weight of the topics addressed. The success of the group often depends on the trust established and the interaction among members:

- Closed groups may feature a curriculum or schedule of topics.
- Closed groups typically set criteria for membership, such as age, gender, or experience with the topic.

Psychoeducational groups, or **curriculum groups**, focus on a specific topic and typically have start and end dates. Psychoeducational groups are usually open, with the stated purpose of teaching a skill or providing information. Topics include

- anger management;
- parenting skills;
- life skills.

These groups follow an evidence-based program whereby the facilitator presents information to the group. Group interaction focuses on the topic.

Process groups focus on the interaction among group members. In process groups, counselors help members process their thoughts, feelings, and behaviors on a deep level. The purpose is to address challenges that members face in the present. Process groups treat issues such as

- depression;
- anxiety;
- PTSD;
- substance use;
- relationship issues;
- other mental illnesses.

Interactions among group members allow them to increase self-awareness and gain insight from other members by sharing experiences and perspectives. Additionally, process groups allow members to practice various skills, such as

- assertiveness;

DID YOU KNOW?

Some states regulate the ratio of group leaders to members (for example, ten to fifteen members for each facilitator). This way, the group size will depend on the number of facilitators available.

- creating boundaries;
- working through conflict.

These groups require a deeper level of trust among their members; therefore, process groups are often closed or semi-closed.

A **homogenous group** facilitates bonding among members based on what they have in common, which provides a focus for the group's purpose. Members of a homogenous group are chosen because they have characteristics or traits in common, such as

- gender;
- age (for example, members who are under eighteen);
- mental health issues (for example, members with a certain diagnosis).

Members of **heterogeneous groups** are chosen for the diversity of their characteristics or traits. Many open groups are heterogeneous: anyone of any age with any issue may participate. This diversity of experiences, backgrounds, traits, and issues that each person brings to the group can help other members.

PRACTICE QUESTION

1. A counselor wants to create a group for parents of children with disabilities to help them learn more about coping and to create a network of people who can support each other through tough times. Which of the following groups would be appropriate?

    A) an open twelve-step group
    B) an open and homogenous group
    C) a closed and heterogenous group
    D) a closed process group

Group Activities and Psychoeducation

Structured activities provide overall structure and routine to an open group. A counselor can use structured activities during a session in a variety of ways.

For example, in an open group, members might use the structured activity format to each say their name and provide a brief update on their progress. Then, there might be a presentation of a relevant topic followed by group reactions and commentary on the topic for a set amount of time. Finally, the group might close with a structured activity, such as each member summing up the session.

This structured method gives group members a sense of stability and trust in the group process, helps them feel comfortable with the routine, and keeps sessions predictable. Structured activities may also be used for

- building trust among group members by helping them get to know each other;
- lessons to keep the progress of the group moving toward its end goal;
- sample situations that members may encounter, which allow them to role-play in group;

- moving a group out of stagnation or resolving a conflict;
- teaching skills;
- engaging new group members.

There are many ways to use psychoeducation as part of the group process. In some groups, the focus is on the presentation of educational materials. Psychoeducation can also be used to normalize and validate a group member's experience. For example, if a member of a substance use group talks about having cravings that feel out of control, the counselor can use psychoeducation to explain the effects that drugs have on the brain and what the brain goes through during the healing process and recovery.

PRACTICE QUESTION

2. A counselor is creating a drop-in group for people who have experienced grief or tragic loss. There is no sign-up process for the group, nor does the counselor have any information about the people who will participate or what they are dealing with. What is the BEST reason to have structured activities in this particular group?

   A) to help group members feel comfortable and welcome by providing a predictable routine
   B) to weed out participants who do not belong in the group
   C) to allow group members to interact with each other in the present and gain insight
   D) to let potential participants know the group is a closed group

Interactions in Groups

There are many ways counselors can manage **leader-member dynamics**. The title of "group leader" can be misleading because group counselors act more as facilitators than leaders. The purpose of a group is to facilitate interactions among group members, and while a counselor may present material or topics for the group to address, the real work takes place when members inspire insight in each other.

Many interactions between leaders and members are positive, but an effective group leader will remember the group's function and resist trying to control all aspects of the group. The following are some ways to keep leader-member dynamics from becoming disruptive to the group:

- Have the members establish group rules and reiterate them at each meeting. When the group creates the rules, the leader is no longer in an authoritative position.
- Defer to the group. For example, if a member challenges the leader's qualifications or reasons for being there, the leader can reflect that question back to the group and ask if anyone else feels that way, why they feel that way, and what impact that has on the group. This takes the focus of discussion off of the leader and back to the members.

- Remind members that the group is not about the leader. This is another skill whereby the group leader reflects the interaction between a member and the leader back to the group.
- Invite the group to decide. If a member's behavior toward the leader becomes too disruptive, it may be appropriate to ask the group to determine if the member's behavior violates group rules and, if so, to act. Deferral to the group puts the power of the member's fate in the hands of the members and not the leader, thus giving group members authority over each other.

Managing leader-member dynamics is similar to the relationship between basketball players and the referee. The action of the game is the ball between the players, but sometimes the ball bounces to the referee. The referee's job is not to take the ball and join the game but to direct the ball back to the players to continue the game. Most groups require a **leader** or **facilitator**:

- For some groups, the counselor acts as the group leader or facilitator.
  - State regulations may require a counselor to be present at a therapy group.
- Some group types require the presence of the counselor, but the counselor may defer group leadership to a member.
- Other groups may not need a counselor as a leader, especially if they are support groups and not therapy groups.
  - Examples include mutual aid groups like Alcoholics Anonymous (AA) or peer support groups.
  - In such groups, it is wise to have someone act as a leader if only to get the group started and ended on time.
  - Chairpersons, coordinators, or facilitators manage logistics and ensure adherence to the group format and rules.

By having a coordinator or facilitator, the groups can remain open to all potential participants, and members and potential participants will know what to expect when they attend. Effective group leaders understand the group's purpose and function, which then determines the level of facilitation the group will require:

- In psychoeducational groups, the leader might be responsible for presenting the material and coordinating discussion afterward.
- In process groups, the leader might be responsible for noticing interaction among members, calling attention to something happening in the group for deeper processing, or addressing issues related to members who are too quiet or too overpowering.
- An effective group leader can facilitate resolutions for therapeutic purposes when conflict arises.

TABLE 6.1. Characteristics and Skills of Effective Leaders

Characteristic/Skill	Definition
Detachment	the ability to keep the focus of the group on the members and not on the leader
Observation	the ability to notice therapeutic events when they happen in a group and point them out
Empathy and encouragement	the ability to draw out group members who are not participating and include them
Reflection and summarization	the ability to rephrase what group members are saying to make a connection with what other members are experiencing
Confrontation and mediation	the ability to recognize conflict or the potential for conflict and guide group members through fixing it themselves
Teaching and clarifying	the ability to add educational information to the group discussion that applies to what is going on in the group and find ways members can use what they learn outside of the group
Management	the ability to keep members on task or focused and help them enforce group rules when necessary

Co-leaders can be very effective in groups since one person cannot notice or address everything that happens. A co-leader can be

- another licensed counselor;
- a counseling intern;
- a peer.

Co-leaders can take on various roles: training new counselors as group counselors, presenting specialized material, or acting as additional observers. Peers, or people further along their recovery journey than other members, can also be very helpful to engage group members.

Before the group session begins, the co-leaders should discuss each of their roles. For example, one co-leader may take the role of lead facilitator while the other observes and interjects, or each co-leader may divide up responsibilities equally.

Although **leader-member interactions** are not usually the focus of group counseling, it is helpful when group members trust the leader. The counselor can promote and encourage interactions between the leader and members through

- introductions;
- self-disclosure;
- asking clarifying questions;
- other counseling skills (for example, reflection, summarization, and attending).

The counselor's role in facilitating the group is to promote and encourage interactions among members. There are several ways to do this:

- Using **direct questioning**, the counselor might ask one group member how he reacted to what another member said.
- To **establish commonality** among members, when one member shares something about a family member who died, for example, the counselor might ask if anyone else has experienced the loss of a family member.
- **Linking** is a technique group counselors use to connect what one member says or experiences to another member to establish a connection, empathy, or understanding.
- **Feedback** in group therapy can be used by the counselor or members to share reactions to another group member—what that person said, did, or shared.
    - In addition to sharing reactions, feedback can include providing encouragement or recommendations.
    - An effective group counselor will facilitate feedback among members but may also use feedback as an instructive tool for the rest of the group.
- **Self-disclosure** is the process of sharing one's perspectives or experiences and generally refers to the counselor's sharing of personal experiences for a therapeutic purpose.
    - Self-disclosure can be useful for establishing a trusting relationship with the group members or for instructive purposes, but it should be used with care.
- Finally, the counselor can bring up **previous information** shared by a member in group to apply to a current situation.
    - For example, if a member shared a coping skill in a previous session that could help someone in the current session, the counselor might ask the first member about what he did and ask if he could explain it again.

Confidentiality in group therapy is held by the counselor, not necessarily the group. This means that the counselor has a legal and ethical obligation to keep what happens or who is a member in the group confidential. The agency hosting the group may have rules regarding group confidentiality that all members will be expected to uphold.

Group members are not legally or ethically obligated to uphold the same standards as the counselor; however, confidentiality is essential for groups to be successful, which is why members need to establish rules of confidentiality. This is one of the first items of business in a new group:

- Counselors should facilitate the creation of confidentiality rules to include how group members recognize each other outside of group and on social media.
- The group should determine the consequences of breaking confidentiality and how such a situation will be handled if it happens.

 HELPFUL HINT

A word of caution when bringing up previously shared information: the counselor cannot bring up information the client shared with the counselor outside the group, which would be a breach of confidentiality.

Another key role of the group counselor is to identify therapeutic moments that occur and point them out to members. The counselor can do this purposefully by asking questions of members and inviting feedback.

For example, if someone shares an experience, the counselor might ask the group if anyone else has experienced something similar or if they have any feedback for that member. The counselor can also do this indirectly by allowing the group to interact and then interjecting on occasion to share an observation of a theme or pattern. The counselor can also use summarization at the end of group sessions to identify patterns and themes that emerged in that session.

PRACTICE QUESTION

3. A member of a process group for people in recovery from substance use says she does not like the group counselor because he is young and never had any substance use issues, so she questions how he can do his job. What is the BEST response the counselor can make?

   A) "If you don't like it, you are free to leave the group."

   B) "All right, I'll find you someone else."

   C) "That's a good point. What do others think about this?"

   D) "There's nothing you can do but accept it."

Group Stages

There are several defined **stages in the group process**:

- forming
- storming
- norming
- performing
- mourning

The **forming** stage of the group process is the start of the group when members join, introduce themselves, and determine their positions in the group. This part of the group process involves establishing the group rules, getting used to the format, and gaining an understanding of what the group will accomplish.

The **storming** stage involves conflict among group members. This can include testing boundaries, ascertaining whether other members really belong in the group, challenging the authority of the counselor, or resisting the way the group has decided to operate. Not every group goes through this stage, but the group's success depends on a healthy resolution; otherwise, members will be stuck in this stage and not get to the group's actual work.

The **norming** stage involves healing and repairing following the storming stage. If there is no conflict within the group, it occurs immediately after the forming stage. This is the stage when group members become comfortable with each other, understand what is expected of them, and settle into the routine of the work.

The **performing** stage describes the phase of real group work being done. The leader's function is reduced because members take on the roles of encouraging interaction with each other. It is in this stage that much of the therapeutic work is accomplished.

The **mourning** stage occurs at the end of the group and begins the process of group termination. During group therapy, members can become close and the end of group can be a sad event. Therefore, to ensure a successful termination of the group, the leader might facilitate an event or ritual to commemorate the successes of the members and to celebrate their accomplishments. Honoring this stage of the group process helps members transition out of the group.

Counselors need to be aware of which stage the group is in to make sure members are ready for a particular intervention. If a proposed intervention is not appropriate for the stage, then it will not be effective. For example, a role-play intervention to teach assertiveness might not be effective during the storming stage because of the level of group conflict; however, adjusting that intervention to teach healthy conflict resolution skills would be appropriate. A counselor should therefore always think about whether members are ready for a particular intervention and if it will help them move toward the stated goals.

PRACTICE QUESTION

4. At the end of a group counseling session, the counselor highlights the way three members achieved deep insight into their issues, and thanked the other four members for helping with validation, feedback, and encouragement of those three members. Which developmental stage is this group likely in?

    A) forming

    B) norming

    C) storming

    D) performing

Attributes in a Group Counseling Context

Group Therapeutic Factors

A counselor demonstrates all of the core counseling attributes in a group context. Important core counseling attributes include

- self-awareness;
- genuineness;
- congruence;
- nonjudgment;
- positive regard;
- active listening;
- attending;
- reflecting;
- empathy.

See Chapter 1, "Core Counseling Attributes," for more details. In addition, the following attributes are important for group counseling:

- facilitation of group topics and group membership
- management of time, rules, and tasks
- observation of group members
- redirection of topics back to the group
- modeling appropriate behavior and healthy relationship skills
- identification of therapeutic moments
- enforcement of group rules
- fairness of treatment of and among group members
- conflict resolution skills
- calling out inappropriate behavior
- facilitating behavioral corrections
- teaching skills and therapy concepts

There are multiple therapeutic events and factors that occur in group therapy that a counselor watches for and facilitates. Group counselors foster the emergence of **group therapeutic factors** by knowing what they are and how to recognize them in a group context. Once a counselor recognizes when these factors occur, it may be appropriate to call attention to them in the group.

Self-disclosure is the sharing of personal information and experiences; it usually refers to the counselor. The purpose of self-disclosure is to further the therapeutic process. Often this is done with the intent to establish trust with the client, to move the client out of stagnation, or to inspire insight.

Self-disclosure can also include the counselor sharing feelings in the present to bring something into awareness. For example, a counselor may disclose feelings of tension within the group to initiate a conversation about conflicts among members.

Self-disclosure among group members is a key component of group therapy and requires that members share their thoughts, feelings, and experiences. The counselor may need to navigate self-disclosures by inviting reticent members to share and limiting the sharing of those who tend to dominate discussions.

Interaction in group therapy refers to the interpersonal engagement among group members. The interaction should not be between members and the counselor but among the members themselves, so that they can learn from each other rather than from the counselor. A counselor who notices how members interact may draw attention to a more quiet member to encourage their participation.

In group therapy, **acceptance and group cohesiveness** refers to members feeling like they belong in the group, that other members accept them for who they are, and that the member relationships are important to them. Group members feel safe and not judged, which results in a healthy environment for therapeutic progress.

When group members come to an understanding of their issues, or if they gain a new perspective or awareness of what they experience, this is referred to as **insight**. The new understanding or perspective helps members see their experience a little differently and even provides what they need to move beyond their issues.

Catharsis refers to an internal experience of change or a sudden realization that leads to a strong emotional reaction. The sudden realization may be associated with something that happened in a person's past or the identification of a triggering event.

Guidance occurs when either the group counselor or other group members provide educational information or advice.

Altruism is an aspect of group therapy whereby group members help each other, thus shifting the focus from themselves to other people. Helping other members provides a sense of value and gratitude among all members, which can improve how members think about themselves. A counselor may point out situations in which one group member helped another in order to draw attention to it and thus magnify the therapeutic effect.

Vicarious learning is learning from the experiences of other people. The self-disclosure of group members allows the other members to hear the good and the bad in the hopes that the listener makes different choices based on the experiences of someone else.

Hope is a strong motivator, and it can fuel a person's desire for change. Without hope, people feel helpless to change their situation. Within a group situation, the **instillation of hope** can come from members who share a common experience and who can show other members that healing is possible. Hearing the stories of someone who has been in the same situation can provide members with inspiration and a model of how healing is possible.

Existential factors involve recognizing what gives life meaning and the shared experience of being human. This may include discussions about big questions surrounding life and death, universal truths, and spirituality. Existential discussion in group therapy can help members come to terms with what they are dealing with by giving it some meaning or purpose outside of themselves.

PRACTICE QUESTION

5. In a highly emotional group session, one member is crying. After a moment of letting him experience his emotions, another member goes over to him and puts a hand on his shoulder. The crying member looks at the second member, and the two make eye contact and smile. The counselor says, "Thank you for reaching out and offering comfort and validation." Which therapeutic factor is the counselor calling attention to?

    A) instillation of hope

    B) existential factors

    C) self-disclosure

    D) altruism

Conflict in Groups

The counselor can use many strategies to facilitate the resolution of **interpersonal conflict in the group setting**. First, the counselor needs to approach all conflicts as if they are a therapeutic opportunity from which group members can learn. Conflict has a way of bringing issues to the surface and inspiring insight; therefore, the counselor should approach conflict with an attitude of curiosity and exploration.

It is essential to focus on the present when doing this in the group. Often, conflict among two or more group members is representative of something else, but that something else cannot be discovered without exploring what is happening in the moment. Counselors should follow certain steps to make the most of conflict:

1. The counselor should first call attention to the conflict and bring it into the present.
2. The counselor should then bring each party's awareness to their individual experiences of the conflict.
3. Group members should be asked to offer their observations and feedback about the conflict.
4. The counselor should guide the parties while they work through the conflict, after which the group processes how it went and what they learned from it.

Group counselors should not let conflict go to waste. Each conflict presents a learning opportunity for group members to not only gain insight into their behaviors but also to learn how to work through conflict in a healthy way.

Counselors must recognize and address harmful group behaviors and intervene if members do not. Often, that intervention includes pointing out the person's behavior and exploring it. This intervention shows everyone that the counselor values the cohesiveness of the group by enforcing group rules and protecting members. If the behaviors violate group rules, then the group must decide whether to enforce the rules and determine the consequences. One method of intervention is blocking. In **blocking**, the group counselor immediately stops a member's behavior if it is

- inappropriate;
- counterproductive;
- harmful to others.

After stopping the behavior, the counselor references the group rules and the reason for blocking the member's behavior. If the member violated the group's rules, the counselor may defer to the group to determine what to do about the member.

For example, if the group decides that name calling is not allowed and a member calls another member an inappropriate name, the counselor should immediately stop the group and block the offending member from continuing.

Unfortunately, a counselor has no power to regulate the behaviors and interactions of members outside of the group; however, part of establishing group rules would include every member agreeing to confidentiality and the way in which people interact outside of the group. If a member violates the agreed-upon rules, then it would be appropriate to address that in the group and let the group decide whether that person is allowed to continue as a member. Additionally, the counselor may speak to members one-on-one, but the most effective interventions occur within the group.

PRACTICE QUESTION

6. What should a group counselor do when there is conflict in group therapy?
   A) call attention to the conflict immediately and help the members work through it
   B) ignore the conflict and address it in a future session when tensions are not so high
   C) speak with the individual group members outside of the group and remind them to work together
   D) bring in a supervisor to deal with the conflict so the counselor does not signal favoritism

CONTINUE

Answer Key

1. B

   An open group would be most appropriate because parents can enter or leave as they please. A homogenous group is suitable because members share the common characteristic of parents of children who have disabilities.

2. A

   Structured activities in an open group—that allow people to participate whenever they want—offer members a familiar routine that does not rely on individual members to keep the group progressing.

3. C

   The counselor acknowledges that the client has a valid point, thus demonstrating empathy, but then turns the question back to the group to facilitate conversation among members.

4. D

   Performing is the stage of group therapy when real work gets accomplished. This session included positive group interactions that contributed to positive outcomes for multiple group members, so the group is likely in the performing stage.

5. D

   Altruism is the act of one group member helping another. This counselor pointed out that one member reached out to another to offer comfort.

6. A

   Conflict in group therapy can be beneficial as a therapeutic learning opportunity. The group should work through conflict in the present.

7 Assessment and Testing

Intake and Interview

Intake Forms

When meeting with a client for the first time, counselors conduct an intake assessment to get to know the client. Clients are often asked to complete intake forms before their appointment and bring them to discuss with the counselor.

Intake forms are kept in the client's chart. These forms enable clients to explain in their own words why they are seeking counseling.

Several versions of intake forms can be used. Standard intake forms are specific to the location where treatment is being offered.

The general categories of information on these forms can include

- personal contact information;
- emergency contact information;
- relevant insurance information;
- list of current symptoms;
- medical concerns and medications;
- current substance use;
- history of mental illness including trauma, suicidal ideation, suicide attempts, and homicidal ideation;
- privacy consents, including consents for prescribing doctors, if relevant.

WELLNESS CENTER
COUNSELING INTAKE FORM

Today's date: _____ Student ID #:_____ Gender:_____

Name: _____ Date of birth: _____

Ethnicity:_____ Education Level: _____ Major:_____

Campus address: _____ City: _____ State:_____ Zip:_____

Home address:_____ City:_____ State:_____ Zip:_____

Phone (h): _____ (email): _____ (cell): _____

Emergency Contact Person: _____ Phone: _____

Relationship to you: _____ Referred by:_____

Do you work:_____ Where:_____ Position:_____

Counseling History

Have you had previous counseling:_____ Dates:_____

Name of counselor:_____

Explain why: _____

Reason for this appointment request today:_____

List any concerns you have: _____

Are you currently taking any medications: What:_____ Why:_____

Have you ever thought about, or attempted suicide:_____

Has anyone in your family, or friends committed, or attempted suicide:_____

If yes who:_____

What are your positives:_____

Figure 7.1. Sample Intake Form

Some treatment centers provide intake documentation for the counselor to complete that serves as a guide for the initial interview. In other cases, the counselor begins by reviewing the categories listed on the client's intake form and expanding on any items that need clarification. Common issues are

- mental health history;
- history of trauma and abuse;
- current substance use;
- suicidal ideation;
- homicidal ideation.

If the client is seeking specialized treatment, the counselor will spend more time exploring the presenting concern rather than areas that do not seem as relevant to the issue. For example, if a client is seeking treatment for depression, the counselor should focus on depression symptoms and corresponding life events rather than other issues.

PRACTICE QUESTION

1. Who completes intake forms?
    A) the counselor
    B) the client
    C) the facility
    D) the administration

Readiness to Change

Most people come to counseling because they want to change something in their lives. The **transtheoretical model (TTM)**, developed by researchers James Prochaska and Carlo DiClemente, offers a useful perspective on the birth and growth of behavioral change. It defines a five-step process that is determined by an individual's readiness or willingness to change:

1. precontemplation stage (not ready to change)
2. contemplation stage (getting ready to change)
3. preparation stage (ready to change)
4. action stage (performing the action that will bring about change)
5. maintenance stage (integrating the action into one's lifestyle and making it habit)

A counselor must determine readiness and willingness to change in all clients. A client's willingness shows how successful she will be in self-managing her condition(s).

PRACTICE QUESTION

2. Gene is a forty-eight-year-old male who wants to stop smoking. He has given some thought to it, but he still enjoys his two-pack-a-day habit and will not listen when his daughter lectures him about quitting. What stage of the transtheoretical model is Gene in?
    A) contemplation
    B) precontemplation
    C) maintenance
    D) action

Initial Interview and Interviewing Techniques

The purpose of a client interview is for the counselor to collect relevant health information to determine if the client is appropriate for a particular level of care and to begin developing the treatment plan.

HELPFUL HINT

Counselors should be mindful of their body language while a client is sharing. If a client feels uncomfortable or as though she is being judged, she is more likely to stop sharing openly.

For the **initial interview**, the counselor will meet with the client individually. Before beginning, the counselor should discuss confidentiality and situations during which confidentiality might be broken. The underlying goal of any interview is to assess the client's concerns and work toward developing an appropriate treatment plan.

A key reason to conduct the **initial interview** is for the counselor to establish a rapport with the client. Establishing a **rapport** means building trust and understanding. A strong counselor-client rapport means the client will feel more comfortable with the counselor and offer more information.

Asking **open-ended questions** allows the client to lead the conversation in a way that is specific to him and his experiences. Open-ended questions teach the counselor more about the client than "yes" and "no" questions. For example, asking a client, "Tell me about your family" will reveal more information than "Do you have any children?" Thoughtful open-ended questions start a conversation.

Motivational interviewing (MI) strategies can be used with clients who are resistant and unsure about engaging in treatment. MI skills include

- open-ended questions;
- reflective listening;
- rolling with resistance;
- summarizing statements.

Using these strategies can help create an environment where clients feel more comfortable talking about their concerns.

At the end of the interview, the counselor should summarize the gathered information and highlight important points for the client to ensure that nothing was missed. The client should be informed of the next steps, given an opportunity to ask questions, and given the counselor's contact information.

In behavioral health interviewing, the client may have a mental disability that prevents productive interviewing. A family member or guardian may assist in obtaining all pertinent information to establish a care plan. This can also include children who need mental health treatment. The care plan will be the foundation to develop a treatment strategy with achievable goals for the client.

DID YOU KNOW?

Rolling with resistance means understanding direct confrontation is not always effective. Rolling with resistance includes avoiding arguments, using reflective listening, and helping the person develop solutions.

PRACTICE QUESTION

3. In which situation should a counselor use motivational interviewing strategies?

    A) The client is lacking external motivation for treatment.

    B) The client has been hesitant but is answering questions truthfully.

    C) The client is unsure if he needs to make a change in his life.

    D) The client sought treatment because she is concerned about her mental health.

Structured Clinical Interview

A structured clinical interview is part of a client's initial intake exam. It is primarily conducted through **client self-report**, when the client describes his symptoms to the counselor based on questions the counselor asks.

There are some standardized structured clinical interviews, like the **Structured Clinical Interview for *DSM-5* (SCID-5)**. The SCID-5 is most commonly used in research settings to screen participants for certain diagnoses that would disqualify them from participating in the study.

There are four main reasons to use the SCID-5:

1. to evaluate for all the major DSM-5 diagnoses
2. to select the population for a study
3. to identify current and past mental health concerns within a study's population
4. to help students and new mental health professionals improve their clinical interviewing skills

Currently, the SCID-5 is only approved for use with adults over eighteen. Some clinics use the SCID-5 as part of their clinical intake. Others use their own version of structured questions, or even use an unstructured format. In either case, the goal is to provide a set list of questions (some open-ended) that can be used to screen for and rule out diagnoses and presenting issues in clients.

There are ten core diagnoses covered in the SCID-5:

1. mood episodes, cyclothymic disorder, persistent depressive disorder, and premenstrual dysphoric disorder
2. psychotic and associated symptoms
3. differential diagnosis of psychotic disorders
4. differential diagnosis of mood disorders
5. substance use disorders
6. anxiety disorder
7. obsessive-compulsive and related disorders
8. feeding and eating disorders
9. externalizing disorders
10. trauma-and stressor-related disorders

The SCID-5 is a comprehensive assessment that can take anywhere from fifteen minutes to several hours. Because it primarily relies on self-report, it may not be an appropriate assessment tool for individuals with significant intellectual issues or an inability to self-report for other reasons (such as poor language ability or highly disorganized thought).

During a structured clinical interview, the counselor relies on both formal and informal observations. A **formal observation** includes items like the content of the responses the client gives to questions.

 HELPFUL HINT

In general, it is not considered best practice to diagnose from only one meeting or assessment. Diagnosis can be ongoing, especially with more complex cases. A diagnosis can change if new information emerges.

Informal observations include the client's body language, affect, and the emotive quality of the client's behavior. Interactional dynamics are an important part of informal observations. **Interactional dynamics** can include not only how a client is interacting with family members during a session but also how she speaks about friends, colleagues, and family members, and even how she interacts with the counselor.

The goal of a structured clinical interview is not to determine a firm diagnosis but rather to have a working diagnostic theory, a good understanding of the client's presenting problem and any environmental factors contributing to the problem, and the foundations for building a treatment plan with the client.

Cultural competence is a key concern in structured clinical interviews. A client who has visions or hears voices that are related to religion or culture should not be diagnosed with hallucinations, especially when these are corroborated by the client's community. Knowing diagnostic standards for cultural differences and having a strong understanding of the client's background are essential for effective structured clinical interviewing.

PRACTICE QUESTION

4. Which of the following is key to a structured clinical interview?
    A) collateral reports from family
    B) client self-report
    C) transtheoretical model
    D) client goals

Other Types of Interviews

There are several specific types of interviews counselors can conduct, including

- the biopsychosocial interview,
- the diagnostic interview, and
- the cultural formulation interview.

Templates for guiding the interview and creating documentation exist for all these types of interviews.

A **biopsychosocial interview** studies the relationship between the client's biological, psychological, and social health.

- Biological effects can include
    - medical health concerns,
    - disabilities, and
    - effects of substance use.
- Psychological health refers to the client's mental health concerns and coping skills.
- Social health includes clients' relationships with others and their families.

 **HELPFUL HINT**

During an initial interview, counselors can use any interview type.

A biopsychosocial interview shows the counselor how these three areas intertwine and impact the client's distress.

A **diagnostic interview** assesses specifically for potential mental health diagnoses. These interviews tend to be more structured to ensure that the necessary information is covered to make an accurate diagnosis.

The **cultural formulation interview (CFI)** is a sixteen-question assessment used to recognize the cultural impacts on a client while assessing for an appropriate diagnosis. The CFI uses open-ended questions to give the client space to talk about his concerns regarding the cultural norms he experiences.

An **unstructured interview** has no standardized questions. This allows the counselor to guide the interview in ways that the counselor believes will lead to the most relevant information. An unstructured interview often allows for a more open discussion about the client's concerns, goals, and motivations.

The main topics covered in an unstructured clinical interview include the following:

- age and sex
- the reason for seeking counseling
- work and education history
- current social activities
- physical and mental health concerns; past and present
- current medications and any drug and/or alcohol use
- family history of mental health and physical health concerns
- the counselor's observations of client behavior during the session (e.g., anxious, detached, euthymic)

PRACTICE QUESTION

5. Which of the following is the BEST interview type to use with a new client in an outpatient mental health clinic?
    A) cultural formulation interview
    B) biopsychosocial interview
    C) diagnostic interview
    D) structured clinical interview

Assessing the Client

General Types of Assessments

A **psychological assessment** is used to assess and treat psychological, psychiatric, and personality disorders as well as developmental delays. Psychological testing can be further categorized into four main types: clinical interview, assessment of intellectual functioning (IQ), personality assessment, and neuropsychological assessment.

The **clinical interview** is a basic but integral component of any psychological testing. Also known as an "intake" or "admission interview," it is generally a comprehensive assessment to collect information about an individual's background and family relationships. Only a licensed clinician may perform a clinical interview.

The **intellectual functioning (IQ test)** is used to measure typical intelligence and is divided into subsections that evaluate verbal comprehension, perceptual reasoning, working memory, and processing speed.

The **personality assessment** was developed to help health care professionals gain better insight into an individual's personality. Two different types of objective tests used to evaluate this are the Minnesota Multiphasic Personality Inventory-2 (MMPI-2) and the Sixteen Personality Factors Questionnaire (16PF).

A **neuropsychological assessment** is used to measure capacity regarding memory, reasoning, concentration, motor skills, and other cognitive elements.

PRACTICE QUESTION

6. Which of the following assessments is the FIRST one a counselor should conduct with a new client?

    A) IQ test
    B) personality assessment
    C) clinical interview
    D) neuropsychological assessment

Reliability and Validity

It is important to understand if the data are reliable and valid. **Reliability** refers to the consistency of the measurement. Take, for example, a performance-scoring system. To be reliable, the system must measure employees in the same manner. Though their scores may be different, *how* they are measured is consistent.

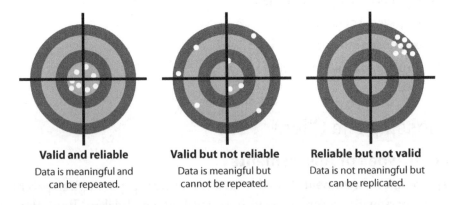

Valid and reliable
Data is meaningful and can be repeated.

Valid but not reliable
Data is meaningful but cannot be repeated.

Reliable but not valid
Data is not meaningful but can be replicated.

Figure 7.2. Reliability and Validity

Validity refers to what is being measured and whether it is relevant. In the example of a performance review, if an employee's performance on a nonwork-related issue is being measured, that item is not valid. It may be a reliable measurement, but it is not accurate or relevant to the actual review.

HELPFUL HINT

The concept of reliability can be thought of in the same way as a person who is reliable. A reliable person behaves as expected every time. A reliable assessment instrument does too.

PRACTICE QUESTION

7. Which of the following is an example of high validity?

    A) a math exam to determine how well the students know the material

    B) an oven that can consistently change temperatures but does not display the correct temperature

    C) using GPA to determine athletic ability

    D) a scale that is five pounds off but always reads the same weight

Mental Status Exam

A **mental status exam (MSE)** is an informal assessment typically conducted during the initial clinical interview. It does not involve formal questions for the client or even a formal scoring method; instead, it is based on the counselor's observations and impressions of the client's behavior and how he presents himself.

Although the MSE is based on the clinician's personal observations, the counselor's goal is not to state her opinion of the client but rather to record her observations objectively and in a fact-based manner. She should not write, for example, "the client has a bad attitude." A more appropriate and objective observation would be, "the client sat in a slouched position during the appointment and gave one- or two-word responses to questions."

The information obtained in a mental status exam is an essential part of the counselor's initial assessment and working diagnosis. She is gathering information about the client's level of interest in treatment, insight into how he perceives his issues and the world, and potential clues that can lead to a formal diagnosis.

Appearance is a common assessment in an MSE. The counselor should observe the following:

- How is the client dressed?
- How does she hold herself? (For example, does she slouch and cross her arms or have a calm and relaxed posture?)
- Is she unkempt and unwashed or meticulously groomed?

Another domain includes **motor behavior**, which relates to a client's physical movements. Excessive fidgeting can be a sign of attention deficit hyperactivity disorder (ADHD) or anxiety disorders, while very slow movement can be a sign of major depressive disorder. Involuntary limb movements or impaired gait may signify physical disorders like Huntington's disease or schizophrenia. Documenting physical movements that seem abnormal will be essential for diagnosing more complex disorders.

Mood is based primarily on the client's self-report. It is the clinician's job to translate the client's self-report into clinically appropriate language:

DID YOU KNOW?

Poor hygiene can be a symptom of several clinical diagnoses, including mood disorders and psychotic disorders.

- **euthymic:** normal or mildly positive mood
- **depressed/sad/dysphoric:** sad, "low" mood
- **anxious**
- **irritable**
- **euphoric/expansive/elevated:** abnormally positive mood

Clinical students often confuse mood with **affect**. While mood is how the client appears to be feeling, **affect** is how the client is presenting. Affect is observed based on the client's facial expressions, posture, reactivity, and vocal quality. (Is it expressive and variable based on speech, more of a monotone, or something in between?) Affect includes the following:

- **normal/congruent with mood:** affect matches described mood
- **labile:** affect swings wildly or is highly variable
- **constricted:** limited range of emotional display
- **blunted:** extremely limited range of emotional display
- **flat:** little or no emotional range displayed

Orientation refers to the client's state of mind. Is he aware of where he is, the date, why they he is in the counselor's office? Clients with poor orientation may be suffering from brain injury, hallucinations, or dementia. Orientation typically assesses the following:

- **orientation to time:** Does she know the day and year?
- **orientation to place:** Does she know where she is, or is she confused?
- **orientation to situation:** Does she know and understand why she is in the counselor's office?

Thought process and form refers to *how* the client thinks and is based on the clinician's observations of the quality of the client's thoughts. Is the client logical with coherent, linear in thought? Or does he display disorganized or tangential thoughts?

- **linear:** coherent, goal-directed, clear
- **tangential:** racing thoughts, jumps from topic to topic, difficult to follow

Categories under thought process and form include

- poverty of thought (having few thoughts);
- blocking (being unable to form thoughts);
- racing thoughts, flight of ideas (having rapid thoughts);
- loose associations (when a person's thoughts are disconnected);
- circumstantiality (when a person is able to get to the point but adds additional details along the way);
- tangentiality (when a person doesn't answer a question even though their thoughts are related to the question asked).

Thought content, on the other hand, refers to *what* the client thinks. Does the client exhibit any signs of hallucinations or delusions? Is she fixating on anything? Thought content includes the following:

- **suicidal/homicidal Ideation:** suicidal or homicidal thoughts, plans, means, and intention to follow through
- **hallucinations:** auditory, visual, olfactory, gustatory, tactile, hypnagogic (having hallucinations upon waking or falling asleep)
- **delusions:** grandeur, jealousy, persecutory, somatic, love, religious
- **obsessions/compulsions:** religious, contamination, fear of losing control of one's actions, sex
- **phobias:** more intense than a fear, consistent and long-term, negatively impact the client's quality of life due to avoidance of everyday activities to prevent having to deal with the fear

Speech refers to the quality of the client's language production. Is it very fast or slow? Is it loud? Speech quality can provide important information about symptoms that relate to schizophrenia, autism spectrum disorder, personality disorders, and more.

- **quality/fluency:** Does the client speak easily or stumble over his words?
- **rate:** Does the client speak very quickly or noticeably slowly? Does the client speak in a monotone, with a clipped voice, or have other unusual vocal inflections?
- **volume:** Is the client's speech noticeably louder or softer than normal?
- **quantity:** Does the client use appropriate and concise words? Does she only offer minimal or monosyllabic words, or does she provide extensive, elaborate detail?

Insight refers to how well the client can describe her own condition and circumstances. For example, a client who experiences hallucinations but is able to express to her counselor that she knows no one else can see them and doesn't believe them to be real would be described as having good insight.

PRACTICE QUESTION

8. Which of the following is an element of a mental status exam?
   A) client's level of insight
   B) case notes from prior counselors
   C) an IQ assessment
   D) client's past drug use

HELPFUL HINT

This list of elements for a mental status exam is not exhaustive. Each clinic will have its own forms or expected observations for MSEs. This list covers the topics that are typically found in the MSE; however, questions and terminology may vary.

Assessment Instruments

An important part of being an effective counselor is understanding how to choose a good assessment. Considering whether the assessment has been tested and approved for a client's age, ethnicity, language, or presenting problem can help a counselor determine what is the best choice to make when assessing a client.

Statistical analysis of large groups of clients and how accurately the assessment measures their symptoms can help the counselor determine the assessment's efficacy. The following are several important statistical factors.

Assessing Trauma

Trauma is an emotional response or reaction to distressing events. Some common exposure events include natural disasters, war, witnessing or surviving violence, witnessing or surviving abuse, witnessing or surviving rape or sexual assault, or being in an accident that leads to hospitalization.

There are four main domains of trauma symptoms.

1. **Intrusion** includes intrusive memories, nightmares, flashbacks, or reactions to triggers.
2. **Avoidance** involves changing one's behavior to avoid certain thoughts, memories, or external reminders.
3. **Negative changes in mood and affect** include memory issues, low self-worth, thoughts that the event was their fault, consistent negative emotions, a sense of detachment, or difficulty feeling positive emotions.
4. **Increased reactivity** includes symptoms like irritability, hypervigilance, elevated startle response, attention issues, sleep issues, and self-destructive behavior.

For a client to be diagnosed with **post-traumatic stress disorder (PTSD)**, he must have been exposed to a traumatic experience, exhibited symptoms across all four domains, and experiencing the symptoms for at least one month.

The **Clinician-Administered PTSD Scale for *DSM-5* (CAPS-5)** is one of the most commonly used assessments for PTSD. It is a structured diagnostic interview with thirty questions. It has high validity and reliability, making it a strong assessment for PTSD. The assessment takes about forty-five to sixty minutes to complete.

The **PTSD Symptom Scale Interview for *DSM-5* (PSSI-5)** is a twenty-four-question semi-structured interview used to assess for PTSD in adults. It is administered by a clinician and used to diagnose PTSD in adults.

The **PTSD Checklist for *DSM-5* (PCL-5)** is a twenty-item self-administered checklist for PTSD symptoms. It can be used to make a provisional diagnosis of PTSD (contingent on further follow-up and assessment by a clinician). It can also be used as a way to monitor symptom severity over time.

The **Clinician-Administered PTSD Scale for *DSM-5*–Child/Adolescent Version (CAPS-CA-5)** is based on the **CAPS-5** assessment, with language and questions geared toward children. It is approved for use with children ages seven and up. Like the CAPS-5, it is a structured clinical interview that lists the symptoms that are key to a PTSD diagnosis; it has thirty questions.

The **UCLA Child/Adolescent PTSD Reaction Index for** *DSM-5* **(UCLA-RI)** is a semi-structured interview for children and adolescents. It covers a client's history of trauma experiences and screens for trauma symptoms based on the four domains found in the *DSM-5*.

PRACTICE QUESTION

9. Suzie was recently bitten by a dog and had to go to the hospital for treatment. Her mother is worried that she may have experienced trauma from the experience. Which of the following is a symptom of avoidance?

   A) Suzie reports frequent nightmares about dogs.

   B) Suzie's mom says that she has been yelling at her brother more often.

   C) Suzie's teacher reports that Suzie has not been paying attention in class.

   D) Suzie refuses to visit a neighbor who has a dog.

Assessing Substance Use

Substance use is the nonmedically warranted consumption of medications or substances such as tobacco, alcohol, or illicit drugs. **Substance dependence** is a deep physical and/or psychological need to use a controlled substance to achieve a feeling of euphoria and/or calmness. **Substance abuse** is the continued use of a medication without medical reason, or excessive and intentional use of a controlled substance (alcohol or narcotics, for example). Finally, **addiction** is dependence on a substance or practice that is physically or psychologically habit-forming to the extent that critical pain and damage result.

The **Tobacco, Alcohol, Prescription medication, and other Substance use (TAPS) Tool** is a four-question screening tool for adults that determines if the client is using tobacco, alcohol, prescription medications, or other substances, and at what frequency in the previous twelve months. It can be self-administered or administered by the clinician.

The **Drug Abuse Screening Test (DAST-10)** is a ten-question assessment to determine drug abuse. It has been approved for adults and older young adults (ages sixteen and up). It can be administered by the counselor or the client.

The National Institute on Drug Abuse (NIDA)-modified Alcohol, Smoking, and Substance Involvement Screening Test (NM-ASSIST) is a clinician-administered online assessment that asks the client about lifetime prescription and illegal drug, alcohol, or tobacco use. If the client indicates any usage, the questions progress to frequency and the degree to which use has negatively impacted the client's life.

The **CAGE questionnaire** consists of four questions that can be worked into an intake assessment or an individual session. CAGE is an acronym for "cut down, annoyed, guilt, and eye-opener."

The **Alcohol Use Disorders Identification Test (AUDIT)** is a ten-item tool that helps counselors recognize when a client's drinking behaviors have become dangerous for their health.

The **Michigan Alcohol Screening Test (MAST)** is a twenty-five-item assessment that helps counselors better understand the lifetime severity of a client's alcohol use. The MAST is often used to help guide treatment plans.

The **Clinical Opiate Withdrawal Scale (COWS)** is an eleven-item screening tool administered by clinicians. It measures objective symptoms of opiate withdrawal such as heart rate, joint pain, stomach issues, goosebumps, sweating, and more. The assessment is used to help clinicians understand the level of opiate dependence and how severe a client's withdrawal symptoms are.

The **Car, Relax, Alone, Forget, Friends, Trouble (CRAFFT)** is a screening tool approved for youth ages twelve to twenty-one to determine substance use. It can be administered by a counselor or through self-assessment. It begins with three questions to determine any level of drug or alcohol use in the previous twelve months. If the client affirms any usage, screening moves on to query about six situations. The final portion is a brief intervention.

The **Drug Abuse Screening Test for Adolescents (DAST-A)** is a modified version of the DAST. It is a twenty-eight-question screening tool to determine adolescent abuse of prescription or illegal drugs, tobacco, or alcohol. It can be administered by the counselor or self-administered.

The **Screening, Brief Intervention, and Referral to Treatment (SBIRT)** is used by clinicians to determine alcohol use. It can be used with adolescents and adults. The client's reported alcohol consumption is placed into different danger levels depending on his weekly consumption, which is then discussed with him, and possible motivation for change is assessed. If the client is amenable, the final part of the SBIRT involves referral to treatment.

PRACTICE QUESTION

10. The counselor is seeing a fourteen-year-old client for the first time. She was referred for missing school and poor family relationships. Her mother suspects she has been using marijuana with friends. Which of the following would be the BEST tool to screen for drug usage?

    A) TAPS
    B) CRAFFT
    C) COWS
    D) SBIRT

Assessing Other At-Risk Behaviors

Counselors have an ethical duty to conduct ongoing assessments for **suicidal** and **homicidal** behavior, **self-injury**, and **relationship violence**. Counselors are legally required to report any serious threats of suicide or homicide to the police for intervention. Self-injury with no suicidal intent and relationship violence are not reportable events, but responsible counseling involves ongoing monitoring and assessment of these aspects of a client's life to ensure safety.

As part of ongoing assessment, counselors have a responsibility to screen for **suicidal** or **homicidal ideation (SI/HI)**—thoughts of harming oneself or others:

- Frequency and duration: How often does the client think about harming herself or others, and for how long?
- Intensity: Are the thoughts fleeting and easy to ignore, or are they pressing and disturbing?
- Plan: Does the client have a plan for how he would kill himself or others, or is it more of a vague wish to be dead?
- Means: If the client has a plan, does she have the means to carry it out? For example, if the client has contemplated shooting herself, does she have access to a gun?
- Intent: How seriously is the client considering enacting his plan? Does he have a specific time and date that he is planning on; does he deny any intent; is it something in between?

HELPFUL HINT

Some people are afraid that asking about suicidal ideation can make a person suicidal. Research shows that this is not true and that assessing for SI can be lifesaving.

Nonsuicidal self-injury (NSSI) is any form of self-injury without intent to kill oneself. The most common forms of NSSI include cutting, burning, and head banging or hitting. Other forms include scratching, hitting oneself or other objects, ingesting harmful substances, and more.

It is important to refrain from judgment or reacting emotionally when assessing for NSSI. Although cutting is the most common form of NSSI, it is important to screen for other types of NSSI behaviors, as they can be easily missed by counselors.

The **SOARS model** is a brief assessment used in clinics to screen for NSSI:

- **S**uicidal ideation: Is the NSSI motivated by or paired with suicidal ideation?
- **O**nset, frequency, methods: When did the NSSI begin; when was the most recent time; how often does it happen; what methods were used?
- **A**ftercare: How are the wounds cared for; has medical attention for the wounds ever been required?
- **R**easons: What prompts or motivates the client to harm herself (emotional release, anger, self-hatred, and so forth)?
- **S**tages of change: Does the client think about stopping; does he want to stop?

Relationship violence, also known as "domestic violence" or "intimate partner violence," occurs when one or both partners are enacting physical, emotional, financial, or psychological abuse on the other partner. Intimate partner violence is dangerous and can be life-threatening. Despite that, it is not reportable except in cases where children witness the abuse or if the abuse is aimed at an older adult.

Important areas of assessment for survivors of domestic violence include

- frequency and duration of attacks (can be helpful to use a calendar);
- type of attack (whether a weapon was used, level of injury);
- partner stability (employment, drug/alcohol use, mental health concerns, suicide threats);
- controlling behavior (money, stalking, controlling who the partner sees);
- attacks on others (children, pets, family members).

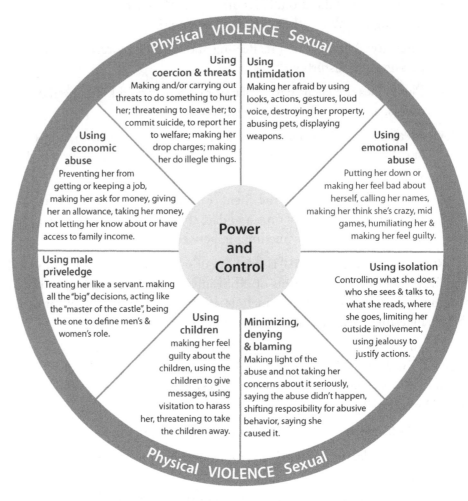

Figure 7.3. The Power and Control Wheel

Safety planning is of paramount importance for clients who experience relationship violence. It often takes a long time for them to leave their abusers. Planning where to go, saving enough money, and childcare are all crucial elements of treatment planning for clients who experience relationship violence.

PRACTICE QUESTION

11. Which of the following is the FIRST thing to determine in assessing for suicidality?

    A) if the client has access to weapons

    B) if the client has any suicidal thoughts

    C) if the client has a specific plan for killing himself

    D) if the client has planned a time and place where she would kill herself

Assessing Depression and Anxiety

Several assessment tools are available to diagnose depression and anxiety, screen for these issues, or measure the severity of symptoms in clients.

The **Suicide Assessment Five-Step Evaluation and Triage (SAFE-T)** helps identify suicide risk in clients. The counselor follows five steps:

1. Identify risk factors that can be changed to reduce the client's risk.
2. Identify protective factors that can be increased to reduce the client's risk.
3. Conduct a suicide assessment to understand the client's thoughts, plans, behaviors, and suicidal intent.
4. Determine the client's risk level and the appropriate response to ensure their safety; intervene as necessary.
5. Document the assessment of the client's risk level with the supporting evidence discussed, the interventions used, and follow-up steps.

The SAFE-T is available as a pocket card or app.

Many assessments exist to screen for depression or evaluate the level of depression in clients.

The psychiatrist David Burns developed the **Burns Depression Test** to screen for depression. The test is meant to be completed by the client. It asks about thoughts and feelings, personal relationships, physical symptoms, and suicidality.

The **Hamilton Rating Scale for Depression (HAM-D)** is commonly used for individuals who already have a depressive disorder diagnosis.

- It measures suicide risk, physical, and emotional symptoms.
- It can be used with both children and adults.
- There are two versions of the HAM-D: one includes seventeen items (HAM-D-17); the other has twenty-one (HAM-D-21).

The **Montgomery-Asberg Depression Rating Scale (MADRS)** is a ten-item tool. It helps the counselor get a better understanding of depressive symptoms in clients who have a mood disorder. Like the Hamilton Depression Scale, it is not used to diagnose; instead, it helps the counselor determine the severity of symptoms. The MADRS should be used with adult clients.

Like the MADRS, the **Zung Self-Rating Depression Scale** measures severity of depression. It is a twenty-item assessment that rates four common symptoms of depression:

1. pervasive effect
2. psychological equivalents
3. psychomotor activities
4. other disturbances

Several assessments are available for diagnosing and screening for anxiety. Some of the more common follow.

The **State-Trait Anxiety Inventory (STAI)** is useful for diagnosing anxiety in adults. Twenty assessment items cover trait anxiety; another twenty questions cover state anxiety. Differentiating between the two types of anxiety helps reveal a client's levels of anxiety on a day-to-day basis (trait anxiety) as opposed to levels of anxiety in response to perceived stressors (state anxiety). The STAI can also help the counselor differentiate between depression and anxiety symptoms in a client.

HELPFUL HINT

Counselors should discuss their recommendations with clients and develop a plan collaboratively before documenting the assessment.

DID YOU KNOW?

The Hamilton Rating Scale for Depression can also be referred to as the Hamilton Depression Scale or the Hamilton Depression Rating Scale.

The **Beck Anxiety Inventory (BAI)** is a relatively quick anxiety screening tool for adults. It can be done verbally during a session or self-reported before a session. In the BAI, the client rates the severity of several physical and emotional anxiety symptoms. This assessment is a good predictor of anxiety disorders, making it a helpful tool when trying to formulate a diagnosis. The BAI produces valid results.

The BAI can also be used to help gauge the client's progress in therapy. Results before and after beginning therapy and/or medications can be compared.

Another anxiety screening tool is the **Generalized Anxiety Disorder 7-item (GAD-7)**, a quick seven-question assessment asking about the severity of anxiety. It is generally self-administered by the client and useful to track treatment progress.

The **Hamilton Anxiety Rating Scale (HARS or HAM-A)** was one of the original anxiety screening assessments. It is administered by a clinician and addresses fourteen categories of physical and psychological symptoms.

Research has found that reliability and validity of the HAM-A is improved when guidance for a structured interview is provided. As a result, the **Hamilton Anxiety Rating Scale Interview Guide (HARS-IG)** was developed. The HARS-IG is considered more reliable and valid.

PRACTICE QUESTION

12. Susan is a client who has been struggling with depressive symptoms since her husband unexpectedly passed away. Since the loss, Susan has been sleeping more than normal, has a depressed mood, and has lost a significant amount of weight. Because of Susan's symptoms, the counselor uses the SAFE-T assessment. What is the correct order of events for this assessment?

    A) document, identify risk factors, conduct suicide inquiry, identify protective factors, and determine risk level/intervention

    B) identify risk factors, identify protective factors, conduct suicide inquiry, determine risk level/intervention, and document

    C) conduct suicide inquiry, identify protective factors, identify risk factors, determine risk level/intervention, and document

    D) conduct suicide inquiry, identify risk factors, identify protective factors, determine risk level/intervention, document

Assessing Personality

Personality assessments are used to tell a counselor about a client's behavior patterns and interpersonal interactions. These can be used to help a counselor determine how to build rapport with a client and choose treatment plans and interventions. They have also been used to assess for career paths. These assessments are a somewhat controversial tool in the world of psychology and counseling because many of them have low reliability and validity, and because one's personality changes frequently throughout a lifetime. The results are usually not shared with the client and are instead used to inform treatment.

Projective tests are assessments in which the client must interpret some type of ambiguous stimuli.

- The most well-known of these is the **Rorschach inkblot test**, which asks clients to describe what they see in an inkblot.
- Similarly, the **Holtzman inkblot technique** uses a client's interpretation of an inkblot to detect personality.
- The **Thematic Apperception Test (TAT)** is a projective test in which the client describes what is happening on different cards featuring people in ambiguous situations.

Overall, projective tests are seen as unreliable because they rely heavily on the counselor's interpretations and have low validity and reliability.

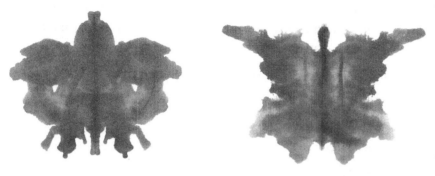

Figure 7.4. Rorschach Tests

Self-report inventories are questionnaires in which people provide information about themselves in response to various prompts. The most common is the Minnesota Multiphasic Personality Inventory-2 (MMPI-2). The **Minnesota Multiphasic Personality Inventory-2 (MMPI-2)** assesses personality traits including

- paranoia,
- social introversion, and
- psychopathology.

The MMPI-2 is not generally used to evaluate people with healthy personalities. Rather, it measures dysfunction within an individual's personality.

The **Sixteen Personality Factors Questionnaire (16PF)** focuses on sixteen fundamental personality characteristics and functions to assist in comprehending where someone's personality may register among those characteristics. The behavioral assessment serves to provide greater understanding of an individual's behavior and causative factors or thought processes behind those behaviors.

The 16PF underwent a factor analysis that distilled the personality traits into five main traits and eventually developed into the **Big Five personality traits**, which measure the client's level of openness, conscientiousness, extraversion, agreeableness, and neuroticism.

The **Woodworth Personal Data Sheet** is regarded as the first personality test. It was developed to screen war veterans for shell shock (now known as PTSD). It is not typically used by clinicians today.

The **Myers-Briggs Type Indicator (MBTI)** is a self-administered questionnaire used to determine four personality factors with opposing domains. The domains include the following:

- introversion versus extraversion
- sensing versus intuition
- thinking versus feeling
- judging versus perceiving

Though widely popular and easy to test online, the MBTI is not generally used by clinicians due to its low validity and reliability.

The **Edwards Personal Preference Schedule (EPPS)** is a series of forced-choice objective questions administered by a clinician. The assessment is designed to illuminate personality through motives and needs and to determine how one would react in certain situations. The assessment has limited validity and reliability and is not a standard personality assessment.

The **HEXACO Personality Inventory (HEXACO-PI)** addresses six characteristics:

1. humility
2. emotionality
3. extraversion
4. agreeableness
5. conscientiousness
6. openness to experience

Scoring for this assessment uses a scale, so the counselor can gauge the significance of the characteristics. However, some critics of the HEXACO Personality Inventory feel that it does not adequately reflect cultural influences.

PRACTICE QUESTION

13. Which of the following personality assessments would be the BEST choice to determine if a client has psychopathic tendencies?

    A) the Edwards Personal Preference Schedule
    B) the Big Five personality traits
    C) the Minnesota Multiphasic Personality Inventory-2
    D) the Rorschach test

Cognitive Functioning Assessments

Certain instruments and assessments are designed to measure psychological functioning. The **Rancho Los Amigos Level of Cognitive Functioning Scale (LCFS)** determines the level of brain function in post-comatose clients and clients with a closed head injury (including traumatic brain injury).

The LCFS focuses on eight areas of cognition (awareness), with each level representing a progression of improvement from brain trauma or damage:

1. No response (level 1)
2. Generalized response (level 2)—reacts inconsistently with no purpose
3. Localized response (level 3)—reacts specifically to various stimuli, with a different response each time
4. Confused-agitated response (level 4)—active but does not comprehend what has happened
5. Confused, inappropriate, nonagitated response (level 5)—less agitated, consistent reactions to basic commands
6. Confused-appropriate response (level 6)—motivated, highly dependent on others, more aware of self and loved ones
7. Automatic-appropriate response (level 7)—acts appropriately in the health care setting and at home; self-aware, oriented to place and time
8. Purposeful-appropriate response (level 8)—independently functions well within the world, has memory of how the past fits with the present and future

The **Mini-Cog assessment tool** is administered in three minutes to screen for cognitive deficiency in older adults. The Mini-Cog is used within the principal health care environment and mainly concentrates on recall abilities. An individual is asked to remember three simple words, then is intentionally distracted by the examiner, and is later asked to repeat the three words.

The **Mini-Mental State Examination (MMSE)** is brief and used to screen for dementia and cognitive functioning in older adults. There are five sections on the MMSE:

1. orientation
2. immediate memory
3. attention and concentration
4. delayed recall
5. language

The MMSE is not to be confused with the mental status exam (MSE) used in clinical intake interviews.

The **Child Development Inventory (CDI)** is a 300-item screening tool that parents complete at home and provide to the counselor. It looks at the child's development in eight areas:

1. social
2. self-help
3. gross motor
4. fine motor
5. expressive language
6. language comprehension
7. letters
8. numbers

DID YOU KNOW?

The Mini-Cog instrument is widely used to assess memory recall for people with Alzheimer's disease.

The CDI also includes the General Development Scale which investigates health, growth, vision, and hearing, as well as a child's developmental behavior.

Cognitive functioning can also be measured by **intelligence tests**. Two main intelligence tests are

- the Stanford-Binet test, and
- the Wechsler test.

French psychologist Alfred Binet wanted to develop a test measuring academic ability in order to determine which students were not learning well in the classroom and who might need special instruction. He assumed that intelligence increases with age and devised a "mental age" measurement. For example, if Bobby, an eleven-year-old, has a mental age of eleven, he is on par with his peers. If his mental age were nine, he would be behind. If his mental age were thirteen, he would be ahead.

Lewis Terman, a professor at Stanford University, used Binet's mental age system to create an **intelligence quotient (IQ)** that links intelligence to a number. To determine someone's IQ, the mental age is divided by the actual age and then multiplied by 100. So, if Bobby's mental age is twelve, his IQ would be 118.

To apply this method to adults, Terman set an arbitrary age of twenty for calculating all adult IQs. Terman developed the **Stanford-Binet IQ test** to determine IQ. Test takers are asked a variety of questions, the answers of which determine a single score.

The other major intelligence test was created by David Wechsler. It is also called an IQ test, although the resulting number is not actually a quotient. Instead, the test is standardized so that the mean (the average of the numbers) is 100, and the **standard deviation** (how spread out the numbers are) is 15 with a **normal distribution** (or bell-shaped curve).

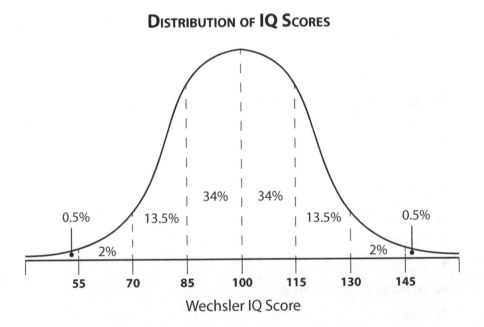

Figure 7.5. Wechsler IQ Score Distribution

A test taker's percentile (relative to the population of test takers) is determined, and the score is based on the number of standard deviations the percentile is from the mean. For example, if Shauna is in the sixteenth percentile, that places her at 34 percent below the mean (fiftieth percentile), which is one standard deviation to the left of the mean. Her IQ score would therefore be 85.

The Wechsler test comes in three different forms:
- Wechsler Adult Intelligence Scale (WAIS)
- Wechsler Intelligence Scale for Children ages 6 – 16 (WISC)
- Wechsler Preschool and Primary Scale of Intelligence (WPPSI)

Each test is composed of different types of questions (verbal and performance on the WAIS, for example). These yield subscores, which, taken together, yield a total IQ score.

PRACTICE QUESTION

14. The first IQ test was developed to determine which of the following?
- **A)** entry into Mensa
- **B)** second grade readiness
- **C)** graduate school readiness
- **D)** possible intellectual disability

Criticisms of IQ Tests

There are several criticisms of the efficacy of intelligence testing of any kind. First, the tests focus heavily on verbal skills. While the Wechsler tests require more manipulation of objects and other such performance skills, the verbal components can skew the scores of those whose verbal skills may not match their intelligence.

Additionally, intelligence tests are often accused of being biased. The questions are constructed on certain cultural norms and are not universal. If the question references information not regularly available to a certain individual, it can unfairly skew the results of the test. Defenders of the test argue that the test has the same validity—and predictive power on, for example, college grades—for all cultural groups. Others claim that the bias runs much deeper, setting up certain groups for success on both intelligence tests and college success, while unfairly impeding others.

PRACTICE QUESTION

15. Why are IQ tests frequently criticized as being biased and not universal?
- **A)** The tests have high validity with GPA.
- **B)** They ignore domains like emotional intelligence.
- **C)** The questions assume certain cultural norms.
- **D)** The questions have low reliability.

Assessing Outcomes

Assessing outcomes is an important part of rigorous therapeutic methods. Outcomes are assessed using **pretest** and **post-test measures**. For example, a client who presents with symptoms of PTSD is given the PCL-5 in the first session to determine the rate of her symptoms. After three months of weekly sessions, she reports having fewer nightmares and is better able to cope with triggers in the community. A new administration of the PCL-5 reveals that she no longer meets the clinical criteria for PTSD. This is considered a positive outcome as a result of treatment sessions with the counselor.

Pre- and post-test measures can also evaluate counseling effectiveness. Some counselors or clinics ask their clients to fill out a weekly, monthly, or termination evaluation that rates their perceptions of the counselor's efficacy. Common questions ask whether the client

- feels understood by the counselor;
- perceives improvement in symptoms;
- feels like the sessions are a good use of time.

PRACTICE QUESTION

16. Assessing a client's symptoms when she starts treatment and when she terminates with her counselor is known as which of the following?

    A) random sampling

    B) pre-test and post-test measures

    C) stratified sampling

    D) case study

Diagnosis

A **diagnosis** is an identified health condition that is based on an assessment by a trained professional. To make a diagnosis, counselors look at the client's symptoms and compare them to the symptoms listed in the *Diagnostic and Statistical Manual of Mental Disorders* (*DSM-5*).

Determining and Using Diagnosis

Because diagnosis is a key component of a client's medical records, clients have the right to know if they meet clinical criteria for a diagnosis. After learning their diagnosis, clients can make informed decisions about their treatment.

Counselors should use language the client can understand when discussing a diagnosis. For example, the way a diagnosis is explained to an adult will be different than the way it would be explained to a child.

Diagnoses are used to help guide treatment. Research has found that specific presenting concerns require different therapeutic approaches. For example, cognitive therapy will not be as effective as using Dialectical Behavior Therapy (DBT) for someone living with borderline personality disorder.

Once a diagnosis is made, the counselor can determine whether additional treatment services would benefit the client. Medication management, as an example, can be an effective intervention for several clinical diagnoses.

Having a clinical diagnosis can significantly change the objectives and goals of a treatment plan. Treatment plans should be in place after the initial interview and continually be adjusted to reflect the client's progress.

Treatment plans allow for further specification and can include goals specific to a diagnosis. For example, clients struggling with obsessive-compulsive disorder may learn new and effective coping skills for their obsessions in the early phases of treatment. Once those skills have developed, the treatment plan can progress to other approaches to respond to the compulsive behaviors that are present. The next chapter discusses treatment planning in depth.

After meeting with a client for an initial interview, the counselor should take time to consider possible diagnoses. The ***Diagnostic and Statistical Manual of Mental Disorders (DSM-5)*** contains twenty-one sections of similar diagnoses. A counselor should get a general idea of which section the client's diagnosis may be in. Then she can begin looking at the specific symptoms for those diagnoses. Every diagnosis has different requirements, all of which are explained in the "Diagnostic Criteria" section for the diagnosis.

Many diagnoses within the *DSM-5* are rated on a mild, moderate, or severe scale, which is determined by the number of symptoms present. This is explained in the "Coding and Recording Procedures" section for each diagnosis in the *DSM-5*. Diagnoses may also have additional specifiers that would be listed in the same section.

The term *co-occurring* refers to the presence of a mental health diagnosis in addition to a substance-related disorder. Some people use alcohol and drugs to cope with symptoms resulting from a mental health condition. As a result, individuals who have co-occurring disorders need to receive treatment for both concerns for the best treatment outcomes.

Dual diagnosis refers to an individual who meets the criteria for two separate diagnoses. Symptoms for both diagnoses must be present at the same time. The term is usually used to describe the presence of a mental health diagnosis and a substance abuse disorder, but it can refer to other disorders. Dual diagnoses can be two mental health conditions, two medical health conditions, or one of each.

Comorbidity is similar to dual diagnosis, but it refers to the presence of more than one health condition. These can be medical or mental health conditions. Each diagnosis section in the *DSM-5* ends with a paragraph explaining the common comorbidities found with that particular illness.

HELPFUL HINT

Counselors may come across dual diagnoses referred to as "co-occurring disorders."

PRACTICE QUESTION

17. A counselor is reviewing initial assessment paperwork before meeting with a new client. The client has been diagnosed with PTSD with dissociative symptoms and major depressive disorder, severe. She received the PTSD diagnosis first. Three years later, she developed depressive symptoms that led to her second diagnosis. Which of the following would BEST characterize her diagnosis?

- A) co-occurring diagnoses
- B) dual diagnosis
- C) comorbid diagnoses
- D) clinical diagnosis

Levels of Care

One of the functions of an initial interview is to determine which level of care is appropriate for clients and their presenting concerns. There are a variety of options, each with its own benefits.

Residential inpatient care programs typically occur within a hospital setting. The goal is to stabilize clients so they can begin receiving treatment for their mental health concerns at a different location:

- Clients receive treatment that can include
  - psychoeducation;
  - individual therapy;
  - crisis intervention;
  - medication management.
- Inpatient programs are appropriate for individuals who have safety risks like
  - recent suicide gestures or attempts;
  - homicidal attempts.
- Inpatient programs are also suitable for clients who need a high level of care, including
  - medication management;
  - drug/ alcohol detox and treatment.

In **partial hospitalization programs (PHP)**, the client attends a structured day program at a treatment facility:

- The program's structure resembles an inpatient program, but the client goes home at night.
- PHPs typically run five days a week for six to eight hours per day.
- PHPs provide clients with safety and structure for most of their day.
- PHPs are appropriate for clients who can safely live at home but still need a thorough treatment program.

- A typical client might have severe mental illness, be compliant with medication, and learning how to manage symptoms behaviorally.

In **intensive outpatient programs (IOP)**, the client attends structured programming for a few hours per day.

- IOPs usually treat addiction, eating disorders, and depressive disorders.
- IOPs typically have a psychoeducational component in addition to group treatment.
- IOPs are appropriate for
  - clients with mild disorders;
  - clients with mild and severe use disorders who have already completed residential treatment programs.

Outpatient treatment (outpatient therapy) is usually recommended to build on what clients learned in other, more intensive programs:

- The duration of an outpatient program varies depending on the presenting concern.
- Outpatient treatment typically follows successful completion of an IOP or PHP.
- Outpatient treatment is typically fewer hours per day than an IOP or PHP.
- Outpatient activities include
  - group therapy,
  - individual therapy,
  - medication management,
  - specialized treatment,
  - psychoeducation, and
  - family therapy.
- Outpatient treatment programs address various mental health concerns, including
  - addiction,
  - childhood behavioral and emotional concerns, and
  - mood disorders.

Psychotherapy is individual counseling between a client and a counselor that

- is appropriate for individuals with a mild mental health concern,
- allows complex clients to maintain a connection to a supportive professional after more intensive treatment,
- includes high-functioning clients, and
- usually consists of weekly or biweekly individual sessions.

Self-help programs generally refer to support groups run by peers rather than mental health professionals:

- Many self-help programs address addiction, but some address other mental health concerns. These include
  - twelve-step programs (Alcoholics Anonymous, Narcotics Anonymous, for example);
  - support for families of addicts (Al-Anon, Nar-Anon);
  - eating and weight management groups (Overeaters Anonymous, Weight Watchers);
  - some grief support groups.
- Activity and attendance rate depend on the client.
- Self-help groups can be used at every level of care.

Treatment programs offer guidelines that can help the counselor decide which level of care to recommend to the client.

PRACTICE QUESTION

18. A client just completed a detox program and an inpatient addiction program to address opioid use disorder. The client has a history of trauma, anxiety, and depression. He has a safe home environment and believes that his mental health concerns triggered his substance abuse. The inpatient program recommended that he attend treatment for a few hours a day, three to four days per week while living at home. Which level of care is the client now entering?

    A) partial hospitalization program (PHP)
    B) intensive outpatient program (IOP)
    C) psychotherapy
    D) outpatient treatment

Answer Key

1. B

    Intake forms should be completed by the client. These forms enable clients to explain in their own words why they are seeking counseling.

2. B

    The precontemplation stage is when the individual is not thinking about behavioral change and is not ready to take steps to change.

3. C

    Motivational interviewing (MI) is ideal for a client who is unsure about a life change (Option C). This client is in the contemplation stage of the transtheoretical model (TTM). Motivational interviewing could help the client find benefits to making changes in his life and encourage thoughtful communication about his hesitations. Option A might be an appropriate answer, but this client may have significant internal motivation. Someone with internal motivation and not external motivation will still be more open to making changes than the client in Option C. Option B describes a client who is actively participating in the interview, and Option D describes a client who seems to have internal motivation for treatment, which would encourage active participation during the interview as well.

4. B

    Client self-report is the backbone of a structured clinical interview.

5. B

    A biopsychosocial interview would be the best interview format to use when meeting a first-time client because it assesses physical health, mental health, and social life. This allows the counselor to determine areas of focus for the treatment plan as well as whether any specialized assessments or interview formats could also be used.

6. C

    A clinical interview, also known as an intake interview, is an informal assessment that makes up the first part of any clinical relationship.

7. A

    Generally, performance on math tests shows fairly accurately how well students understand the material, which makes it a valid measure of student knowledge.

8. A

    A client's level of insight, or how aware she is of the content of her thoughts, appearance, behavior, and condition, is a key part of a thorough mental status exam.

9. D

   Refusing to interact with anything that may remind the client of the traumatizing event is a sign of avoidance.

10. B

    The Car, Relax, Alone, Forget, Friends, Trouble (CRAFFT) is the only assessment that is endorsed for use with adolescents and screens for drug usage.

11. B

    The first step in assessing for suicidality is to determine if the client has any suicidal thoughts.

12. B

    When using the SAFE-T, the counselor begins by identifying risk factors that can be changed to reduce the client's risk. Next, the counselor determines what protective factors can be increased to reduce risk. This is followed by a suicide assessment that looks at the client's thoughts, plans, behaviors, and suicidal intent. Once the counselor has all the information needed, the client's risk level can be determined and an appropriate response to ensure the client's safety can be formulated. After discussing recommendations with the client and developing a plan, the counselor should document the assessment of the client's risk level with supporting evidence discussed, the interventions used, and the recommended follow-up steps.

13. C

    The Minnesota Multiphasic Personality Inventory-2 (MMPI-2) scores and assesses for negative personality traits associated with psychological disorders, including areas such as paranoia, antisocial behaviors, depression, and more.

14. D

    Alfred Binet first developed his IQ test at the request of the French government to determine which students might have an intellectual disability as a basis to require separate classroom instruction.

15. C

    The main criticism of IQ tests not being universal is that the questions are culturally biased toward the test makers.

16. B

    Using pre-test and post-test techniques determine if an intervention has caused a change in symptoms or behavior.

17. C

   The client has comorbid diagnoses because more than one disorder is present. Option A can be ruled out because neither disorder is a substance use disorder. Option B is incorrect because the client received the diagnoses at separate points in her life. If she had developed symptoms of both disorders at the same time, then Option B would be correct. "Clinical diagnosis" (Option D) simply refers to an identified health condition as determined by professional assessment.

18. B

   The client is entering an intensive outpatient program (IOP). A partial hospitalization program (PHP) can be ruled out because the treatment recommendation is only a few days a week. Psychotherapy is generally one or two short sessions per week and would not meet the recommended level of care from the referrer. Finally, the situation describes more intensive scheduling than a typical outpatient program. After completing the IOP, the individual would likely be encouraged to continue with outpatient treatment.

8 | Research and Program Evaluation

Research in Counseling

A central premise in the counseling field is that everything is supported by research, starting with the basic counseling skills that everyone is taught. Those skills have been researched, and best practices for using them have been developed. The assessments used in counseling to evaluate and diagnose a client's condition are all based on research that confirms the assessment's validity and reliability. The interventions used for particular diagnoses are also researched to create evidence-based practices for how to use them effectively. In this way, research creates a foundation of knowledge that supports the methods, approaches, and interventions used with clients; however, not all research is appropriate for all situations and clients, so a competent counselor must understand how to read and critique published research to inform counseling practices.

Counselors should know that research on mental health is built on the work of previous researchers to expand the body of knowledge—one study is not enough to draw conclusions. Additionally, the body of knowledge for counseling is supported by research in other fields, such as social work, psychiatry, medicine, and nursing. Therefore, counselors need to expand their source materials to ensure they are getting the biggest picture possible.

Counselors also need to understand how to critique specific studies. For example, knowing the differences among the various types of research designs affects how the results can be applied. **Research designs** are strategies that are used to answer research questions using data based on observation or experience. Counselors must also read the methodology used to determine how participants were chosen for a study, the number of participants, and how the study was conducted.

The counselor should understand the basics of reading the results of studies, especially the differences among significant results, statistically significant results, and clinically significant results. These factors all work together to help the counselor understand whether the conclusions drawn by the researchers are appropriate for what the counselor needs to know.

Needs assessments evaluate individual, organizational, and community needs:

- At the individual level, a needs assessment evaluates a client's current functioning and status across multiple domains.
  - Individual needs assessments determine which services and resources a client needs.
- Organizational needs assessments determine whether the population it serves requires services.
  - Managers and administrators use organizational needs assessments to determine whether anything has to change to meet the organization's needs.
- Community needs assessments evaluate the entire population of the community to determine the strengths and challenges it faces.
  - Community needs assessments reveal which services a community's members can benefit from.

Counselors use data and data analysis to determine client progress and evaluate outcomes. Data collected from more formal assessments can provide a numerical picture of client needs:

- Formal assessments like the Beck Depression Inventory determine the severity of a client's symptoms.
- Assessment instruments can be used at various intervals in the counseling process to show the client the changes in symptom severity.
- Analysis of that data can tell the counselor if the interventions were successful or if a certain symptom cluster still needs work.

There are multiple strategies for ensuring the ethical and culturally relevant implementation of conducting, interpreting, and reporting the results of research and program evaluations. Guidelines include

- the impartial recruitment of participants;
- recruiting participants who represent the population culturally and demographically;
- providing participants with informed consent and the ability to opt out;
- confidentiality and privacy;
- securing an ethical review to ensure the absence of bias and the elimination of risk to participants;
- treating all participants with dignity and respect during the research;
- reporting all results truthfully, regardless of the outcome;
- addressing limitations of the research; and
- submitting the research for peer review.

PRACTICE QUESTION

1. An agency is deciding whether to offer a group counseling program for single pregnant women. What should the agency do before creating the program?
   - **A)** conduct a needs assessment
   - **B)** hire an expert consultant
   - **C)** start the group and see who shows up
   - **D)** evaluate previous programs

Statistical Concepts and Methods Used in Research

Counselors must stay current on research trends in mental health counseling and understand the statistical concepts and methods used in research. Research involves a combination of qualitative and quantitative approaches. Some studies use mixed methods:

Qualitative research addresses how and why things happen. This research relies on interviews, focus groups, and other open-ended evaluation techniques. In an effort to explore a topic more deeply, qualitative research generally involves fewer participants. While this research can lead to statistical results, the methods used to achieve these results must be reviewed before applying them in practice. The results of qualitative research can often lead to more questions.

Quantitative research relies more on numbers and data points that can be measured and quantified. This form of research uses standardized assessments and methods of measuring behavior and may involve experimental conditions. Quantitative research presents results using numerical data.

Counselors should ask several questions when reviewing research to inform the practice:

- How old is the research?

It is important to consider when a study was conducted and when it was published. There is often a significant period between the actual study and the publication of the results, which may influence the applicability of the results. For example, a study conducted between 2013 and 2015 and published in 2020 may not be relevant due to social and cultural shifts that may have occurred since its completion.

- How many participants were involved, and what were their characteristics?

Studies involving few participants tend to be less generalizable than those with large groups of participants. Furthermore, characteristics such as age, race, gender, geographic location, and socioeconomic status of participants can impact results. A counselor looking for research on depression treatment in adolescents from a particular cultural group would not find relevant information in a study about older adults in a different cultural group. When deciding whether the research applies to their clients, counselors should consider if the participants are representative of their client population.

- What methods were used in the research?

If a study reports significant positive results but does not compare the methods to a control group, the results may not be as positive as they seem. Or, if a study purports to be about children with ADHD, the researchers must show how they determined that the participants have ADHD. Examining the methods of the study will help counselors determine if its results make sense.

- What are the limitations of the study?

Limitations presented at the end of the study are researchers' comments that reveal flaws in the research and address how the study could have been improved. These comments may call attention to issues that might have limited the research, such as using a small number of participants or focusing on only one cultural group.

Research can be stated in terms of statistically significant results and clinically significant results. Statistically significant results do not always mean that the results are clinically significant or clinically appropriate.

- Over how many months or years did the study take place?

The period over which a study is conducted can impact the validity of the results. For example, a study on addiction treatment may only evaluate the results for the duration of the treatment and for a short time following it. Addiction, however, can be a lifelong challenge, so a counselor should question whether positive results after a short period could be sustained after a longer period.

- What other studies support the research?

Strong research is that which has been replicated under either the same or different conditions. When deciding between two evidence-based practices, the one with fifteen different studies will likely be more valid and reliable than the one with only two studies.

PRACTICE QUESTION

2. A counselor is considering several group therapy treatment options while planning an intervention group for women with addictions in prison. Using knowledge of statistical concepts in research, which would present the strongest research picture?

   A) one research study of a group intervention that evaluates women with addiction in an urban setting over ten years

   B) multiple studies that evaluate the intervention of women with addictions that took place seven years prior with no further research conducted

   C) a study of a group that used a similar intervention in one women's prison located in a foreign country

   D) several research studies of an addiction group intervention evaluated in several women's prisons over the past five years that include follow-up studies after the women were released

Developing and Evaluating Counseling Programs

Agencies, businesses, and schools that offer mental health services use evaluation to determine the effectiveness of their counseling programs. **Program evaluation** determines whether the services offered uphold the program's mission, goals, and objectives.

Program evaluation is a form of research that focuses on a program rather than people to determine if the program is achieving its stated goals and what it needs to become more successful. Many organizations use program evaluation strategies to determine the efficacy of programs. Common examples include tobacco cessation education or public health efforts. Program evaluation may be conducted by employees of the program or by a third party.

Experimental and quasi-experimental designs are appropriate for research but not for program evaluation. The quantitative approach may also be inappropriate for program evaluation. Qualitative approaches in research may include case studies, in-depth interviews, or focus groups. Program evaluation can also use these methods, but the focus is on the participant's experiences with the program.

Descriptive design can be used in program evaluation through the use of surveys, for example. Correlational design is not appropriate for program evaluation because it requires multiple variables. With program evaluation, no variables are being manipulated.

In program evaluation, data must be gathered from multiple sources. For example, it is important to engage with stakeholders at all levels of a program to gather enough data on the services offered, how they are received, and how the program could improve. The data are then analyzed to create a list of recommendations for program improvement.

Evaluation is not limited to the program level. **Self-evaluation** helps reveal whether counseling interventions and programs have helped clients achieve their goals. In self-evaluations, clients consider how the counseling intervention impacted their lives and whether they have achieved their stated goals.

Peer assessment and **peer evaluations** are effective in group counseling settings and for the counselor. Peer evaluation helps members encourage each other through interactive feedback. A counselor might invite a colleague to visit the group and provide feedback on the counselor's skills and techniques.

Outcome measures reveal the impact of therapy and interventions. In counseling, outcome measures are determined during the assessment process and are based on the client's goals. Counselors often use formal outcome measures by employing the same assessment instruments used during intake to demonstrate quantitatively that a client's symptoms have improved.

There is a saying in counseling that treatment planning "should begin with the end in mind." Therefore, when clients present for therapy with symptoms of depression, for example, a counselor might ask them what their lives would be like without depression. Clients might say they would sleep more, exercise, eat right, and spend more time with family and friends. These become treatment goals and the basis for outcome measurement.

Counseling education programs are evaluated by the **Council for Accreditation of Counseling and Related Educational Programs (CACREP)**, the counseling education accreditation board. This body establishes a set of competencies that counseling professionals should be able to demonstrate upon completion of a counseling education program.

To earn **CACREP accreditation**, the educational program must demonstrate that it meets the accreditation standards. Many state licensing boards require that an applicant attend a CACREP-accredited school, which streamlines the licensing process because the CACREP accreditation board has verified that the school's program teaches the required evidence-based competencies.

PRACTICE QUESTION

3. What is the primary difference between research and program evaluation?
    A) One is more expensive than the other.
    B) One focuses on people, the other on programs.
    C) One is more important to science than the other.
    D) Counselors read research, not program evaluation.

Evidence-Based Practice

Evidence-based practice describes methods and interventions used by counselors that are supported by research and professional best practices. Evidence-based practice creates a standard of client care, beginning with a comprehensive assessment of the client's presenting problems. That assessment informs a diagnosis, which must be backed up with evidence that the client meets the criteria; this includes using formal assessments and clinical interviews. The diagnosis then informs the treatment plan—a list of goals and objectives for addressing the symptoms associated with the diagnosis.

$$\text{assessment} \longrightarrow \frac{\text{diagnosis}}{\text{formal assessments + clinical interviews}} \longrightarrow \text{treatment plan}$$

Figure 8.1. Evidence-Based Practice

To meet the goals and objectives, the counselor uses evidence-based therapeutic interventions supported by research as valid approaches for the specific diagnosis. Counselors are expected to abide by evidence-based practices while also receiving the proper training to implement evidence-based interventions.

Many evidence-based manualized treatments target specific diagnoses and specific clients. Evidence-based manualized treatments present interventions with step-by-step modules that counselors can use with clients to ensure program fidelity or adherence to the proper use of the intervention.

Evidence-based practice holds counselors to a professional standard of care and builds public trust between the counseling profession and potential clients. Counselors should therefore not use treatment intervention methods that are not supported by research for a particular diagnosis.

PRACTICE QUESTION

4. Evidence-based practice includes standards of care informed by research that begins with which of the following?

    A) a comprehensive assessment of a client that yields a diagnosis

    B) determining which treatment a client needs

    C) consultation with the client's previous providers

    D) researching available treatments for the client's diagnosis

Answer Key

1. A

   A needs assessment will help the agency determine if such a program would fulfill an unmet need in the community.

2. D

   This option includes several best practices in research, including studies on the same population the counselor works with, the same setting, multiple studies with a large number of participants, and an evaluation of how well the treatment serves the clients after they leave prison. Not only is this collection of studies valid for the application the counselor is considering; it also shows positive results over a long period, thus increasing the likelihood that the counselor's clients will benefit from the intervention.

3. B

   Research focuses on people, whereas program evaluation focuses on programs.

4. A

   The first step in the process of evidence-based practice is conducting a thorough assessment of the client. Formal assessments and clinical interviews should be used to demonstrate that the client meets the criteria for a specific diagnosis. Once a diagnosis is made, then a treatment plan can be created.\

9 CPCE Practice Test

1. A colleague prefers conducting unstructured clinical interviews, rather than structured interviews using the SCID-5. What are some of the typical topics covered in an unstructured clinical interview?

   A) enjoyable activities, exercise routine, and eating habits
   B) career goals, finances, and dating history
   C) social activities, physical and mental health history, and drug and alcohol use
   D) sources of guilt and shame, legal history, and leisure activities

2. You are running a group counseling session for professionals who are struggling with mental health concerns. Two group members have been contributing open-ended questions, which you feel is inappropriate. How can you appropriately encourage group participation?

   A) ask members to use their own experiences when sharing
   B) ignore the behaviors because the members are participating
   C) wait until another group member shares an observation
   D) ask the two members to not attend the next session

3. You offer a family therapy program in your addiction treatment program. As part of this, you provide psychoeducation about the disease concept of addiction, recovery, communication, and healthy boundaries. A common boundary concern is when a person takes on a caretaker role with a loved one who is struggling with an addiction. This role may involve some enabling. How would you describe this relationship pattern?

   A) codependency
   B) gaslighting
   C) controlling
   D) dependence

4. A counselor at an outpatient mental health program is developing a treatment plan for a new client. She has included the client's background, diagnosis, treatment goals, objectives, and interventions. What else should be added to the treatment plan?

   A) dates and times of sessions
   B) a timeline for therapy
   C) the client's informed consent
   D) discharge referrals

5. Helena has worked as a customer service representative for a local grocery store chain for one month. She began seeing you about three months ago when she was unemployed. Since she began working, her reported anxiety symptoms have decreased. Helena shared that she felt uncomfortable after a conversation with a coworker who said that she is unqualified for her job and that he thought she was given the job for other reasons. She explained that when he said this, he pointed to her body. She immediately felt uncomfortable and found an

excuse to walk away. Which term BEST describes Helena's experience?

- A) jealousy
- B) workplace harassment
- C) condescending behavior
- D) sexual assault

6. A counselor is interviewing a new client who is on public assistance. She discloses that she is getting as much money as she earned while working. Furthermore, she says it is ridiculous for people to work when they can get public assistance and not work. How should the counselor respond?

- A) refuse to talk about this with the client
- B) strongly disagree with the client's statement
- C) agree with the client
- D) tell the client that this subject is dependent on each person's values

7. You have just completed an intake interview with Sarah, a fourteen-year-old girl whose mother brought her in for an assessment after her school counselor expressed concern about her behavior. Over the school year, Sarah has lost a significant amount of body weight and has a low weight compared to her peers. She discussed with the school counselor her anxiety about gaining weight and the negative impact these thoughts have on her functioning. Sarah shared that she only eats when she is hungry, usually has one piece of fruit for each meal, and drinks water throughout the day to stay hydrated. Sarah did not appear to recognize the significance of her behaviors and weight when she met with her counselor. Which diagnosis would you choose after learning her symptoms?

- A) avoidant/restrictive food intake disorder
- B) anorexia nervosa, restrictive type
- C) anorexia nervosa, binge eating/purging type
- D) bulimia nervosa

8. You have been working with Ally for six months regarding her depressive symptoms. She has been in a committed relationship for four months and is having a hard time relating to her partner's family relationships. Ally is an only child who has a strained relationship with her family, and her partner is close with her parents, siblings, and extended family. Ally's partner wants to spend more time with Ally at family events compared to earlier in their relationship when it was just the two of them. Ally and her partner have agreed to a couples session. Which of the following would be the MOST helpful topic to explore?

- A) boundaries
- B) healthy communication
- C) values clarification
- D) long-term goals

9. You are working in an addiction treatment program with Martha, who has been diagnosed with alcohol use disorder and binge eating disorder. You have training and experience as an addiction counselor but no exposure to eating disorder treatment since earning your degree three years ago. Which of the following should you do?

- A) talk to your supervisor about your competency with this client
- B) work with the client individually and focus on her addiction
- C) work with the client and research eating disorder treatment
- D) refer her to a colleague with more experience in eating disorder counseling

10. Elijah and Mary are developing a blended family. Both are divorced, have had time to process and move on from their divorces, and have children from their previous relationships. They are working on defining new roles, boundaries, and expectations within their blended family. Which stage of Carter and McGoldrick's stages of Remarried Family Formulation are they in?

- A) entering the new relationship
- B) conceptualizing and planning a new marriage and family
- C) moving into the same residence
- D) remarrying and reconstituting a family

11. Elijah and Mary are discussing with you what they think their new boundaries should be, specifically as concerns dividing responsibilities between themselves. Which boundary issue would address this concern?

- A) membership
- B) space
- C) authority
- D) time

12. You were asked by your supervisor to conduct a personality assessment for a new client. You choose one that has thirty items and several uses. This assessment can be used to make a diagnosis of PTSD within the last month, lead to a diagnosis of PTSD at a different point in a person's life, and assess for PTSD symptoms over the past week. This tool aligns with the *DSM-5* criteria for post-traumatic stress disorder. Which assessment will you use?

    A) Global Psychotrauma Screen
    B) PTSD Checklist for *DSM-5* (PCL-5)
    C) Posttrauma Risky Behaviors Questionnaire
    D) Clinician-Administered PTSD Scale for *DSM-5* (CAPS-5)

13. During your group session, you notice that Eddie has been quiet and shared very little. He does appear engaged while others are talking by making eye contact and nodding. You do not know Eddie and his case well, but you would like to encourage group participation. Which of the following would you consider?

    A) put him on the spot in group
    B) talk to him individually after group
    C) facilitate a group activity
    D) give him a week to get comfortable

14. You have recently begun facilitating a group for individuals struggling with depressive disorders. Their previous group leader unexpectedly fell ill and was unable to provide closure and ease the transition to you. You have noticed that group members have limited participation and are not as active as they were before. Which of the following could help encourage members to participate?

    A) play an icebreaker game
    B) conduct a meditation exercise
    C) lead guided imagery
    D) request a new counselor

15. A fifty-seven-year-old man has been meeting with a counselor to address his alcohol dependence and has cut down on his drinking over the past few weeks. He arrives at his appointment sweating, says that he has been vomiting, and has a noticeable tremor in his hands. What should the counselor do?

    A) call 911, even if the client refuses to consent, as he is likely detoxing and may experience seizures or possibly death
    B) explain the possible dangers of alcohol withdrawal and collaborate with the client to decide whether to seek medical help
    C) encourage the client to withstand the uncomfortable symptoms for a few days, as they will likely pass after the painful detox process
    D) encourage the client to decrease his alcohol intake more slowly, as he will be less likely to experience such serious withdrawal symptoms

16. You work in an outpatient addiction treatment center and are meeting with a new colleague to discuss the use of session fading in your treatment program. How can you explain session fading to this professional?

    A) As clients progress in their recovery and satisfy their treatment plan goals, their treatment schedules include fewer sessions.
    B) As clients progress in their recovery, the group counselors allow them to have more active roles in the group.
    C) During clients' last three months of counseling, they are required to attend fewer group therapy sessions.
    D) During clients' last month of treatment, they only need to attend individual counseling sessions.

17. You are running a group therapy session that focuses on relapse prevention skills for individuals in early recovery. Some group members have just completed an inpatient rehab program; others have recently relapsed. Some individuals will be in this group longer than others, and new members will be joining. Which therapeutic approach would work BEST for your group?

    A) motivational interviewing
    B) cognitive behavioral therapy
    C) solution-focused brief therapy
    D) behavioral therapy

18. You are a school counselor who has been meeting with an eight-year-old boy, Max. Max was referred to you by his teacher after she noticed that he was having a hard time in class.

Max has been in the foster care system and was recently adopted by his foster parents. Max has shared that he is happy with his adoptive parents and is trying to find his place in the family. Max's teacher told you that he appears to make "silly" mistakes in his work when he knows the correct answers. He has a hard time staying focused during lessons and is sometimes unaware when the teacher calls on him. The teacher has noticed that his folders are messy, which makes it hard for him to find his work. Which diagnosis would you investigate?

A) adjustment disorder

B) attention-deficit/hyperactivity disorder, inattention presentation

C) autism spectrum disorder

D) attention-deficit/hyperactivity, combined presentation

19. Counselors who work with clients with a history of trauma and PTSD are at an increased risk of developing what?

A) post-traumatic stress disorder

B) major depressive disorder

C) complex trauma

D) secondary trauma

20. You are working with Nina, a twenty-two-year-old female who has been struggling with suicidal ideation while coping with her recent diagnosis of bipolar disorder. Nina has shared that she has thoughts about death daily and finds that by evening, her thoughts turn to a desire to die. She has had passive thoughts about suicide recently, and this concerns her. You validate her concern and work to develop a safety plan. She has agreed that keeping a small card with her safety plan in her wallet would be ideal. What is something that could be written on her safety card?

A) her employer's phone number

B) list of mental health concerns

C) phone number for a supportive person

D) phone number for her ex-partner

21. Nina calls you and shares that she is currently struggling with suicidal ideation. She explains that she has had a tough day and feels like giving up. Nina lets you know that she is home alone and has access to prescription medications that she has been thinking about taking. She is tearful and says that she called because she does not want to die but does not know what else to do. How should you proceed?

A) tell her you are concerned about her safety and will be calling for a wellness check

B) tell her you are concerned and that you can meet with her individually tomorrow

C) tell her you are concerned and encourage her to call her close friends for support

D) tell her you are concerned and encourage her to use her emotion regulation skills

22. You are working with a new client, a child, in your mental health practice. The parents meet with you to discuss their concerns about their child. The mother explains that compared to her other children, this child does not seem to be learning as quickly. For example, he started speaking right before his third birthday, has a difficult time with his fine and gross motor skills, and has a BMI in the fifteenth percentile. You give the parents an at-home assessment to complete and bring to the next session. Which assessment have you chosen?

A) Ages & Stages Questionnaires (ASQ)

B) Battelle Developmental Inventory Screening Tool, 2nd ed (BDI-ST)

C) Child Development Inventory (CDI)

D) BRIGANCE Screens-II

23. You have been working with Adrien at an inpatient addiction treatment program for two and a half months. He has successfully met his treatment goals and is expected to complete this program in two weeks. After speaking with Adrien about his goals after treatment, you have both agreed that he would benefit from continuing in treatment. Adrien states that his days have little structure since he is unemployed, and he is worried about being bored at home. He reports having a healthy home environment that is sober and supportive of his recovery. Which treatment option would provide him with a structured environment that will allow him to focus on his recovery?

A) outpatient treatment program

B) intensive outpatient treatment program

C) aftercare programming

D) partial hospitalization programming

24. You are facilitating an LGBTQIA+ group for adolescents in your area. Which of the following would be the MOST appropriate topic for your session?

    A) identifying safe, enjoyable hobbies and interests
    B) psychoeducation about medication-assisted therapy
    C) psychoeducation about family dynamics
    D) identifying triggers for self-harm

25. Which of the following behaviors is MOST likely to encourage your group members to talk to you?

    A) be available before or after the group session
    B) provide them with your email and phone number
    C) consistently arrive on time for group
    D) have a snack during the group

26. You have been working individually with Scott in an outpatient addiction treatment program. He has been in treatment for ten months and has twelve months of sobriety. Scott was in an inpatient treatment program for eight weeks before outpatient treatment. Which of the following factors BEST supports the decision to complete his treatment?

    A) He has maintained sobriety in his toxic home environment.
    B) He has made changes to his routine and friendships and uses healthy coping skills.
    C) He has not missed an individual session since he started treatment.
    D) He has paid off the remaining balance of his copays.

27. You have been working individually with a transgender woman throughout her transition. She originally came to you with anxiety and depressive symptoms, and throughout your time together she has been responsive to CBT techniques and new coping skills. She currently reports feeling "much better" regarding her mental health. She wants to continue treatment for support, as she is still adjusting to the many changes in her life. She has limited social support and has been working hard to make healthy connections with individuals in the LGBTQIA+ community. What treatment recommendations could you suggest to her?

    A) biweekly individual sessions with you
    B) medication-assisted therapy
    C) an LGBTQIA+ support group
    D) volunteering at a local youth center

28. Alana is a client in an outpatient addiction treatment program. She began treatment three weeks ago to get sober from opiates and has been attending individual and group counseling and twelve-step meetings. In an individual session, Alana shared that she is only attending treatment because she wants to avoid criminal court for a possession charge. She lives with her partner, who actively uses opioids, and she works in a pub where her coworkers use drugs during their shifts. Which type of challenge has she been experiencing?

    A) consequences of addiction
    B) barriers to sobriety
    C) failure to comply with treatment
    D) lack of motivation

29. You are running a family therapy program for family members with a loved one attending an inpatient rehab program. Which of the following is an appropriate psychoeducation topic for this group?

    A) different methods of substance use
    B) financial cost of addiction
    C) the disease concept of addiction
    D) common mental health concerns

30. Which of the following behaviors could a group leader model to group members to encourage active listening?

    A) drinking his coffee
    B) chewing gum
    C) nodding his head
    D) playing with a pen

31. Sandra has brought her son to meet with you because she has concerns about his behaviors. Josh is six and began attending school one month ago. When Sandra tries to leave after dropping him off, Josh gets angry and hits his teacher as she tries to lead him into the building. Josh's teacher shared that when he gets into

the classroom, he becomes sad, is unable to concentrate, and does not interact with his peers. Sandra has a different experience with Josh at home and describes him as demanding and always close. Based on the information, which diagnosis should you consider?

A) social anxiety disorder
B) specific phobia
C) generalized anxiety disorder
D) separation anxiety disorder

32. Rudy began working with you a year ago when he was experiencing depression. He met the criteria for major depressive disorder and has recently begun struggling with his symptoms again. You decide to use a depression screener at your next session to investigate the severity of his depressed mood, guilt, suicidal ideation, insomnia, work and interests, retardation, agitation, and anxiety. Which assessment are you planning to use?

A) Burns Depression Test
B) Hamilton Depression Scale
C) Montgomery–Asberg Depression Rating Scale
D) Zung Self-Rating Depression Scale

33. Your clinical experience focuses on working with adults, but today you were asked to help with an intake session for a child. Which of the following interventions can be used with children to encourage sharing?

A) play therapy
B) open-ended questions
C) role-playing
D) guided imagery

34. You are meeting with a forty-eight-year-old Black man with suicidal ideation. He was recently discharged from an inpatient psychiatric program and given a major depressive disorder diagnosis. He shares that since he has been home, his mood has improved and he has more energy than before. He lives with his wife of twenty-seven years, and his children are independent. He works in construction about sixty hours per week. Before he was discharged, he struggled to identify protective factors and was asked to sign a no suicide contract form.

What suicide risk factors should you pay close attention to?

A) He is at a higher risk of suicide because of his work schedule.
B) The client is Black and therefore, statistically, has a higher suicide risk.
C) Having adult children who have moved out of the home puts him at a higher risk.
D) He is unable to identify protective factors.

35. When meeting a reluctant client for the first time, what is the counselor's BEST approach?

A) set firm conditions for the client and get him involved
B) take the initiative to tell the client about your personal background and beliefs so that you can put him at ease
C) enable the client to express his feelings and ideas, while discerning that time and effort are required to build relationships
D) get the client to agree with your ideas so that no problems arise

36. A counselor is discussing how group members should act when they see each other in public. What is the BEST way to approach this?

A) The group should decide together what to do.
B) Group members can never acknowledge each other.
C) It does not matter what they do.
D) Members must act friendly toward each other in public.

37. You are meeting with a new client who was referred by her primary care physician. Ann is a twelve-year-old female who has been lashing out verbally at teachers over the past year. Ann's parents report similar behaviors at home and explain that they do not know how to help her. Ann's mother says that there are usually four to five outbursts each week between school and home. Even when Ann does not have an outburst, she is irritable. Ann's mom feels like she is "walking on eggshells" when Ann returns home from school because she never knows how Ann's mood will be. Based on the information, which diagnosis will you investigate?

A) borderline personality disorder
B) disruptive mood dysregulation disorder

C) attention-deficit/hyperactivity disorder

D) bipolar disorder

38. Which of the following accurately describes quantitative research?

    A) It relies on data that can be measured.

    B) It is not intended to be applied to practice.

    C) It uses a small number of participants.

    D) It investigates how and why things happen.

39. You have been meeting with Josh for three months. Josh has been married for two years; he and his wife have a one-year-old daughter. Josh shared that they have been struggling to adjust their family dynamics since their daughter was born. He shared that his wife came from an intact home, whereas he was raised by a single father. Josh explained that his wife feels that he has been "stepping on her toes." He recognizes the role his home environment has on his behavior and is trying to be mindful of this. Which of the following would be MOST helpful for him?

    A) journaling his feelings

    B) couples counseling

    C) emotion regulation skills

    D) empathy and support

40. Which of the following is a body movement or gesture that could demonstrate that you are reacting negatively to what your client has shared with you?

    A) maintaining eye contact

    B) shifting in your seat

    C) maintaining your posture

    D) keeping neutral facial expressions

41. Bianca has been struggling with depressive symptoms since her divorce. She has been working more to supplement her income and feels guilty for not spending much time with her teenage daughter. Bianca is concerned because her daughter has been talking about needing to lose weight. She becomes anxious when Bianca tells her she is perfect the way she is and responds by pointing out her "problem areas." Bianca noticed that her daughter has less energy, which she believes is the result of not eating properly. At her daughter's last physical, her doctor encouraged her to gain some weight, as she was underweight. Which diagnosis is MOST appropriate for Bianca's daughter?

    A) restrictive food intake disorder

    B) anorexia nervosa

    C) binge eating disorder

    D) bulimia nervosa

42. A client is referred by a mental health court for wraparound services, and the counselor is required to report weekly to the care team. Which of the following is NOT appropriate to share with the care team?

    A) client's appointment attendance

    B) client's diagnosis and treatment plan

    C) details of the client's trauma history

    D) reported side effects of prescribed medication

43. You have been facilitating a process group for individuals in recovery from a variety of substances. You have learned that several members have been socializing outside of the group session, but they have not included all members. How can you explain this as a concern to your group?

    A) that it breaks group confidentiality

    B) that socializing can isolate group members

    C) that there is no counselor present

    D) that it takes away from the group contributions

44. You just completed an intake session for Yasmin, a twenty-nine-year-old female who identifies as bisexual. Yasmin shares that she was raised in a religious home and that her family stopped talking to her when she told them she is bisexual. Since then, she has had difficulty building meaningful relationships and is worried that if she lets someone truly get to know her, that person will choose to end the relationship. Her goal is to learn to build healthy relationships with others. When discussing her treatment options, you talk about the benefits of having a corrective emotional experience and how she can try this approach in counseling. How would you describe a corrective emotional experience to Yasmin?

    A) similar to cognitive restructuring, modifying the way she perceives her family's response to her sexuality

B) working to repair the relationship she has with her family and processing their reactions during her sessions

C) developing an open therapeutic relationship in which she can be her true self and feel supported

D) working through the emotions she has been holding on to regarding her family's reactions and moving on

45. Studies reveal that alcoholism has negative effects on interactions with a person's family, friends, and society. What is a counselor's primary responsibility when working with clients with a history of alcoholism?

A) finding the point of origin of the drinking problem, formulating a diagnosis, and creating a viable treatment plan

B) providing clients with addiction psychoeducation to help them understand how their addiction affects their loved ones

C) encouraging clients to consider a family therapy program so every family member can receive help

D) helping clients get their family, friends, and other associates to be supportive of their recovery efforts

46. You are running a relapse prevention group in an outpatient addiction treatment program. One of the group rules is that members do not come to group impaired. When the group begins, you observe that a member appears impaired. You ask her to step outside, then have another staff member take her to the doctor on staff for assessment. Which behavior are you demonstrating?

A) blocking
B) linking
C) facilitating
D) creating safety

47. Which of the following is necessary for a client to give informed consent?

A) must be physically present for the practice or study

B) must understand the associated risks of participating

C) must receive financial compensation for participating

D) must give verbal consent, not written

48. Marcyanna is a forty-three-year-old female who was referred to you by her priest. She is reluctant to speak with you and explains that she has been meeting with her priest weekly for two years and does not see how you could help her. She was diagnosed with major depressive disorder about two years ago and ignored the recommendation of mental health counseling. She continues to struggle with some symptoms, specifically: lethargy, poor concentration, and a lack of appetite. She reports that her priest has helped her with her feelings of guilt and worthlessness through prayer and guidance. As you discuss treatment options with Marcyanna, which of the following would you recommend?

A) individual therapy only
B) medication-assisted therapy only
C) medication-assisted therapy and individual counseling
D) medication-assisted therapy and group counseling

49. You are meeting with a client who has been arguing with his parents daily about his behaviors. Adam is a sixteen-year-old male who does not feel that he needs to tell his parents every detail about his life. His parents have asked him to go to counseling because they are unhappy that he will not talk to them about his friends and romantic interests. When you meet with Adam, he appears resistant to counseling and says that you are "on his parents' side." He expresses frustration with his parents, raising his voice and making harsh comments about them. His parents joined the session for about ten minutes, which resulted in an argument between them and Adam. You maintain a calm demeanor and give Adam the space he needs to verbalize his frustration once his parents leave. Which skill BEST describes your behavior in this situation?

A) conflict tolerance
B) mindfulness
C) confrontation
D) patience

50. During your second session with Adam, you ask him what he feels he might get out of counseling. He is unsure, but he would appreciate his parents backing off. Adam explained that he talks to his parents about his classes, sports teams, interests, and hobbies; however, he does not want to "gossip," as he sees it, about his friends or any romantic interests. What is an appropriate resolution skill to work on with Adam?

    A) mindfulness
    B) deep breathing
    C) communication
    D) distress tolerance

51. A counselor meets with a client whose son has been diagnosed with childhood diabetes. The client is disturbed and anxious about her child's condition. What is the BEST way to help this client?

    A) focusing on how the client can help her child
    B) completing a psychological assessment of the client to determine if she can care for the child
    C) referring her to a better paying job
    D) telling the client to calm down because if she is in a hysterical state, she will not be any help to her child

52. You work at a family therapy practice specializing in preventive approaches and are providing psychoeducation classes for parents with teens who are presenting with behavioral concerns. Which form of prevention are you providing?

    A) universal prevention
    B) selective prevention
    C) indicated prevention
    D) primary prevention

53. Sam is a new client who has been in therapy since his PTSD diagnosis. He did not benefit from CBT or DBT and is specifically seeking an EMDR counselor. You were recently certified in cognitive processing therapy and have no experience with EMDR. How would you proceed?

    A) ignore the client's request and begin CPT work
    B) explain why CPT is better and begin CPT work
    C) refer Sam to a colleague who is certified in EMDR
    D) end the initial session since you cannot provide treatment

54. You began working with a single mother, Lucy, and her fourteen-year-old daughter Erin. Lucy reached out for counseling because she gets overwhelmed with the frequency of arguments that she and her daughter have. Lucy was honest and shared that they both get angry and hostile and say mean things. Lucy is looking for ways to decrease the amount of conflict she and Erin have. What would be MOST helpful for both mother and daughter?

    A) discussing body language
    B) emotion regulation skills
    C) walking away
    D) journaling

55. You recently began working with a new client, Paulo, a twenty-six-year-old gay man. He struggles with worrying, becomes fixated on issues, and has difficulty moving past them. Paulo shared that his partner did not respond to his text message quickly like he usually does, and Paulo began to worry that he had done something wrong and that his partner was going to leave him. Paulo also struggles with concentration, fatigue, and feeling on edge. His partner has pointed out that he is irritable when he gets "worked up." After exploring Paulo's history with these symptoms, you learn that they started when he was around sixteen. Paulo came out to his parents when he was fifteen, and they sent him to a conversion camp to "get well." When Paulo returned, he pretended that the camp was successful to appease his parents. He began to notice the same symptoms when he would worry that his parents would catch him in a lie. What do you suspect Paulo is struggling with?

    A) childhood trauma
    B) post-traumatic stress disorder
    C) generalized anxiety disorder
    D) major depressive disorder

56. You are meeting with a young adult who was referred by her school counselor. The paperwork identifies concerns about periods of high

energy, lack of sleep, and risk-taking behaviors, followed by a period of low energy, suicidal ideation, and feelings of worthlessness. Based on this information, which interview should you conduct?

A) biopsychosocial interview
B) diagnostic interview
C) cultural formulation interview
D) intake interview

57. You and your group coleader are running the first process group of the day in an addiction treatment rehab. A client named Jeanine began complaining about the care she has received. Agitated, she made negative comments and judgments about other group members. What is the BEST course of action?

A) redirect the group to change topics
B) ask her to step out with your coleader while you process the experience with the group
C) have the group engage in a box breathing exercise followed by processing the experience
D) wait to see what other group members' reactions and responses are before acting

58. One of your clients, Bethany, is talking to you about her new job. She was surprised to find that some of her male colleagues were unhappy about her working there. She explained that when she arrived, she was being dismissed when she introduced herself. Bethany believes the reason for her colleagues' attitude is that she is a female. She shares that she has been struggling with anxiety on her way to work and would like to focus on that during her session. What approach would you use to help Bethany?

A) focus on emotion regulation
B) cognitive restructuring
C) empty chair technique
D) improving communication

59. John, twenty-two, has been struggling with restlessness, irritability, and sleep disturbances for the past five months. The counselor suspects that he is struggling with generalized anxiety disorder. John shared that he will be starting a master's program in the fall and is overwhelmed with everything he needs to accomplish beforehand. He has tried meditation exercises, deep breathing, and walking as coping skills. Which strategy could help John with his anxiety symptoms?

A) focus on coping skills to manage his anxiety in the moment
B) break down what he needs to do into smaller pieces
C) focus on coping with depressive symptoms
D) provide psychoeducation about the stages of change

60. You are working with the parents of a five-year-old boy whose teachers have concerns about his behavior. The parents feel that he is simply a unique free spirit; his behaviors do not concern them. The teachers insist that the child be evaluated. Both parents have their own approaches to parenting. What are some age-appropriate strategies you could recommend to them for managing their child's behaviors?

A) explain cause and effect
B) be consistent in their parenting
C) begin family therapy sessions
D) ignore the teacher's concern

61. Your private practice office is in a building with an elevator, which has a pass code to deter people from using it excessively. You have an initial intake with an individual who is unable to walk long distances due to medical concerns. How would you proceed?

A) refer the client to a different practice
B) have the meeting on the first floor
C) provide the code to the client before the session
D) see if he can use the stairs before providing the code

62. Jace is a senior in high school who has been experiencing an increase in his energy levels. His parents have noticed that he has been sleeping less and is practicing soccer more than usual. Even with the physical exercise, he is going to bed later and waking earlier in the day. When his dad helps him practice, he notices that Jace feels great about his skills and talks more than usual. Jace has been telling his dad about his goal of playing at college and the steps he will take to improve his skills. Jace's primary care physician recommended that he meet with

you for an assessment since these changes have been present for the past five days. Which diagnosis would be the MOST appropriate?

   A) manic episode
   B) hypomanic episode
   C) bipolar II disorder
   D) cyclothymic disorder

63. You have a session with a twenty-four-year-old male who was referred by his school counselor. He has been struggling with anxiety symptoms and shares that he has become very close with his male best friend. He is worried that his feelings of friendship are romantic interest. He explains that his parents are openly against being gay, and he is worried that they would disown him. Which characteristic would be the MOST helpful for your client?

   A) consistency
   B) patience
   C) bias
   D) unconditional positive regard

64. Jean is a thirty-two-year-old woman who began seeing a counselor three years ago when she became suicidal. In therapy, Jean has learned that her depressive symptoms are connected to her history of trauma. Previous counselors have tried using DBT and CBT without lasting results. Which of the following would be the BEST approach to try with Jean?

   A) motivational interviewing
   B) exposure therapy
   C) EMDR
   D) solution-focused therapy

65. You just had a third session with a couple who has been married for seven years. Lance and Beth both feel unappreciated and that they go above and beyond without any recognition of their efforts. They are both unhappy in their marriage and have felt this way for about six months. You suggested they make a contingency contract to recognize and reward the other person's efforts. They agreed and said they would think about what they would like to include in the contract. Which therapy is this technique a part of?

   A) emotion-focused therapy
   B) behavioral couple therapy
   C) cognitive behavioral couple therapy
   D) person-centered therapy

66. You are an intake counselor at an outpatient drug rehab program. After meeting with a young woman who has been struggling with opioids, you decide that she meets the criteria for opioid use disorder, severe. Part of your role is to determine if she is appropriate for the level of care you provide, and, if so, to develop a treatment plan. You are concerned that she has continued to use opioids and is unable to stop. As a result, you conclude that she needs a different level of care. Which level of care would be the MOST appropriate, given the diagnosis?

   A) detoxification program
   B) inpatient rehab program
   C) partial hospitalization program
   D) intensive outpatient program

67. Lucas is a high school junior who was asked to join a group for at-risk students because his teachers are concerned he may be using substances. He has come to a few group sessions but participates very little. The counselor followed up with him after the most recent session, and Lucas shared that he does not think he will get anything from the group and is concerned that his friends will see him go into the guidance office each week. Which group stage is Lucas in?

   A) orientation
   B) transition
   C) work
   D) consolidation

68. Luis is a twenty-eight-year-old male who has been struggling with anxiety for about a year. Recently, he cannot think of a day when he has not felt anxious. Luis identifies feeling restless, fatigued, and irritable, and he struggles to concentrate at work. You diagnosis him with generalized anxiety disorder. What is the minimum number of symptoms Luis must have for criterion C to meet diagnostic criteria?

   A) one
   B) two
   C) three
   D) four

69. A counselor is reviewing the limitations of confidentiality with new clients. What is a limit clients should be aware of?

  A) Their spouse can have limited access to their records.
  B) Their emergency contact can have limited access to their records.
  C) Their records may be viewed during a state or federal audit.
  D) Their records are not protected by confidentiality in death.

70. You are running a relapse prevention group in an outpatient addiction treatment program. The group members have either recently completed an inpatient rehab program or have had a recent relapse after a period of sobriety. Based on the population of your group, which of the following would be the MOST appropriate topic for psychoeducation?

  A) coping skills for depressive symptoms
  B) emergency mental health services
  C) the disease concept of addiction
  D) the benefits of Narcotics Anonymous

71. Theresa was married to her husband for thirty-four years before he was killed by a drunk driver eight months ago. She had been a stay-at-home mom in her younger years, and there had been no need for her to work as her children grew. Theresa's children are concerned about her since their father's passing because she has not accepted that her life is going to change now that he is gone. After looking through Theresa's finances, her oldest child saw that there was not enough money for her to maintain her current lifestyle. He encouraged her to consider returning to work or changing her lifestyle. Theresa has not made any changes to her routine and refuses to talk to her children about returning to work. The children are also concerned because she tends to focus on their father throughout the day, which contributes to extreme sadness and feelings of helplessness. She blames herself for her husband's death because he was on his way to pick up her medication from the pharmacy when his vehicle was struck. What do you suspect Theresa is struggling with?

  A) major depressive episode
  B) denial
  C) adjustment disorder
  D) complicated grief

72. Which of the following is an example of a counselor-imposed barrier to treatment?

  A) using EMDR for a client with generalized anxiety disorder
  B) maintaining a consistent treatment schedule for clients
  C) closing the office on a recognized federal holiday
  D) having more than one office available for appointments

73. A counselor is working with a client who has similar problems as several other clients. Which action is MOST appropriate for the counselor to take?

  A) let the client know she has problems that many others have
  B) try to learn if this client's problems have any significant differences
  C) talk about this situation with a coworker
  D) handle it like any other case

74. You have noticed that several members in your group get defensive when you talk about your observations of their continued unhealthy behaviors. How can you encourage members to be more open to receiving feedback?

  A) role-play receiving feedback
  B) discuss emotion regulation skills
  C) allow them to provide feedback to each other
  D) discuss healthy communication skills

75. You just finished a session with Declan, a forty-six-year-old man who has experienced significant changes in the past few weeks. Declan's wife had an affair, which led to their mutual decision to get a divorce. When Declan looked over his finances, he realized that he cannot afford to continue with his debt payment schedule on his salary alone. Declan has a history of major depressive disorder and shares that he reached out to you because his symptoms have started to return; specifically, his lack of appetite, insomnia, fatigue, feelings of hopelessness, and suicidal ideation. Declan denies having any intent or means for suicide at this time. What is your treatment recommendation?

   A) individual counseling
   B) medication-assisted therapy (MAT)
   C) counseling and MAT
   D) inpatient mental health program

76. At the beginning of a session, you give your client a questionnaire that investigates four areas of her life: her energy source, how she processes information, how she approaches decisions, and her preference for structure. You hope the assessment can help provide some validation and insight for the client regarding her thoughts and behaviors. What assessment have you given your client?

   A) Myers–Briggs Type Indicator (MBTI)
   B) Holtzman inkblot technique
   C) HEXACO personality inventory
   D) Birkman Method

77. You are working in a family therapy clinic and are meeting with Tim and Mary, the parents of a thirteen-year-old named Susie. Tim and Mary have been concerned about Susie's behaviors since her aunt died unexpectedly two months ago. Since then, Susie has stopped spending time with her friends, and her grades have dropped significantly. They also recently found a pack of cigarettes and empty beer bottles in the garage. Tim and Mary denied that any of these behaviors were present before the family's loss. They shared that when they tried talking to Susie about their concerns, she became angry and missed the points they were trying to make. Which of the following exercises would allow you to model ideal behaviors that Tim and Mary could use to share their concerns with Susie?

   A) journaling
   B) meditation
   C) role-playing
   D) empty chair technique

78. Jack is a seventy-two-year-old veteran who enlisted in the Navy during the Vietnam War. After his tour, he returned home and began working in the kitchen of a local prison. Since the war, he has struggled with flashbacks and depressive symptoms. He has been able to cope by staying distracted with work and raising his children. Now that he has retired and his children have grown, his depressive symptoms have increased. Specifically, he has been struggling with a low mood, insomnia, and a lack of interest and pleasure. What treatment approach would be MOST effective to treat his symptoms?

   A) psychodynamic therapy
   B) solution-focused therapy
   C) eye-movement desensitization and reprocessing therapy
   D) gestalt therapy

79. Which of the following accurately describes qualitative research?

   A) It relies on data that can be measured.
   B) It is not intended to be applied in practice.
   C) It uses many participants.
   D) It investigates how and why things happen.

80. You are working in an outpatient addiction treatment program and facilitating a closed group for individuals who completed an inpatient treatment program. Over the past two weeks, one group member has struggled with her mental health and sobriety. Since then, she has returned to the inpatient treatment program. What is the BEST way to begin processing the change in the group?

   A) ask for the group's opinion of the member who left the group
   B) ask how having this member leave makes them feel
   C) ask if they saw any signs that the member was struggling
   D) inform them that the member is no longer in the group, and proceed as normal

81. Johnathan sought counseling after learning that his wife of thirteen years had been having an affair for the past four months. He owns a construction business that causes him to work long hours and take trips out of town a few times a month. Johnathan still loves his wife and wants to try to move past this. After providing support and validation, you discuss the pattern of stages that spouses typically experience after learning of their partner's infidelity. What are these three stages?

   A) shock, moratorium, forgiveness
   B) emotional roller coaster, moratorium, trust-building

C) emotional roller coaster, trust-building, forgiveness

D) shock, emotional roller coaster, trust-building

82. You are involved in a new medication trial for alcohol use disorder. Your results show that this medication is effective for opioid use disorder. It is then determined that a new study should be conducted to investigate the medications used for opioid use disorder to ensure that your study has what?

   A) reliability
   B) validity
   C) generalizability
   D) effective treatment

83. In your work as a counselor, you gravitate toward a client-centered approach. This is evidenced by the fact that you do not judge clients for what they say during sessions and continue to support them despite your personal beliefs and opinions. Which of the following concepts are you using?

   A) congruence
   B) unconditional positive regard
   C) transference
   D) unbiased mindset

84. One of your current clients sent you a friend request on social media. How should you proceed?

   A) block the request
   B) ignore the request
   C) wait until your next session
   D) consult with your supervisor

85. You are a high school counselor who has been meeting individually with a sophomore who recently started identifying as nonbinary. The student shared this with a friend, who then shared it with other students. This quickly led to bullying, which worsened the mental health symptoms the student was already struggling with. This student shares that they come from a religious household that is not supportive of the LGBTQIA+ community and often speaks negatively about them. The student has been struggling with feelings of hopelessness and thoughts of suicide. What should you assess for?

   A) bullying concerns
   B) safety concerns
   C) academic concerns
   D) abuse at home

86. You are meeting with a new client who identifies as a different gender, race, and ethnicity from you. How can you encourage acceptance?

   A) display genuineness
   B) show your anxiety—this is your first client from this background
   C) ask closed questions to learn more
   D) move around in your seat frequently

87. You are conducting an initial assessment with a client who identifies with a different ethnicity and religion than you do. How would you proceed?

   A) refer the client to a colleague who shares his ethnicity
   B) cancel the appointment
   C) conduct the initial assessment
   D) speak with your supervisor for guidance

88. You are reviewing your parent-skills training material to help a new family with their child's problematic behaviors. Which of the following terms might you find in such material?

   A) cognitive behavioral family therapy
   B) functional family therapy
   C) parent-child interaction therapy
   D) operant conditioning

89. What should a counselor do when a client complains of medical problems?

   A) ignore such problems because they are beyond the scope of her responsibilities
   B) inform the client that she recognizes his problems but will not address them
   C) recommend that the client suspends therapy and visits a physician instead
   D) make referrals to the proper sources for treatment

90. Theo is a young man who you began working with when he was struggling with depressive symptoms. He has struggled to find motivation for his work responsibilities and, as a result, was

disciplined and eventually let go. Theo used this as an opportunity to focus on his mental health and now feels that he is in a healthier space. He wants to start looking for a new job but is still struggling to maintain motivation. Which of the following topics would be appropriate for psychoeducation?

A) medication compliance
B) DBT skills
C) importance of self-care
D) effective goal setting

91. You are conducting an intake interview with John, who was referred by his primary care physician due to his concerning mental health symptoms. When John met with his doctor, he presented with disorganized speech and diminished emotional expression. On the referral form, John describes hallucinations and seeing family members who have died. He told his doctor that he had been seeing family members for about five weeks, and his wife reported that the other symptoms the doctor observed started around the same time. Despite these symptoms, John has not experienced a major depressive episode, manic episode, or hypomanic episode. His wife said that he had not been using alcohol or other drugs. Based on the information, which diagnosis should you investigate during your session with John?

A) brief psychotic disorder
B) schizophreniform disorder
C) schizophrenia
D) schizoaffective disorder

92. You are working in an outpatient addiction treatment program and recently received a referral for a new client who just completed an inpatient rehab program. Sam was diagnosed with alcohol use disorder while at his inpatient rehab program. During your session, you learn that Sam has limited social support because his family and friends do not know how to respond to him identifying as demisexual. How can you help him regarding his friends?

A) discuss coping skills for his distress
B) provide psychoeducation about sexuality
C) improve his communication skills
D) focus on his addiction treatment

93. A counselor is discussing goal setting with a client—specifically, the difference between intrinsic and extrinsic motivation. Which of the following is an example of intrinsic motivation that the counselor could share?

A) receiving a bonus after a year of work at a new clinic
B) working out because it is fun and feels good afterward
C) making the honors list after working hard at school
D) buying a nice house in a desirable neighborhood

94. Which of the following can be done during supervision to help you understand your limits regarding cases you take?

A) self-assessment
B) self-reflection
C) trainings
D) self-care practices

95. You are running an intensive outpatient program group. A group member shares that she received Narcan last night after relapsing and overdosing on heroin. She denied seeking medical attention. Your clinic has a medical staff member present when it is open. What is the BEST action to take?

A) process her relapse and continue with the group
B) consult with your supervisor after the group session concludes
C) focus on relapse prevention skills
D) escort her to meet with the medical staff for assessment

96. You are meeting with a couple for their first session. From their intake assessment, you determine that both bear some of the responsibility for the verbal abuse in their relationship. They agree that they have poor emotion regulation skills and could improve their communication skills as well. Which treatment approach is recommended?

A) psychoeducation and couples counseling
B) psychoeducation and family therapy
C) psychoeducation and individual counseling
D) individual counseling and family therapy

97. Which of the following behaviors could demonstrate genuineness to a client?
    A) warm and open body posture
    B) closed posture
    C) inconsistent eye contact
    D) fidgeting in chair

98. You are starting a new group session with individuals who are struggling with substance use. While establishing the group rules and norms, you discuss how you, the counselor, will act when you see group members in public. What is the BEST explanation of what they can expect?
    A) You will wave only.
    B) You will wave and say hello.
    C) You will talk to them like a friend.
    D) You will not acknowledge them unless they have given you permission to do so.

99. You are working with the parents of a young girl who has begun acting out and not doing her schoolwork. They need suggestions for how to stop her negative behaviors from progressing. You tell them that research shows that children who have a particular belief system are less likely to use tobacco, alcohol, and drugs. What is this belief system?
    A) religion
    B) spirituality
    C) moral code
    D) philosophy

100. You are conducting a brief mental status exam in a category that offers the options of tearful, depressed, mood-congruent, and flat. Which area are you looking at?
    A) behavior
    B) speech
    C) affect
    D) thought process

101. During an interview, a curious client asks several questions about the counselor's private life. How should the counselor respond?
    A) refuse to answer such questions
    B) answer the questions fully
    C) explain that your primary concern is with her problems and that discussion of your personal affairs will not help meet her needs
    D) explain that it is the responsibility of the interviewer to ask questions and not to answer them

102. Mark is a sixteen-year-old boy with depressive symptoms. He does not share much in therapy and appears uncomfortable. His mother brought him to counseling after his teachers told her about an essay he wrote that appears to glorify suicide. Which of the following could help build trust with Mark during sessions?
    A) using open-ended questions
    B) reflecting on his mother's input
    C) providing suicide psychoeducation
    D) family sessions with his mother

103. Anthony has arrived fifteen minutes late for his session. This is the first time he has been late in the five months you have been working with him, so you allow him to continue. He tells you that a car on the highway got a flat tire and blocked one of the two lanes. When you asked Anthony if he considered stopping to help, he said no because he assumed someone else would. What is this social theory called?
    A) social impact
    B) functionalist theory
    C) conflict theory
    D) bystander effect

104. A counselor works in an outpatient addiction treatment program with several clients who are enrolled in a drug treatment court program. The counselor must communicate with the clients' appointed court personnel regarding their progress in treatment. What is the BEST approach for sending updates?
    A) send the report two weeks early
    B) include all intimate details from sessions
    C) share with the clients what information will be included in the report
    D) allow the clients to choose which drug screens to submit

105. You are working with an individual who has been having a hard time communicating with her partner. She shares that she always feels

defensive, which you believe contributes to her inability to shift her perspective. During your session, you discuss emotion regulation skills that can help her manage her emotions better in the moment, which will allow her to better communicate her thoughts and emotions. Which of the following is an emotion regulation skill you could recommend?

A) box breathing
B) ignoring the conflict
C) matching her partner's tone
D) screaming

106. During a mental status exam, your client begins talking about the role the sun plays in her behavior. She explains that when the sun is in the sky, it controls her behavior, which contributes to her inability to focus on work during the day. When the sun goes down in the evenings, her control returns, so she is able to focus on her work. How would you describe her thought content?

A) delusion
B) hallucination
C) obsessions/compulsions
D) other

107. Joan is a seventeen-year-old female you have been working with for one year, after her school counselor referred her for therapy. Joan has been struggling with depressive symptoms for a year, and symptoms such weight loss and her inability to concentrate were noticed at school. She is tired all the time and has no appetite. Though she has been in therapy, she continues to struggle with her symptoms. Based on the information, which diagnosis should you assess for?

A) major depressive disorder
B) major depressive episode
C) persistent depressive disorder
D) premenstrual dysphoric disorder

108. At the end of a one-hour interview with a client, she begins to discuss another issue that will take additional time to consider. You have another client scheduled shortly after this interview. What is the BEST way to proceed?

A) finish the initial interview and schedule a second appointment with that client to discuss the new issue
B) skip the next client's appointment and allow the current client to continue, using all the time she needs to explain the new issue
C) ask the client to give a clear rationale for why she feels the need to talk about the new issue near the end of the interview
D) let the client know that her scheduled hour has expired, and you have someone else to meet

109. Evidence-based practice refers to what?

A) using interventions that are proven through research to be effective
B) recommendations for health and wellness goals
C) rigid criteria to meet medical necessity requirements
D) systemically developing statements that serve providers in determining care

110. You receive a referral for a new client, a twenty-eight-year-old male who has been having difficulty at work. He has received a written warning for not completing his tasks as expected and is now experiencing anxiety symptoms and significant worry about losing his job. In the paperwork, he notes having difficulty sleeping, specifically, waking up several times at night and not feeling rested in the morning. The sleep difficulties started almost four months ago and occur four to five nights a week. Which diagnosis would you investigate?

A) generalized anxiety disorder
B) hypersomnolence disorder
C) insomnia disorder
D) central sleep apnea

111. Several group members have been showing their reactions while others are sharing. This has led to a shift within your group and a decrease in group participation. You have decided to discuss the benefits of being nonjudgmental in group sessions. Which of the following reasons would be the MOST important to discuss?

A) It makes everyone feel safe.
B) It keeps the group going.
C) It keeps the group on track.
D) It allows group to end early.

112. You have been working with Laura for three months. She became a stay-at-home mother about four years ago when her children were born. She has been missing her career but feels guilty because she loves her time with her kids and feels that she should be grateful she is able to stay home with them. Which skill would be appropriate to use with Laura?

    A) unconditional positive regard
    B) summarizing
    C) reflective statements
    D) self-disclosure

113. You are discussing with a colleague why you prefer the SCID-5 to other assessment tools. Which reason could you give to support your preference?

    A) It is required when giving a diagnosis using the *DSM-5*.
    B) It streamlines the intake process.
    C) It saves time.
    D) It ensures that counselors are checking for the most common diagnoses.

114. You are working as a school counselor and have been meeting regularly with a high school junior named Aleida, who has recently increased her self-awareness regarding her academic abilities, social skills, and emotions. This has allowed her to set realistic goals for her future and work with you on improving her emotion regulation skills. What has Aleida successfully developed?

    A) idealization
    B) realization
    C) intrinsic understanding
    D) planful competence

115. You run a support group at a college counseling center for students with social anxiety. During your first group session, members establish their rules. What is a benefit of group rules?

    A) Establishing rules can make members feel more comfortable.
    B) Rules are meant to be used as criteria for discharge.
    C) Rules are more of a guideline for group members.
    D) Making rules can be an icebreaker activity.

116. A counselor works in an inpatient treatment program for individuals dealing with trauma and post-traumatic stress disorder. He runs a group that teaches mindfulness, interpersonal effectiveness, emotion regulation, and distress tolerance. What is the treatment modality for this treatment program?

    A) EMDR
    B) CPT
    C) DBT
    D) CBT-E

117. You are working with a college student who has poor sleep hygiene. Ryan sleeps for only five hours and often struggles to pay attention in school. After deciding that he would benefit from receiving psychoeducation about sleep, you discuss sleep cycles. How many stages are there in a sleep cycle?

    A) three
    B) four
    C) five
    D) six

118. A couple requests help to improve their seven-year marriage. When the counselor asks them about their goals, they begin to argue. The husband says that his wife nags him too much about chores. The wife states that her husband is lazy. What should the counselor do?

    A) assist them in establishing treatment goals to help them learn to improve their communication and resolve conflict
    B) recommend that they each attend individual sessions with you to set separate goals to work on until they are ready to work together in a session
    C) assist them in setting a goal to help them resolve their arguments about household responsibilities
    D) recommend they receive individual treatment to help them work on individual issues

119. You are working with Lucia, a forty-two-year-old female, for her depressive concerns. Lucia's elderly mother moved into her home so that Lucia could provide support for her. In Lucia's family, this is a norm, and she has been expecting this to happen for some time after

noticing her mother's mobility declining. Lucia's husband does not agree with this transition and feels that Lucia should move her mother into a nursing home. Which of the following could help Lucia with her husband's resistance?

   A) telling Lucia that you can only provide emotional support for her, not her mother
   B) encouraging her to do what feels right
   C) encouraging a couples counseling session
   D) encouraging her to move her mother into a nursing home

120. Sandra has recently completed detox at your inpatient rehab facility and will be joining your process group. She has a history of post-traumatic stress disorder and has sought treatment for her alcohol addiction. Which approach would be recommended, given her dual diagnosis?

   A) completing her alcohol addiction program with a referral for PTSD treatment once she is discharged
   B) completing her alcohol addiction program and meeting with a psychiatrist for an assessment of her PTSD
   C) completing a PTSD treatment program with a referral for outpatient addiction treatment after discharge
   D) completing her alcohol program and DBT program at the same time during inpatient treatment

121. You have been working with Richard for approximately six months regarding his concerns with his marriage. Richard shares that he and his wife argue frequently and have been unhappy with their marriage for over a year. He would like to work through this tough patch and has been trying to understand his wife's perspective, be an active listener, and avoid blaming. Richard feels that these strategies have positively impacted his relationship. What skills has Richard been using with his wife?

   A) coping skills
   B) dialectical behavior therapy skills
   C) conflict resolution skills
   D) communication skills

122. Lucas chose to attend addiction treatment rather than serve a jail sentence for a recent drug-related arrest. As a condition of his deal, he must provide an update from the treatment provider to the court once every eight weeks. Lucas does not like these updates and believes his treatment should be kept private. How can the counselor comply with his deal while maintaining a therapeutic rapport?

   A) omit from the report the challenges Lucas has faced in the past eight weeks
   B) exaggerate the details of his progress in the past eight weeks
   C) be truthful, and review the report with Lucas before sending it
   D) allow Lucas to fill out his own progress forms for the court

123. Three members appear to be struggling with engagement during your group session. They have been closing their eyes, slouching, and making noises that communicate their discomfort. How would you describe this type of behavior?

   A) intellectualizing
   B) withdrawing
   C) reframing
   D) aggressive

124. A counselor is meeting with a new client for the first time. Nader shares that he has never been in counseling and appears uncomfortable: he cannot sit still, is bouncing his leg, and says he is having trouble concentrating. The counselor takes a few moments to explain what Nader can expect from his session and how it can help guide the counselor's work with him. Which intervention is this?

   A) normalizing the client's experience
   B) validating the client's experience
   C) psychoeducation
   D) therapy road map

125. Jia started therapy when her youngest child began attending college. Jia has her master's degree in journalism and had a successful career as a journalist. When she and her husband wanted to settle down, she decided to stop working to become a stay-at-home mother. This quickly became her identity, and Jia began to disengage from her hobbies and interests. When Jia's youngest started college, Jia began

struggling with the idea of an empty nest. She does not enjoy her hobbies and has not wanted to return to writing. She has also been sleeping more than usual and has noticed that her clothes are fitting more loosely. Which diagnosis would you investigate?

   A) adjustment disorder
   B) major depressive disorder
   C) disruptive mood dysregulation disorder
   D) dysthymia

126. A client has been referred to you by another agency. You have reviewed the case extensively, but the client begins to relate lengthy details about his situation. Which statement BEST exemplifies why this is a good or bad idea?

   A) It is a waste of time because the details are in the report from the previous agency.
   B) It is beneficial because the other agency may not have included some key details in the report.
   C) It is neither good nor bad.
   D) It is beneficial because it is important to build a relationship with the client by listening to his concerns and showing personal attention.

127. You are working in an outpatient addiction treatment program and are meeting with a new client, Sam, who recently completed a local inpatient addiction rehab program. You learn that Sam does not have sober support: his close family and friends struggle with their own addiction issues. Sam would like to find other options for support. What is an appropriate recommendation?

   A) social media connections
   B) group therapy
   C) Alcoholics Anonymous
   D) a dating app

128. You are meeting with a client who you suspect has a substance use disorder, and you want to use an assessment that is more thorough than the CAGE questionnaire. You decide on an assessment with ten questions rated on a zero-to-four scale. Once all the questions are answered, you add them to get a risk level regarding the presence of a substance use disorder. Which assessment are you using?

   A) Drug Abuse Screening Test (DAST-10)
   B) Alcohol Use Disorders Identification Test (AUDIT)
   C) Michigan Alcohol Screening Test (MAST)
   D) Alcohol, Smoking, and Substance Involvement Screening Test (ASSIST)

129. When adults leave their parents' home, one of the main goals is to develop a "solid self." Which of the following BEST describes this goal?

   A) developing oneself financially
   B) developing one's own relationships and friendships
   C) developing one's own views and beliefs
   D) developing healthy coping skills

130. Which of the following does NOT describe beneficence in client care?

   A) an obligation to do good for the client
   B) providing informed consent
   C) the act of telling the truth
   D) removing the client from harm's way

131. You are running a group therapy session in an outpatient treatment program and notice that group members are hesitant to be vulnerable in their sessions. Which exercise would help create trust within the group?

   A) develop group rules together
   B) use icebreaker exercises
   C) call on group members to share
   D) avoid processing group exercises

132. You are providing a psychoeducational session for parents who want to learn how to support their LGBTQIA+ child. One of the parents asks you to provide an example of cisgender. What is the MOST appropriate response?

   A) an individual who was born a female and identifies as male
   B) an individual who was born a male and identifies as female
   C) an individual who was born a female and identifies as neither male nor female
   D) an individual who was born a male and identifies as male

133. You are working as a counselor in an inpatient addiction rehab program. When should you begin planning to discharge your clients?

   A) during their intake
   B) halfway through treatment
   C) one month before discharge
   D) two weeks before discharge

134. You have been working with Michael for three weeks. He was encouraged to seek professional help by his wife when she noticed that he had been withdrawing from his family and friendships. Michael was in a billiards tournament league and has stopped attending the matches. Additionally, he missed his son's last three soccer games. Michael shares that he has been struggling with feelings of hopelessness, fatigue, and passing thoughts of death. Based on the information, which mental health diagnosis should you assess for?

   A) bipolar disorder
   B) cyclothymic disorder
   C) major depressive disorder
   D) hypomanic episode

135. You are working in private practice and meeting with a new client. A brief review of the categories on his intake forms reveals issues with his social life, medical health, history of mental health concerns, and important relationships. Based on this information, what type of interview should you conduct?

   A) biopsychosocial interview
   B) diagnostic interview
   C) cultural formulation interview
   D) intake interview

136. You began working with John when he started struggling with anxiety. He experiences panic attacks and feels anxious throughout the day. John denied having a history of any mental health concerns, including anxiety, until he was diagnosed with prostate cancer six months ago. His symptoms have negatively impacted his job, which is what led to him meeting with you. He reports becoming "consumed" with fear about his treatment and how his family is being impacted by his health. Based on the information, what anxiety diagnosis is appropriate?

   A) panic disorder
   B) generalized anxiety disorder
   C) anxiety disorder due to prostate cancer
   D) panic attacks

137. Your client Samantha has had depressive symptoms for two months: a depressed mood, loss of interest in hobbies and friends, and sleeping more than normal. She is drinking six to eight beers after work four to five days a week. Samantha feels guilty about driving to work while impaired and working the full day not feeling well. She explained that in the past, she drank one to two drinks on occasion. Based on the information, which idea should you discuss with your supervisor?

   A) refer her to an inpatient addiction treatment program
   B) refer her to a counselor who is in recovery
   C) refer her to your supervisor for assessment
   D) continue working with her and monitoring her alcohol use

138. You have been working with Adell for five months after the unexpected loss of her husband. Adell shares that she is able to find some happy moments in her day, but most days she stays in her home. Which of the following could be a helpful referral for Adell?

   A) grief support group
   B) psychiatrist
   C) volunteer centers
   D) family time

139. A counselor facilitates a family therapy program at an outpatient addiction treatment program. The beginning portion of the program focuses on psychoeducation. Which of the following topics would be the MOST appropriate for that client population?

   A) overview of common mental health concerns
   B) the disease concept of addiction
   C) therapeutic interventions like EMDR
   D) the effectiveness of medication-assisted treatment

140. You have been working with Zane since he lost his job. He has been struggling with feelings of worthlessness, hopelessness, and sadness.

He enjoyed his job as an art teacher, but his position was cut due to budgeting. He now feels concerned about paying his rent and student loans. Zane has taken this loss as a reflection of his performance, despite receiving several offers for personal references for future job applications. Which cognitive behavioral therapy technique could be helpful for Zane?

- A) cognitive restructuring
- B) guided discovery
- C) journaling and thought records
- D) successive approximation

141. The idea of congruence is associated with which therapeutic approach?

- A) cognitive behavioral therapy
- B) solution-focused brief therapy
- C) person-centered therapy
- D) family therapy

142. Gillette has been in your aftercare group since completing an inpatient rehab program for alcohol use disorder. She is active in the sessions and has made progress in her recovery. Lately her sharing has been focused on how she can apply the skills she has learned to her recovery and processing her challenges and successes. Which of the group stages would BEST describe Gillette's experience?

- A) orientation
- B) transition
- C) work
- D) consolidation

143. Mary, a former client, is returning to therapy. She was receptive to talk therapy and needed a safe place to talk through her thoughts and worries. She did not have any diagnosable mental health concerns when you worked with her in the past, and she decided to stop meeting with you when she was doing well. At Mary's first session in a year, she shared that she has been having panic attacks since she lost her job when the COVID-19 pandemic began. She worries about paying for her children's education and other expenses. Mary stated that she has had three panic attacks and worries about the "what ifs" for another one. Since her panic attacks, Mary spends hours each day searching for side job opportunities, which has negatively impacted her sleep. She does not have any known medical concerns and denies the use of drugs and alcohol. What diagnosis is the BEST fit for Mary's symptoms?

- A) unspecified anxiety disorder
- B) generalized anxiety disorder
- C) obsessive-compulsive disorder
- D) panic disorder

144. You are meeting with a new client for an intake interview at an outpatient addiction treatment program. While conducting the assessment, it becomes clear that the client is struggling with alcohol use and depressive symptoms. What is the BEST therapeutic strategy for this client?

- A) treat the client's addiction concerns and then address the depressive symptoms
- B) treat the client's depressive symptoms first, followed by addiction treatment
- C) treat the presenting addiction, then reassess for depressive symptoms
- D) treat the addiction concerns and the mental health concerns at the same time

145. You are the director of a mental health practice. What is an example of advocacy you could participate in for client concerns?

- A) creating a social media account providing psychoeducation on coping skills
- B) lobbying for laws that protect the liability of client safety
- C) talking to your colleagues about your concerns
- D) encouraging your colleagues to make phone calls and emails regarding your concerns

146. You are in an individual session with Jay, who tells you about an argument he had with his wife. He explained that his wife said he does not spend time with her, which made him angry. He said that he has been working overtime to buy a new car because the family vehicle keeps breaking down and is unreliable. When you ask him how he felt when she made that comment, he said "frustrated, unappreciated, and overwhelmed." He shared that he feels like he cannot please her. Which strategy could you recommend to Jay?

- A) walking away
- B) improving his communication skills

C) stop working overtime
D) delaying the vehicle purchase

147. Before meeting with two new clients, you are reviewing the initial paperwork and see that their concerns stem from infidelity. When you work with clients on infidelity, you use an integrated approach developed by Snyder, Baucom, and Gordon. The model is based on which three stages?

   A) dealing with the impact of the infidelity, exploring the context and finding meaning, moving on
   B) dealing with the impact of the infidelity, exploring the context and finding meaning, forgiveness
   C) exploring the reason for the infidelity, exploring the context for the infidelity, forgiveness
   D) full disclosure of the infidelity, dealing with the impact of the infidelity, finding meaning again

148. You have been working with a client with major depressive disorder for five months, reviewing and updating the treatment plan every four sessions. Which event would be an important reason to update the treatment plan?

   A) persistent hopelessness and guilt
   B) continued suicidal ideation
   C) hospitalization for suicide attempt
   D) persistent lack of energy and insomnia

149. You have been working with Jonah, who has been in a domestic partnership for nine years. Jonah has discussed several times that his partner has been physically abusive, leaving him with bruises. After this occurs, his partner buys an expensive gift as an apology and promises to get help. Everything seems fine for a week or two, but then his partner becomes aggressive and eventually abusive again. To the best of Jonah's knowledge, his partner has not gotten help for his anger issues. Which of the following would be an appropriate psychoeducation topic?

   A) emotion regulation skills
   B) the cycle of violence
   C) antisocial personality education
   D) self-defense skills

150. You have been working with Sally for a month and are focusing your treatment on her struggle with anxiety symptoms. After deciding that it would be helpful to use an assessment to gauge the severity of her symptoms, you choose a twenty-one-item tool that has Sally rate the severity of her symptoms. Examples of symptoms assessed include feeling hot, unsteady legs, and feeling shaky or unstable. After Sally has rated her symptoms, you can add the numbers to see if they fall into a low, moderate, or potentially concerning category. Which assessment have you selected?

   A) generalized anxiety disorder seven-item (GAD-7)
   B) Beck Anxiety Inventory (BAI)
   C) State-Trait Anxiety Inventory
   D) Hamilton Anxiety Rating Scale (HARS)

151. You have been working as a school counselor and have been meeting individually with a student named Bianca, whose family immigrated to the United States from Mexico. During her session, Bianca shared that she yelled at a peer on the school bus because her peer was making jokes about her parents' inability to speak English. Bianca was disciplined for the argument; the peer was not. She reported feeling intimidated by the principal and was unable to explain what her peer had said. Which skill would be important for Bianca to work on?

   A) emotion-regulation skills
   B) walking away
   C) tolerating ignorance
   D) advocating for herself

152. According to Hayes and Hayes, there are four concerns that should be discussed within a blended family for everyone to move forward in a healthy manner. You have been working with two adolescents whose mother is remarrying after divorcing their father two years earlier. The children have verbalized resentment toward their mother's fiancé, think he is a bad man, and fail to see any positives that can come out of the relationship. When asked about what supports these beliefs, they struggle to give concrete examples of him being a bad person. The children report that their father is a wonderful man, and they do not understand why their mother wanted to leave him. Which of Hayes and

Hayes's concerns would you focus on with these two adolescents?

- A) learn healthy and effective communication patterns
- B) provide education regarding the new family structure
- C) allow children to move through stages of grief associated with their parents' divorce
- D) encourage them to let go of the "myth" that the new partner is bad

153. You are working at a college campus student counseling center. When your clients arrive late, it disturbs your schedule for the rest of the day because you have been giving them the full session length. How might you address this concern?

- A) do nothing and continue having full sessions when clients arrive late
- B) develop a zero-tolerance policy for tardiness
- C) talk to your supervisor about having shorter sessions when clients arrive late
- D) add "buffer" time to your schedule to allow for clients' lateness

154. You have been providing individual therapy in an outpatient addiction treatment program. One of your clients who struggles with anorexia nervosa shared that she is five months pregnant. When you assess her disordered eating patterns, she told you that she has been struggling more recently because of the changes to her body due to pregnancy. She denied sharing this with her ob-gyn and explained that she is worried about being judged because she understands the importance of having a healthy diet while pregnant. How would you proceed?

- A) have her call her ob-gyn in your presence
- B) refer her to an inpatient hospitalization program
- C) refer her to a nutritionist
- D) increase the frequency of her sessions

155. A counselor working at an inpatient addiction rehab program plans to give a psychoeducational lecture to the program participants. What would be an appropriate topic for this lecture?

- A) vocational opportunities
- B) coping with trauma
- C) nutrition
- D) relapse prevention

156. Philippe is a thirty-six-year-old male who has been struggling with depressive symptoms. He identifies as a successful businessman, explaining that he graduated at the top of his class with an MBA and was immediately hired by a Fortune 500 company, where he has earned several promotions. When he is at work, he is busy and active, but when he goes home to his empty townhome, he struggles with sadness and loneliness. He shares that he does not have much social support or enjoyable leisure activities and explains that his days are repetitive: wake up, work, go home, watch television, eat dinner, and sleep. Which recommendation would be beneficial for Philippe?

- A) focusing on his success
- B) bringing work home
- C) exploring leisure activities
- D) thinking about his strengths

157. Person-centered therapy should take place in a supportive environment created by a close personal relationship between counselor and client. The general direction of the therapy is determined by the client, while the counselor seeks to increase the client's insight and self-understanding through informal questions. Three attitudes on the part of the counselor are central to the productivity of person-centered therapy. They are congruence, unconditional positive regard, and what?

- A) complimentary
- B) positive reaction
- C) empathy
- D) coerciveness

158. You are providing therapy for a child whose parents are both women, Carla and Meg. He has been having difficulty in school and is getting bullied because he has two mothers, and classmates have called him "wimpy" because he does not have a dad in his life. Carla and Meg are concerned about how their son is internalizing these messages. He has been withdrawing from his sports team and is not spending as much time with his friends as he used to. Additionally, his teachers have contacted his mothers

expressing concern about his grades dropping. How would you proceed?

A) assess for depressive symptoms
B) assess for bipolar disorder
C) assess for trauma
D) assess for mood disorders

159. You are reviewing a client's referral paperwork before an intake interview. Sandra is a twenty-eight-year-old woman who has been struggling with a depressed mood for about two and a half years. During these moods, she has a hard time controlling her eating habits, sleeps more than normal, and feels hopeless. She was unable to recall any time longer than three weeks that she did not struggle with her depressed mood. No symptoms of a manic or hypomanic episode, psychotic disorders, or substance use disorders were noted in the paperwork. Based on the information, which diagnosis should you investigate during your intake interview?

A) disruptive mood dysregulation disorder
B) major depressive disorder
C) persistent depressive disorder (dysthymia)
D) premenstrual dysphoric disorder

160. You are meeting with a new client for an intake assessment. Luke is a sixty-eight-year-old man who recently lost his wife to cancer. They had a long and happy marriage filled with children and grandchildren. Luke describes his wife as his best friend and shares that he feels lost without her. While he is relieved that she is no longer in pain, he feels selfish for missing her as much as he does. You have decided to use cognitive behavioral therapy in your sessions. Which approach would be MOST effective?

A) empty chair technique
B) exposure therapy
C) sand tray therapy
D) reframing thoughts

ANSWER KEY

1. **C**

   The main topics covered in an unstructured clinical interview include the following:
   - age and sex
   - reason for seeking counseling
   - client's work and education history
   - client's current social activities
   - any physical and mental health concerns, past and present
   - current medications and any drug and/or alcohol use
   - family history of mental health and physical health concerns
   - the counselor's observations of a client's behavior during the session (for example, anxious, detached, euthymic)

   While the topics listed in Options A, B, and C may come up in an interview, they typically occur within the counselor's investigation into the common areas.

2. **A**

   You can encourage members to talk about their experiences, what they have learned, and what helped them when they were struggling. Focusing on this can help them stay out of the counselor role while in the group session.

3. **A**

   Codependency is a common unhealthy relationship behavior found among individuals who are struggling with an addiction. The codependent person tends to focus on the individual who is struggling, which leads to the codependent person putting her needs on the back burner. This behavior can also enable the individual in active addiction.

4. **B**

   The main components of a treatment plan include a brief client background, diagnosis, problem list, treatment goals, objectives, interventions, timeline, method of evaluation, and tracking progress. In this scenario, option B is the best choice.

5. **B**

   This is an example of workplace harassment. Different companies have different ways to report these incidents, but a counselor can work with Helena to process her experience and help her feel validated about her reaction. The following behaviors are considered workplace harassment:
   - offensive jokes and comments
   - physical abuse and threats of abuse
   - insults, humiliation, derogatory slurs, and name-calling
   - abusing authority

6. **D**

   While it is your responsibility to discuss the client's viewpoint, it is equally important that the client grasp society's viewpoint. Counselors should not disclose their personal ideas. It is best to help the client understand the consequences of willfully not accepting employment and explain societal work values.

7. **B**

   The symptoms align with a diagnosis of anorexia nervosa, restrictive type. The specifier of "restrictive type" is appropriate because Sarah eats only one piece of fruit for each meal, which means she is restricting. Sarah is not engaging in behaviors related to binge eating/purging type.

8. **C**

   A values clarification exercise can help Ally and her partner gain a better understanding of what is important to them and the differences they may have. This can be used to facilitate a conversation about what they would like their relationship to look like.

9. **A**

   You should discuss with your supervisor your ability to ethically provide treatment. Individuals with co-occurring disorders have more success if they receive treatment for both concerns at the same time. If you cannot provide a particular treatment, you should refer the client to the appropriate professional.

10. **B**

    The second of the three stages involves individuals accepting their new roles in the relationship. This requires patience, open communication, and working on boundaries within the family. Elijah and Mary both need to establish boundaries with previous partners and family regarding co-parenting.

11. **C**

    Authority refers to new boundaries that define the responsibilities among adults. These can include who is responsible for discipline or financial concerns, and identifying new decision-making processes. Navigating all of these boundaries can help ease the transition for a blended family.

12. **D**

    The Clinician-Administered PTSD Scale for *DSM-5* (CAPS-5) can take from forty-five to sixty minutes to complete and can be used for clinical purposes as well as research. The assessment aligns with criteria B, C, D, and E for post-traumatic stress disorder. Additionally, this assessment looks at the duration of symptoms, the symptoms' level of distress on the client, and the impact the symptoms have on the client's social and occupational functioning.

13. **B**

    Since you do not have a rapport with Eddie, you should talk to him outside of group and explore barriers impacting his participation. Once you have learned more, you can work together to develop a plan to increase his participation.

14. **A**

    Icebreaker games can facilitate discussion that feels safe. Once safety is established within the group, members are likely to participate more.

15. **B**

    Vomiting and tremors do not necessarily indicate a medical emergency, but they do signal withdrawal. The counselor should explain the possible risks of alcohol withdrawal to the client and discuss whether he wants to seek medical treatment. The client should be encouraged to consult with a medical professional if these symptoms occur again.

16. **A**

    Session fading is a strategy whereby the number of sessions decreases as clients accomplish goals on their treatment plans. This could be reflected in the number of individual, group, and psychoeducational sessions they are asked to attend.

17. **C**

    Solution-focused brief therapy (SFBT) applies in this situation because it is effective in three to ten sessions. In a relapse prevention group, members can identify their goals and determine which solutions have helped them before. This approach can also help members identify plans to address any barriers they face in working toward their goals.

18. **B**

    It would be appropriate to assess for attention-deficit/hyperactivity disorder (ADHD), inattention presentation. While Max has four symptoms reported by his teacher, six are needed to make an accurate diagnosis. Margaret Keyes published a study in the *Archives of Pediatrics & Adolescent Medicine* that discusses the higher rates of ADHD among adopted children compared to their non-adopted peers.

19. **D**
Secondary trauma resembles post-traumatic stress disorder (PTSD) and is more likely to occur when counselors have a poor self-care routine. Secondary trauma can significantly impact the counselor's ability to provide mental health services.

20. **C**
A safety plan can include the phone numbers for supportive people in Nina's life as well as the 988 Suicide & Crisis Lifeline. Other common information on safety cards includes protective factors and coping skills.

21. **A**
Nina should be evaluated at the local hospital. She is distressed and has verbalized a plan as well as intent to follow through with the plan. The fact that she called you is a positive sign, and you can say so when you talk to her about calling for a wellness check. It is appropriate to keep her on the phone while contacting the authorities.

22. **C**
The Child Development Inventory (CDI) is a three-hundred-item screener that parents can complete at home and give to the counselor. This tool looks at the child's development in eight areas, including social, self-help, gross motor, fine motor, expressive language, language comprehension, letters, and numbers. The CDI also includes the General Development Scale, which investigates the child's health and growth, vision and hearing, and development behavior.

23. **D**
At a partial hospitalization program (PHP), Adrien would attend treatment for six to eight hours a day. For many, this form of treatment can be a bridge from inpatient treatment to returning home. Adrien is a candidate for a PHP program since he has a healthy and supportive home environment. While the other three options are possible, they will not provide Adrien with the structure that he is seeking for his routine at home.

24. **A**
A helpful group exercise would be to identify hobbies and interests to promote mental health. This can also help group members learn more about each other while enhancing your group cohesiveness. Not all clients will be affected by addiction or self-harm, so options B and D are not the best choices. Psychoeducation about family dynamics could be helpful, but it will not help group members to connect as well as option A.

25. **A**
All of the options can help you build rapport with group members, but being available to them before and after sessions gives them a consistent opportunity to speak with you individually. This is more effective than communicating via phone and email because you will not miss important body language cues. Being on time for the group can help members feel that you are dependable, but you will not have time to speak with them individually if you arrive right when the group starts. Snacking during group can be a distraction and serve as a barrier to participation.

26. **B**
Treatment is completed when the client has shown growth and achieved identified treatment goals. Since Scott is in treatment for an addiction, he should be able to effectively manage stressors and triggers, have healthy sober support, and not struggle with other mental health concerns.

27. **C**
With her mental health symptoms being manageable, she would likely benefit from engaging in an LGBTQIA+ support group, where she would be with individuals who can relate to her and validate her thoughts and experiences. Individual counseling could occur biweekly; however, this would not change her support system as a support group would.

28. **B**
Everything Alana has listed is a barrier to sobriety. She does have extrinsic motivation to stay sober (pending legal charges). Even though her motivation is extrinsic, she is

still attending sessions and meetings, so she is compliant with treatment. The term *consequences of addiction* usually refers to negative consequences that might push a person to addiction treatment (for example, loss of relationships, financial insecurity, or career and/or health problems).

29. **C**
Family programming in an addiction setting commonly provides education about the disease concept of addiction. This can help family members better understand how addiction changes the way the brain works and the challenges this can cause. Additionally, this would be an ideal time to discuss how the family could support their loved one's recovery efforts.

30. **C**
Body cues, such as nodding your head and making eye contact, show the speaker that you are listening. Counselors who are mindful of their body language can help show group members what is expected during a session.

31. **D**
The behaviors Sandra has described are associated with separation anxiety disorder, although it is imperative to better understand Josh's symptoms before providing an accurate diagnosis. For example, does his distress stem from being worried about not being with his mom when he is at school? Is he worried that he would lose his mom? The behaviors may be caused by his anxiety and not knowing how to manage his emotions in a healthy manner. The four-week period matches the criteria for this diagnosis and has a significant impact on Josh's functioning at school.

32. **B**
The Hamilton Depression Scale is a commonly used tool for individuals with a depressive disorder diagnosis. It is also referred to as the Hamilton Rating Scale for Depression and the Hamilton Depression Rating Scale. This tool can be used with both children and adults and currently comes in two versions: one with seventeen items, the other with twenty-one. The Montgomery–Asberg Depression Rating Scale is a ten-item tool that can be used to gain a better understanding of depressive symptoms in those who have a mood disorder. The Zung Self-Rating Depression Scale is a twenty-item assessment that rates four common symptoms of depression: pervasive effect, psychological equivalents, psychomotor activities, and other disturbances.

33. **A**
Various forms of play therapy are appropriate for children. Depending on their ages, children may not understand the concept of role-playing and may have trouble focusing during a guided imagery exercise.

34. **D**
Option C is not the main focus for the counselor. Suicide rates are statistically lower among Black individuals, so Option B is incorrect; however, the client should still be monitored for his suicide risk. The most concerning part of the client's suicide risk is his inability to identify protective factors, which can include future goals and relationships.

35. **C**
It is important to be open and friendly but remain professional. Remember that patience is an important attribute in a counselor.

36. **A**
Each group will be different; some groups may not want to acknowledge each other, while others may not mind. Regarding addiction treatment process groups, members may encounter each other at outside support groups like Alcoholics Anonymous or Narcotics Anonymous. Therefore it can be helpful to have an agreed-upon response to seeing each other.

37. **B**
Ann is likely living with disruptive mood dysregulation disorder. She is experiencing verbal rages in more than one setting, and these outbursts have been occurring for the past year. The minimum requirement for outbursts for this disorder is three per week, and Ann's mother reports that they are more frequent than that. This diagnosis can only be

made for individuals between the ages of six and eighteen.

38. **A**
Quantitative research uses standardized assessments and measurable data to investigate behaviors. Important components of this research include the methods that are used, limitations of the study, and whether other research supports its findings.

39. **B**
A couples counseling session would allow Josh and his wife to identify their roles within their family and create new boundaries. Additionally, they could receive feedback about what changes could be made to their communication patterns to make them more effective.

40. **B**
Shifting in your seat while a client is sharing can reveal that you feel uncomfortable emotionally.

41. **B**
Bianca's daughter appears to be struggling with anorexia nervosa. A further assessment is necessary to make a proper diagnosis. The key signs of anorexia nervosa include food intake restriction, intense fear of gaining weight, behaviors that prevent weight gain, and disturbance in one's perceived body shape or weight. Young adults and teenagers struggling with an eating disorder may not be getting the proper nutrients to grow and develop.

42. **C**
The goal of the care team is to help the client through the process. Disclosures should only include the information focused on the client's progress. Disclosing the details of the client's trauma history is not relevant to care coordination and would be a breach of the client's confidentiality.

43. **B**
When socializing members exclude other members, this can affect the group's sense of safety by making members feel like they are outsiders. Because of this, processing groups tend to discourage socialization.

44. **C**
Corrective emotional experiences require that the individual has a similar experience with the opposite outcome for a difficult situation. This applies to romantic relationships, friendships, or family relationships.

45. **A**
The counselor's primary responsibility is to provide a full range of assistance, including creating a treatment plan with a diagnosis and goals.

46. **A**
Blocking occurs when a counselor stops a behavior that could harm the group. An impaired group member violates the rules and expectations. Having the member assessed by a medical professional is an added measure to ensure her safety.

47. **B**
To provide informed consent, the client must understand the risks associated with participating, the potential benefits, the procedure, and the possible consequences. Most states require that an informed consent be signed and dated rather than offered verbally.

48. **C**
While working with her priest has been beneficial, Marcyanna has continued to struggle. The long duration of her struggle highlights the importance of a holistic approach to which she has not been previously exposed. Therapeutic interventions could be used during individual therapy, and medication could help her manage her other continuing symptoms. Research has shown that the combination of therapy and medication is an effective treatment regimen for depression. You can encourage Marcyanna to continue meeting with her priest if she finds that his support has a positive impact on her symptoms.

49. **A**
Maintaining composure while Adam expresses his frustration and argues with his parents can help strengthen your rapport with him since he will see that you do not automatically side with his parents, as he may have been expecting.

50. **C**
By improving his communication skills, Adam can learn to more effectively explain to his parents the boundaries he wishes to have in their relationship and the reasons why. It appears that Adam has been open with his parents about his interests and schooling, but he wants privacy when it comes to his social supports.

51. **A**
Having the client focus on helping her child is the main objective. This is best accomplished by helping her solve the problem while alleviating her fears concerning the diagnosis.

52. **B**
Selective prevention focuses on working with at-risk groups on concerns that could be preventable. This could include teen substance use and other problematic behaviors. Universal prevention provides prevention efforts for a larger-scale population. Indicated prevention aims to minimize concerns that have already begun.

53. **C**
The ethically responsible counselor respects the client's wishes and would refer Sam to a professional trained in EMDR. Though you can discuss the benefits of the therapy you are trained in, the client ultimately decides which therapy to use.

54. **B**
Healthy responses to conflict include remaining calm and clear in your communication. If both individuals are quick to anger, they would likely benefit from learning coping skills for their distress that they can use when they argue. This can help Lucy and Erin work toward healthier communication patterns.

55. **C**
While Paulo's experience at the conversion camp could have been traumatic, the symptoms describe generalized anxiety disorder. The symptoms are not applicable for a post-traumatic stress disorder (PTSD) diagnosis or major depressive disorder. According to the Trevor Project, 13 percent of LGBTQIA+ youth report being exposed to conversion therapy, over 75 percent of which occurred under the age of eighteen.

56. **B**
The symptoms described are associated with bipolar disorder, which indicates the need for a diagnostic interview. A structured interview assessing the client's symptoms would allow you to identify a diagnosis.

57. **B**
Since you have a coleader, you can ask him to step out with Jeanine while you stay and process what happened with the group. Other members may have various reactions, including anger, empathy, and confusion. It would be unhealthy for the group if Jeanine continued talking negatively about other members during the session. The colleague who steps out with Jeanine can provide her with one-on-one support and try to understand what contributed to her behavior.

58. **A**
Sexism in the workplace is an unfortunate experience that many women deal with. For Bethany, the first step would be to improve her emotion regulation skills so that she can cope with her anxiety symptoms that arise in the moment. Once she is able to better cope, you can talk about other approaches she can take to try to respond to her negative experience.

59. **B**
When it comes to goal setting, it can be helpful for clients to break down a larger goal into smaller pieces, which can make the goal feel less overwhelming. John might explore which specific aspects of beginning his master's program are distressing. For example, are his concerns related to housing, finances, time management, or employment? Breaking down John's concerns will also help

the counselor understand which issues are causing him the most distress.

60. B
Consistent expectations and consequences help children learn to behave appropriately. When each parent has different parenting styles, their children may feel like they can act differently with each parent.

61. C
If the client has a physical condition that hinders his ability to use stairs, he should receive reasonable accommodations to allow him access. Providing the code before the session will make it easier for the client to get to therapy.

62. B
The symptoms fit the criteria for a hypomanic episode. A hypomanic episode is not as severe as a manic episode; for example, a hypomanic episode is minimally four days long, whereas a manic episode lasts at least one week. Hypomanic episodes do lead to changes in behavior, but hospitalization is usually not required as it might be for those in a manic episode. Additionally, individuals in manic episodes can engage in dangerous behaviors, whereas Jace has focused on improving his soccer skills.

63. D
This client would benefit from being in an environment where he feels comfortable and safe to explore his sexuality and the concerns he has about his family's support. He may not have other people in his life who can give him a safe place to talk about his thoughts, feelings, and struggles. A counselor practicing positive regard projects an attitude of acceptance of the client as a person and understands that seeing every person is worthy of dignity and respect.

64. C
Eye movement desensitization and reprocessing (EMDR) is an evidence-based approach to treating trauma. With EMDR clients can experience a decrease in their symptoms, replace negative thought processes, and reduce their responses to triggers.

65. B
There is an abundance of research on behavioral couple therapy when it comes to effective couples counseling. Behavioral couple therapy can help a couple improve their relationship by using specific and effective techniques. Strategies of this form of therapy include modeling, positive reinforcement, and shaping.

66. A
Based on the client's diagnosis and presentation, she should be referred to a detox program. Being in a safe environment can allow her to fully detox so she can then engage in a treatment program. Withdrawal symptoms can interfere with a person's ability to fully participate in a treatment program, which is why detox programs contain more psychoeducational groups than process therapy groups do. While the symptoms of opioid withdrawal are not fatal, the combination of symptoms such as vomiting, sweating, and diarrhea can lead to health concerns such as dehydration. Detox programs include 24/7 medical supervision to monitor for health crises.

67. B
Since Lucas has begun his group therapy sessions, he is past the orientation stage. He is in the second stage, where he questions the value he will gain from participating while also having concerns about others learning that he is in the group.

68. C
The *DSM-5* requires that an adult have a minimum of three of the following symptoms to satisfy the requirements. Children must have one symptom.

- restlessness or feeling keyed up or on edge
- being easily fatigued
- irritability
- muscle tension
- sleep disturbances (difficulty falling or staying asleep, or restless, unsatisfying sleep)

69. C
Limits to confidentiality include

- being reviewed during a state or federal audit,
- sharing records for record keeping and billing purposes,
- sharing records with a supervisor or colleagues for consultation that would benefit the client,
- sharing records if the counselor is concerned clients may harm themselves or others,
- sharing records in a medical emergency,
- sharing records if the client discloses abuse that falls into required mandated reporting,
- sharing information if the client brings another person into the session, and
- a court requiring that a counselor disclose client information.

70. **C**
The disease concept of addiction can help group members gain a better understanding of factors that can contribute to a relapse and how to cope with triggers. While the other topics would be beneficial, they may not be as relevant as option C.

71. **D**
Theresa is likely struggling with complicated grief regarding the sudden loss of her husband. She has been dealing with guilt, sadness, and feelings of helplessness for a significant period of time. Another sign of complicated grief is that she has made little change to her routine and has not accepted that she needs to change her lifestyle to accommodate her financial situation.

72. **A**
Using a therapeutic approach or intervention that is not effective for the client's diagnosis is a counselor-imposed barrier. The use of eye movement desensitization and reprocessing (EMDR) is effective for clients with trauma or post-traumatic stress disorder (PTSD)—not anxiety disorders. Counselors should always work within their scope of practice and only use interventions for which they have proper training.

73. **B**
Although problems among clients may be similar, every situation is unique and may require a different solution. Counselors must learn as much as possible about each client before working on a solution.

74. **A**
Role-playing exercises can help you show group members how they can receive feedback and respond in a nondefensive manner. Additionally, you could talk about emotion regulation skills that might help them cope with their initial reactions.

75. **C**
Research has shown that the most effective approach for treating major depressive disorder is the combination of counseling and medication-assisted therapy. Declan would likely benefit from grief work for the loss of his marriage, as well as supportive counseling while he adjusts to the inevitable changes.

76. **A**
The Myers–Briggs Type Indicator (MBIT) investigates if a client is an extrovert or an introvert, a sensor or an intuitive, a thinker or a feeler, or a judger or a perceiver. The assessment will determine a personality type that helps you understand how a client sees the world. There are sixteen personality types possible with this assessment.

77. **C**
Role-playing during your session with Tim and Mary would show them how they can effectively communicate their concerns with their daughter. It would also allow you to give them feedback on the communication skills they have learned from you.

78. **C**
Eye-movement desensitization and reprocessing (EDMR) therapy is an evidence-based practice effective for treating symptoms associated with post-traumatic stress disorder (PTSD). According to the Veterans Affairs website, the prevalence rate of PTSD among older adults ranges from 1.5 to 4 percent. Since Jack's coping skills have served as a distraction for his symptoms, it is understandable that when these distractions

are not available, his symptoms become more distressing.

79. D
Qualitative research aims to investigate how and why things happen. It focuses on a small number of participants, which allows topics to be further explored than other forms of studies. Results from these studies tend to produce additional topics for research.

80. B
When a group member leaves a closed group, other members will inevitably be impacted. They can feel a variety of emotions ranging from worry and sadness to relief. While processing this transition, it is important to focus on the individuals who are still in the group and what this change means for them.

81. B
The three stages are emotional roller coaster, moratorium, and trust-building. These do not necessarily occur in this order, and some people may regress at times, which is fine. Everyone's experience is different, so their healing processes will be different as well. Emotions experienced can include anger, sadness, and isolation. Individual therapy can provide Johnathan with a safe place to feel, sit with, and begin to process his emotions regarding his wife's infidelity.

82. B
The original study was designed to study the effects the medication had on those living with alcohol use disorder. For the study to be valid, it must be designed to investigate those struggling with opioid use disorder.

83. B
Unconditional positive regard is a mindset used by client-centered counselors. This concept helps build therapeutic alliances because it creates an environment where clients feel safe talking about things they may not have previously felt comfortable talking about. Being mindful of your body language and facial expressions plays a role in unconditional positive regard.

84. D
Unless you are using a social media account as a psychoeducational platform, being friends with clients online can change your relationship's dynamics and harm your therapeutic alliance.

85. B
It would be appropriate to assess for the student's safety. This can include a suicide assessment and checking for protective factors. The Trevor Project estimates that an LGBTQIA+ teen attempts suicide every forty-five seconds. Knowing the statistics for suicide within the LGBTQIA+ community, it is necessary to stay proactive with these clients and continually assess for mental health concerns.

86. A
Being genuine can help your client feel more comfortable despite any differences you may have.

87. C
Canceling appointments based on a client's demographics is unethical. The best option is to proceed with the scheduled appointment. If you have concerns about working with clients with different backgrounds than yourself, you should process this with a supervisor.

88. C
Parent-child interaction therapy (PCIT) uses a two-stage process to look at children's behaviors. This approach is appropriate for children who are between two and seven and exhibit disruptive behaviors. This therapy addresses the relationship between the child and caregivers, as well as the forms of discipline that are used.

89. D
A counselor must know when to seek the help of a professional in another discipline and refer the client to this source. The counselor must also coordinate activities with the other professional.

90. **D**
Theo would likely benefit from learning about the difference between long- and short-term goals. Aspects of healthy goals, which include making sure that the goals are attainable and realistic (for example, SMART goals), can also be discussed.

91. **B**
A diagnosis of schizophreniform disorder can be made when a client has experienced at least two of the following symptoms for at least one month. One of the symptoms must be one of the first three options:
- delusions
- hallucinations
- disorganized speech
- grossly disorganized behaviors or catatonic behaviors
- negative symptoms (diminished emotional expression or avolition)

Additionally, several mental health diagnoses must be ruled out, including schizoaffective disorder, major depressive disorder, and bipolar disorder with psychotic features. This means that the symptoms associated with schizophreniform have not occurred at the same time as the disorders mentioned, or are present for only a short period. Medication and substance use must also be ruled out as a cause.

92. **C**
Discussing sexuality can be difficult if a person's loved ones and friends are not understanding or have a history of making hurtful comments about members of the LGBTQIA+ community. To improve Sam's communication skills, you could try a role-playing exercise to practice verbalizing his thoughts. This would also allow you to discuss coping skills that could help him if the conversations do not go as planned.

93. **B**
Extrinsic motivation comes from sources outside of the self, such as material rewards, validation or acclaim from others, and recognition. Intrinsic motivation is internally powered, making outside recognition irrelevant.

94. **A**
Self-assessments can help counselors understand their limitations when it comes to which mental health concerns they are competent to work with.

95. **D**
All of the options are appropriate in this situation; however, the first priority should be the client's well-being and safety. Since there is a medical professional in the office, the client should be evaluated to see if further medical attention is necessary.

96. **A**
Since the couple is struggling with verbal abuse and have identified emotion regulation as a growing point, they would benefit from psychoeducation about coping skills for their emotions. Couples counseling can give them a safe place to talk through their experiences with the counselor's guidance to aid in effective communication. Couples counseling will also allow them to try out new communication skills that they can use outside of therapy. Couples who do experience violence need to be carefully screened before engaging in couples counseling. Other treatment approaches include gender-specific counseling, group, or individual counseling.

97. **A**
Body language can send significant messages to a client. If a counselor makes inconsistent eye contact or moves frequently in his chair, he might seem uninterested in what the client is sharing.

98. **D**
To respect confidentiality, the counselor should not acknowledge group members in public without their consent.

99. **B**
In addition to decreasing the risk of tobacco, alcohol, and drug use, spirituality can also lessen depressive symptoms in youth, according to a 2008 study by Abraham Verghese.

100. C

The category of affect relates to how people express the emotions they are feeling. It is important to determine whether clients are acting in ways that are congruent with how they say they are feeling.

101. C

The best way to handle the situation is to remind the client that the two of you are focusing solely on her problems. A discussion of your personal affairs will not be useful in resolving any of her issues.

102. A

Using open-ended questions can help Mark share more than "yes" or "no" answers. Even if his answers are short, he can still lead the discussion. While he may benefit from some psychoeducation, it does not need to be the focus of the sessions.

103. D

The bystander effect is a social phenomenon that occurs when one person or a group of people assume that someone else will help because there are others around. When people see something happen among a group, it is easy to assume that others have observed the same thing and will take action. This eases some of the responsibility, a concept known as diffusion of responsibility, that is felt by the so-called bystanders.

104. C

When clients' treatment influences their legal issues, lack of trust can be a barrier. The counselor should build trust with the clients by being open and honest about what information is shared with the court. Information regarding urinalysis screens, attendance, and participation may be shared; however, personal details of the clients' sessions should not be included unless they are directly relevant.

105. A

Box breathing is an emotion regulation skill that your client can use in the moment to lessen her emotional reaction. Avoidance would not do her any good, nor would matching her partner's tone of voice. Screaming may be one way to cope but would not be appropriate in the moment since her partner could interpret this as an act of aggression.

106. A

The scenario describes delusional thought. According to the *DSM-5*, there are four types of delusions: bizarre delusions, non-bizarre delusions, mood-congruent delusions, and mood-incongruent delusions. This client is exhibiting mood-incongruent delusions, which are not impacted by her mood. Her theme tends to include control and nihilism.

107. C

Persistent depressive disorder, also known as dysthymia, can be diagnosed in children and adolescents who experience depressive symptoms most days for at least one year. This disorder can be diagnosed in adults who experience a depressed mood most days for a minimum of two years. For children, the depressive symptoms must be present for one year for a diagnosis of dysthymia. Joan should be monitored for depressive episodes that can occur, including suicidal ideation.

108. A

Counselors must stick to their appointment schedules. Appointments should stay intact and only be interrupted if an emergency has arisen. When clients have additional issues to discuss, a new appointment should be scheduled to address those concerns.

109. A

Evidence-based practice refers to the use of interventions proven by research to be effective.

110. C

Insomnia disorder is the correct option to explore. The giveaway is that this client is not getting adequate sleep and is reporting frequent waking at night. He has begun to experience negative consequences from the lack of proper sleep. To be diagnosed with an insomnia disorder, an individual must have a hard time falling asleep or staying asleep, or wake up earlier than intended. This change will negatively impact one or more areas of functioning. The sleep disturbance must be present for a minimum of three months, at least three days a week.

111. A
While maintaining a nonjudgmental environment can help keep the group on a productive path, the most important thing is that everyone in the group feels safe.

112. A
Laura is having an internal struggle between wanting to return to work and wanting to be a good parent. This is a common dilemma for women in similar situations, and she would benefit from having a safe, judgment-free environment where she can explore her thoughts and emotions.

113. D
There are four main reasons to use the SCID-5:
1. to make sure the counselor is evaluating for all the major *DSM-5* diagnoses
2. to help select the population for a study
3. to help identify current and past mental health concerns within a study's population
4. to help students and new mental health professionals improve their clinical interviewing skills

114. D
Planful competence occurs among families with adolescents and is strongly influenced by the child's environment and caregivers. Research has shown that healthier children have both parents equally involved in their upbringing.

115. A
Group rules can help members know what to expect and what is expected of them. They address concerns such as late arrivals, missing group, interacting outside of group, having food and drinks in the group, and managing cross talk.

116. C
This counselor runs a dialectical behavior therapy (DBT) skills group that helps clients learn the skills they can use to reduce their distress while in treatment and after returning home.

117. B
Sleep cycles have four stages that can last from 90 to 120 minutes. Once one sleep cycle ends, the cycle begins again. People's bodies respond differently to each of the sleep stages.

118. A
The counselor should guide the couple to set treatment goals to improve communication. This will help them learn new skills they can use to address disagreements as well as other problems in their relationship.

119. C
While you provide Lucia with emotional support, you can also offer a counseling session with her husband. This way, you could help both individuals express their thoughts and concerns in a healthy manner with the goal of improving their understanding of each other. With improved understanding, the couple can work to determine which option is right for them and their family.

120. D
The best outcomes for people with a dual diagnosis require that both conditions receive treatment at the same time. Dialectical behavior therapy (DBT) is an evidence-based practice effective for treating post-traumatic stress (PTSD). In an addiction rehab setting, Sandra would likely be engaged in specialized group sessions as well as addiction groups, with one counselor providing the trauma treatment and another one providing the addiction treatment.

121. C
The behaviors Richard has been using are examples of conflict resolution skills. Other skills include being patient with the other person, remaining unbiased, keeping calm, avoiding lecturing, being mindful of one's body language, and observing other people.

122. C
Embellishing or neglecting relevant information is unethical. Reviewing the report with Lucas before sending it can open a dialogue about his concerns. For example, he may feel that he made progress in an area that is not mentioned in the report.

123. B
These group members appear to be withdrawing from the group session, evidenced by their body language and nonverbal communication. As a leader, you could use skills such as redirecting to try to shift these behaviors to encourage group participation.

124. C
The counselor is providing Nader with psychoeducation about his intake assessment. It makes sense that he would be apprehensive if he has never been in therapy before and is unsure what to expect. All clients will come to sessions with an expectation of what they will experience; unfortunately, this expectation is not always accurate or helpful. Taking time to explain the process can also help build rapport with Nader.

125. B
Jia may be struggling with major depressive disorder. While some adults rejoice at the idea of an empty nest, many others struggle with the transition from raising their children to supporting them as they become independent. This can be a time to encourage Jia to learn more about herself, her interests, and her passions.

126. D
Listening to the client talk about his situation in his own words can help you get to know him and his case better.

127. C
Support groups, such as Alcoholics Anonymous and Narcotics Anonymous, help individuals in recovery make connections with other people in recovery. Individuals who are active in these groups are encouraged to work closely with a sponsor who can provide guidance and support in their recovery. Group counselors often advise against building relationships with other group members because it can change the dynamic of the group. A support group in a clinical setting would be an exception to this.

128. B
The Alcohol Use Disorders Identification Test (AUDIT) was developed by the World Health Organization (WHO) and is used to identify individuals whose drinking behaviors have become concerning for their health. Scoring for this assessment includes lower risk, increasing risk, higher risk, and possible dependence.

129. C
The main goal of the leaving home phase of the family life cycle is to develop one's own identity, which includes beliefs and convictions. Younger people tend to be influenced by those around them, whereas during this stage, one can make decisions without the influence of others.

130. C
The term *beneficence* relates to the ethical principle of doing what is in the client's best interest; the term *veracity* describes a commitment to being truthful.

131. A
Having the group work together to develop rules or norms can help create an environment where members feel safe. They can address their concerns, such as keeping what is said in group sessions private, which can help members feel that they are all on the same page.

132. D
Cisgender is used to describe individuals who identify as the sex they were assigned at birth

133. A
Discharge planning should begin at the time of intake. While a client may expect to be in treatment for a certain length of time, things change. Starting to plan at intake gives you ample opportunity to talk with your clients about their thoughts for discharge. Depending on the setting you work in, discharge planning can include continued mental health treatment at a different level of care.

134. C
Individuals struggling with major depressive disorder often withdraw from their relationships or lose interest in activities they previously enjoyed.

135. A
The categories listed would best be addressed during a biopsychosocial interview. *Biopsychosocial* is made up of the terms *biology*, *psychological*, and *social*.

136. C
Anxiety disorder due to prostate cancer is the best choice because John's symptoms are directly caused by his medical diagnosis, and he has no history of mental health concerns. A medical exam, lab work, and a verbal history will determine an individual's history of mental health concerns. A key component of this diagnosis is that symptoms significantly impact a client's social life, work, and other important areas of functioning.

137. A
Samantha's alcohol drinking has undergone a significant change, and she has driven and worked while impaired. She would likely benefit from an inpatient co-occurring treatment program and a medically supervised detox.

138. A
Adell may find that attending a grief support group is helpful. In such a group, she would be able to connect with other individuals who can relate to her grief and normalize her experience. This is different from meeting up with her friends, because a support group is guided by a counselor and focuses on members' experiences with grief and loss.

139. B
For a family therapy program in an addiction setting, the most appropriate topic is the disease concept of addiction. There are many misconceptions about both addiction and recovery. Providing family members with a solid understanding of how addiction changes the way our bodies work and effective treatments can help families navigate their future together. Sessions on medication-assisted treatment (MAT) could be helpful for some clients, but not every client will have a family member using MAT.

140. A
Cognitive restructuring and reframing can help Zane adjust his negative thought patterns that automatically assume that he lost his job because of his performance. Colleagues offering personal references for future job opportunities is evidence that he did well at his job. If Zane can change his negative automatic thoughts into healthier thoughts, he will see a positive shift in his depressive symptoms.

141. C
Congruence is a term used by psychologist Carl Rogers when he was developing person-centered therapy. Rogers defined congruence as genuineness that is needed for a counselor to provide unconditional positive regard and empathy.

142. D
Gillette is in the final stage of group therapy, where she applies what she has learned in group to her everyday life. For some outpatient aftercare groups, this may mean that she is almost finished with the group.

143. D
The symptoms described align with panic disorder. After Mary had several panic attacks, she became worried about having more panic attacks, and she changed her behavior as a result of her concerns (searching for side jobs to the extent that her sleep is interrupted). It is important to rule out any medical conditions, mental health conditions, or substance use that could be causing her panic attacks.

144. D
Research has shown that the best approach is to treat both addiction and mental health concerns at the same time. Individuals struggling with dual diagnosis often have intertwined symptoms. For example, the client's depressive symptoms could lead to cravings and triggers, which would challenge her sobriety. By providing mental health treatment in conjunction with addiction treatment, the client will learn to manage her mental health symptoms in a healthier manner.

145. B
Counselors can lobby for law changes when they find concerns to fight for, including laws

and regulations regarding professional and client safety concerns.

146. B
Jay would likely benefit from improving his communication patterns. This can include learning to cope with the negative emotions that arise, as well as communicating his thoughts in a way that avoids placing blame on his wife.

147. A
The 2008 model for working with infidelity from Snyder, Baucom, and Gordon lists three stages that do not have to be progressive. The order of the steps will depend on the clients and their experiences with infidelity. This approach will help both individuals learn skills for emotion regulation and decision-making. As with other couples' intervention strategies, the overall goal is to help them strengthen their relationship and see the other side of their negative experience.

148. C
Treatment plans should be reviewed frequently and revised when needed. A new problem or a crisis, such as hospitalization for a suicide attempt, requires a treatment plan to be revised. Treatment plans are also revised when a diagnosis changes, if clients resolve problems on their own, or when clients make notable progress in sessions.

149. B
The cycle of violence would address the several stages that can help Jonah identify the pattern within his partner's behaviors, including being abusive, buying a gift as an apology, a honeymoon phase, and a repeated tension buildup.

150. B
The Beck Anxiety Inventory (BAI) is an anxiety screening tool that can be completed fairly quickly. It can be done orally during a session or self-reported before a session. The symptoms included in the BAI are effective predictors of anxiety disorders, which make this a helpful tool when trying to formulate a diagnosis. The BAI can gauge progress after the client completes it a second time, and the results are compared once the client has begun therapy and/or medications. The BAI has been found to produce valid results.

151. D
Focusing on advocating for herself can help prepare Bianca for a variety of future situations when it will be important to clearly communicate her experience and explain her actions.

152. D
While it sounds like the children need a safe space to grieve the loss associated with their parents' divorce, their concern about their mother's fiancé being a bad man appears to be a personal thought lacking supportive evidence. They seem to hold their father in the highest of regard, which would make any man their mother dates look inferior despite his behaviors.

153. C
Talking to your supervisor before making any changes will provide feedback on the logistics of the concern and the feasibility of your proposed solution.

154. A
The main concern should be for the health and welfare of your client. If she is apprehensive about telling her doctor about her mental health struggles, having you in the room while she talks to her doctor can help her feel supported. If she does not want to call with you in the room, you can talk to your supervisor about contacting the doctor yourself, provided you have the necessary Health Insurance Portability and Accountability Act (HIPAA) consents.

155. D
Relapse prevention is an appropriate psychoeducational topic for an addiction rehab program. While some of the participants could benefit from the other topics, all participants are engaging in treatment for an addiction concern.

156. C
Exploring leisure and enjoyable activities can pinpoint interests that Philippe can add to his routine to bring him some enjoyment. This

could include exercise, art, reading, yoga, meditation, journaling, or joining a sports recreational league. Choosing a social leisure activity such as a sports league could also provide him with an opportunity for social connection outside of the workplace.

157. C
For person-centered therapy to be successful, the counselor must create a supportive environment and be as open, nonjudgmental, and empathetic as possible.

158. A
Due to the symptoms and the bullying, it is important to assess for depression. Once you have a better understanding of his difficulties, you can determine how to move forward and help him.

159. C
Persistent depressive disorder is the appropriate diagnosis for individuals who have been struggling with major depressive disorder for over two years. It is important to rule out symptoms of manic and hypomanic episodes that would indicate the presence of bipolar I, bipolar II, or cyclothymic disorder.

160. D
Reframing negative thoughts, such as Luke's sense of being selfish for missing his wife, would be beneficial. Knowing how thoughts can impact feelings and behaviors, working to change Luke's thoughts would likely have a positive impact on his feelings and behaviors.

Online Resources

Trivium includes online resources with the purchase of this study guide to help you fully prepare for your CPCE exam.

Practice Test

In addition to the practice test included in this book, we also offer an online exam. Since many exams today are computer based, practicing your test-taking skills on the computer is a great way to prepare.

Review Questions

Need more practice? Our review questions use a variety of formats to help you memorize key terms and concepts.

Flash Cards

Trivium's flash cards allow you to review important terms easily on your computer or smartphone.

From Stress to Success

Watch "From Stress to Success," a brief but insightful YouTube video that offers the tips, tricks, and secrets experts use to score higher on the exam.

Reviews

Leave a review, send us helpful feedback, or sign up for Trivium promotions—including free books!

Access these materials at
https://triviumtestprep.com/cpce-online-resources

Made in the USA
Middletown, DE
10 January 2025

69184575R00124